Selected Issues in
Equity
Compensation

Fifth Edition

Selected Issues in Equity Compensation

Fifth Edition

Edited by Scott S. Rodrick

The National Center for Employee Ownership
Oakland, California

This publication is designed to provide accurate and authoritative information regarding the subject matter covered. It is sold with the understanding that the publisher is not engaged in rendering legal, accounting, or other professional services. If legal advice or other expert assistance is required, the services of a competent professional should be sought.

Legal, accounting, and other rules affecting business often change. Before making decisions based on the information you find here or in any publication from any publisher, you should ascertain what changes might have occurred and what changes might be forthcoming. The NCEO's Web site (including the members-only area) and newsletter for members provide regular updates on these changes. If you have any questions or concerns about a particular issue, check with your professional advisor or, if you are an NCEO member, call or email us.

Selected Issues in Equity Compensation, 5th ed.
Edited by Scott Rodrick; indexed by Pam Chernoff
Book design by Scott S. Rodrick

The National Center for Employee Ownership
1736 Franklin Street, 8th Floor
Oakland, CA 94612
(510) 208-1300
(510) 272-9510 (fax)
Web site: www.nceo.org

Originally published as *Stock Options: Beyond the Basics* in September 1999.
    Second edition August 2000. Third edition January 2003.
New edition, titled *Selected Issues in Stock Options*, January 2004.
Second edition of *Selected Issues*, titled *Selected Issues in Equity Compensation*, February 2005. Third edition January 2006.
Fourth edition January 2007. Fifth edition February 2008.

ISBN-10: 1-932924-41-8
ISBN-13: 978-1-932924-41-1

Contents

3. State Securities Law Considerations for Equity Compensation Plans 103

Matthew Topham

4. Preparing for an Initial Public Offering 123

Mark A. Borges

7.   Underwater Stock Options and Repricing Strategy   201

Daniel N. Janich

8.   Stock Options in Divorce   217

William Dunn and Donna Yip

Preface

More and more companies are realizing that their employees are their most important asset. To attract, retain, and reward employees, many companies use stock options and related plans, often in "broad-based" programs that include most or even all employees. Our standard introductory guide for company owners, managers, and advisors is *The Stock Options Book,* which covers a multitude of issues relating to stock options and stock purchase plans.

This book goes a step beyond *The Stock Options Book* with extensive information on crucial issues such as administration, securities laws, and divorce. It is not a comprehensive overview like *The Stock Options Book* but rather is more selective and detailed. It is not meant to be an introduction to the field or to be a guide to all advanced issues.

We hope you find this book useful and that it inspires you to become more involved with stock plans. To read about the other information resources that we at the National Center for Employee Ownership (NCEO) offer, including many other publications on stock plans, communicating to employees, and creating an ownership culture, visit our Web site at www.nceo.org or see the back of this book.

Fifth Edition

This book was originally titled *Stock Options: Beyond the Basics* and then was reissued as *Selected Issues in Stock Options* in 2004 to avoid confusion with the title of another NCEO book. With the addition of more material on plans other than options (mainly ESPPs, as in the final chapter), the second edition of the reissued book was retitled to *Selected Issues in Equity Compensation,* a title we retain with this fifth edition.

In this edition, every chapter (except chapters 7 and 8, where the authors did not find it necessary) as well as the glossary has been revised to bring the book up to date (as of the end of 2007) with recent developments.

CHAPTER

1

Administering an Employee Stock Option Plan

Mark A. Borges

Contents

OR MANY YEARS, STOCK OPTIONS have been a popular non-cash means for compensating employees. While many corporations grant stock options primarily to their senior management as an integral component of their executive compensation programs, a growing number of companies grant stock options at various levels within the organization. Moreover, broad-based employee stock option programs that award stock options to all or substantially all employees, long used by smaller businesses, are now used by larger corporations as well. Even though corporations must recognize an expense for stock options for financial reporting purposes, option use continues to be widespread.

Befitting their popularity, employee stock options are one of the most comprehensively regulated forms of equity compensation. A multitude of complex and, at times, confusing tax, accounting, corporate, and securities laws affect the adoption, implementation, operation, and administration of employee stock option plans. These laws are supplemented by an array of other provisions, ranging from the detailed requirements of the national stock exchanges to the general common-law principles of contracts. While the terms and conditions of individual employee stock option plans vary from company to company, the characteristics of all employee stock options are heavily influenced by the various rules that govern their use.

The laws, regulations, and other principles governing employee stock options are well-documented elsewhere. Less understood are the administrative considerations that arise in maintaining an employee stock option plan. This chapter discusses the more common administrative aspects of employee stock options.

Recent revelations about stock option backdating and growing concerns about option grant timing practices have heightened the interest in the administrative aspects of employee stock option plans. Companies seeking to avoid potential backdating problems should ensure that they have implemented and adhere to well-designed policies and procedures for both the grant and exercise of their stock options.

1.1 Establishing the Plan

When a company decides to implement an employee stock option plan, management will commission the preparation of a formal plan document. Typically, the plan's structure, as well as its specific terms and conditions, will be determined in consultation with the company's legal counsel, accountants, and outside compensation or benefits specialists. Factors taken into consideration in designing the plan will include the cost to the company and to proposed participants, the projected dilution of shareholders' ownership interests, the potential liquidity alternatives for participants, and the income tax, securities law, and financial accounting consequences to participants and the company from the operation of the plan.

Most employee stock option plans allow for the grant of both nonstatutory (nonqualified) stock options and incentive stock options. This permits flexibility in granting the appropriate form of option to intended recipients, while maintaining an effective limit on the total number of shares of stock available for issuance under the plan. (The rules governing incentive stock options stipulate that the stock option plan must state the maximum number of shares of stock available for grant under the plan.) Typically, the company's legal counsel will prepare the plan documents. Once management is satisfied with the plan's design and structure, the plan will be presented to the company's board of directors for consideration and adoption. Because under the corporate laws of most states, the board of directors must authorize any issuance of shares of the company's stock, board approval is generally required before the implementation of an employee stock option plan.

Following adoption by the board of directors, the employee stock option plan then is submitted to the company's shareholders for approval. Shareholder approval is required if the company's securities are listed on a national stock exchange (such as the New York or American stock exchanges or the NASDAQ Stock Market). In addition, shareholder approval may be a requirement under state corporate law or the company's charter documents. Even if shareholder approval is not required, there may be distinct advantages to obtaining shareholder approval of the plan. The preferential tax treatment afforded by the Internal Revenue Code (the

"Code") to incentive stock options is available only if the stock option plan has been approved by the company's shareholders. In addition, the exclusion from the deduction limitation of Section 162(m) of the Code for "performance-based" compensation requires that a compensation plan or arrangement be approved by shareholders. In addition, compliance with certain provisions of the federal securities laws may be made easier if the plan has been approved by shareholders.

1.2 Granting Options

1.2.1 Policies and Procedures

Many companies establish formal policies and procedures to facilitate the efficient administration of their employee stock option plans. Formal policies enhance the plan administrator's ability to operate the plan consistent with the company's objectives for its equity compensation program. They also enable the plan administrator to resolve problems that may arise during the life of the plan. Formal guidelines for processing stock option grants can serve as an effective means for ensuring that all company procedures are properly followed.

A formal grant process, as well as specific procedures for processing option grants, can also be an effective means of eliminating the risk of option backdating, either due to deliberate efforts to manipulate option grant dates or timing or due to incomplete or inconsistent grant practices.

A comprehensive stock option plan policy should address:

- How option recipients are to be determined.
- How the size of stock option grants (number of shares) is to be determined.
- Which type of stock options to grant: incentive stock options (ISOs) or nonstatutory stock options (NSOs).
- How often stock options are to be granted.
- When stock options will be granted.
- How the vesting schedule is to be determined.
- How stock option grants are handled in special situations.

A written procedure should address the following:

- The company's internal grant approval process.
- How the option exercise price will be determined.
- The grant transaction recordation.
- The grant agreement preparation and completion process.
- Inter-departmental communications.

1.2.2 Plan Participation

Under an employee stock option plan, both the selection of recipients and the timing of grants are typically reserved to the discretion of the board of directors or appropriate board committee. Companies use a wide variety of different approaches and policies for determining which employees should receive stock options. In some instances, only members of senior management are eligible to receive stock options. Other companies will grant stock options to all managers. Still other companies grant stock options to all employees, regardless of their job descriptions.

Some companies grant stock options to all newly hired employees, while others grant options only to employees who have completed a specified term of service with the company. Stock options are frequently used as a form of merit bonus, in combination with or in lieu of a salary increase or in conjunction with a promotion. It is not uncommon for a company to make periodic (for example, annual) uniform stock option grants to all employees.

In view of the high degree of investor interest in the timing of stock option grants, companies have begun to establish a fixed schedule for when options will be granted during the year. In some instances, this schedule will be preannounced by the company. Other companies have elected to restrict the grant of stock options to predetermined time periods, such as during a specified period following the release of the company's quarterly or annual financial results.

1.2.3 Number of Shares Granted

Under an employee stock option plan, the number of shares of stock to be granted under option to each employee is typically determined by the board of directors or appropriate board committee. Companies use a wide variety of different approaches and/or policies for determining the size of a stock option grant. Typically, a company will establish guidelines for determining the number of shares of stock to be subject to each stock option grant. The number of shares of stock may be determined on an employee-by-employee basis, by job classification, or based on the company's overall performance over a specified period of time. The number of shares of stock also may be determined as a percentage of the employee's annual salary.

1.2.4   Internal Approval Process

In order to grant stock options, generally a company will find it beneficial to establish internal approval procedures. The exact nature of these procedures will vary from company to company. In any event, the procedures should address such matters as who will be recommended for a stock option grant, the size of the recommended grant, and whether any special terms and conditions will be attached to the grant. These decisions are usually made by the human resources department and/or other benefits personnel, possibly with input from various management-level employees. For example, in the case of newly hired employees, the hiring manager may provide the first level of stock option grant approval. For merit grants, an employee's direct supervisor may provide the stock option grant recommendation.

Next, all grants, regardless of origin, will be incorporated into a formal proposal to be submitted to the company's board of directors or appropriate board committee for review and approval. If the board of directors has delegated responsibility for stock option grants to a subcommittee of the board, such as the compensation committee or a special stock option committee, the recommendations will be considered and approved. Alternatively, the committee may make its own recommendations, which will be submitted to the full board for review and final approval. Stock option grants generally become effective as of the date of board action (although the terms of the plan and/or the specific grant authorization may provide otherwise). Under the New York Stock Exchange's corporate governance listing standards, the compensation committee of a listed company is responsible for making recommendations to the board of directors with respect to the company's "Section 16 officers" (other than the chief executive officer), including incentive compensation plans and equity plans, such as a stock option plan. Compensation for employees who are not Section 16 officers may be set, but need not be set, by the compensation committee.

In view of the high degree of investor interest in the timing of stock option grants, a company should document the entire internal approval process, including the grant date, the number of shares subject to the award, the exercise or purchase price, and the identity of the intended optionee. The company also should consider documenting the identities of the persons who authorized the award, and the related authorization date. This authorization should be reflected in the board or committee meeting minutes or in a written consent in lieu of a meeting. To the extent that the company delegates responsibility for option grants to an executive officer (or group of executive officers), there should be restrictions on the scope of this authority (for example, limits on the size of awards and/or permissible optionees). In addition, the board of directors should regularly audit the activities resulting from this delegated responsibility to ensure that this authority is not being misused.

Companies should also make sure that their internal control system covers the administration of their stock option plan. The principal areas that should be incorporated in the control system include both grant procedures and reporting grants and awards within the company, particularly with respect to interdepartmental communications. Finally, these procedures should be routinely evaluated and tested to ensure they contain no material deficiencies.

1.2.5 Grant Agreement

Most companies document a stock option grant by preparing a formal grant agreement. The grant agreement for a stock option is a written document that specifies the terms and conditions of the stock option grant. The grant agreement typically contains the following:

- The correct name of the grant recipient (the "optionee").
- The effective date of the stock option grant.
- The type of stock option (ISO or NSO).
- The number of shares of stock covered by the option.
- The option exercise price.
- The vesting schedule for the shares of stock covered by the option.
- The expiration date of the option.

In addition, the agreement usually sets out the procedures the optionee must follow to exercise the stock option, the permissible forms of payment of the option exercise price, and other related matters. Since the agreement usually will also set out the obligations of the optionee in connection with the receipt and/or exercise of the stock option as well as any restrictions imposed on the option or the option shares, most companies require that the optionee sign the grant agreement. A company should set a time limit within which an optionee must sign and return the grant agreement; the company should address whether there is to be a penalty for failure to return an executed agreement.

When the grant of the stock option is formally approved, typically multiple copies (at least two) of the grant agreement will be transmitted to the employee for signature. One copy is to be retained by the employee for his or her records. The plan administrator should include a copy in the employee's file, and, if desired, a third copy should be sent to the company's legal counsel.

Other documents may be distributed along with the grant agreement. A copy of the stock option plan, a summary thereof, or a plan "prospectus" is usually provided to the employee. This may be required by federal and/or state securities laws. Additionally, it may be helpful to distribute such items as a form of stock option exercise notice, an escrow agreement (if appropriate), and a question-and-answer memorandum or fact sheet that answers the most frequently asked questions about stock options and contains instructions on exercise procedures. If the company maintains an internal employee Web site, some or all of these documents or information may be posted to Web pages that the optionee can access. It may also be more efficient to require that optionees acknowledge receipt of this documentation electronically.

1.2.6 Option Exercise Price

Typically, the exercise price of an employee stock option will be equal to the fair market value of the granting company's stock on the grant date. Occasionally, a stock option plan will permit the option exercise price to be less than fair market value (for example, 85% of the fair market value of the granting company's stock on the grant date). However, such provisions are becoming less common because an option with an exercise price below fair market value may be considered to involve a deferral of compensation subject to Section 409A of the Code.

Most stock option plans stipulate how fair market value is to be determined. There are many methodologies employed to set fair market value for a public company, including (1) the closing price of the granting company's stock on the grant date, (2) the closing price of the granting company's stock on the date preceding the grant date, (3) the average of the high and low trading prices of the company's stock on the grant date, (4) the average of the high and low trading prices of the company's stock on the date preceding the grant date, and (5) the average trading price of the company's stock for a specified period (for example, 20 trading days) before the grant date. In the case of a privately held company, fair market value is frequently based on a formula prescribed by the company's board of directors or an external appraisal of the company's value.

1.2.7 Vesting

Generally, an employee earns the right to exercise his or her stock option and purchase the option shares over a specified period of time. (Occasionally, a company will permit an employee to exercise his or her stock option immediately at any time after the date of grant, subject to a right of repurchase in favor of the company should the employee leave the company before a specified date.) The process of earning the option shares is commonly referred to as "vesting." The vesting period set forth in the grant agreement is commonly referred to as the "vesting schedule."

Stock options typically are not exercisable immediately upon grant, but become exercisable either in one lump sum after a specified period of time or in cumulative increments. Generally, a vesting schedule will provide that at the completion of designated intervals, a predetermined percentage or ratio of the option shares are earned and become available for purchase by the employee. These interim dates are called "vesting dates." Typically, vesting is measured from the date a stock option is granted; however, some companies measure vesting from the date the employee was hired or commenced providing services to the company or some other specified date.

A company will adopt a vesting schedule that best suits the incentive or other objectives of its employee stock option plan. Many plans provide for annual vesting schedules; that is, the option shares will vest in equal annual installments over a period of several years (typically, three, four, or five years). In certain parts of the U.S., monthly or quarterly vesting schedules are used. With the adoption of Statement of Financial Accounting Standards No. 123 (revised 2004) (commonly known as "FAS 123(R)") as the accounting standard for stock-based compensation, it is becoming more common for options to become exercisable or vest upon the achievement of a specified company performance goal, such as achievement of a specified earnings-per-share, revenue, or profitability target. Like options that are subject to service-based vesting requirements, options subject to performance-based vesting may become exercisable either in one lump sum after a specified performance goal has been satisfied or in cumulative increments as multiple performance goals are met.

1.2.8 Term

When a stock option is granted, the grant agreement will specify the date the right to purchase the option shares will expire. This period of time within which the stock option must be exercised is referred to as the "option term." Typically, stock option terms range between five to ten years from the date the option is granted. Occasionally, the expiration date of a stock option will be measured from the date the option shares vest. Once the stock option term has expired, the employee may no longer purchase the option shares.

In the case of an incentive stock option, the maximum permitted option term is ten years. If the employee owns stock possessing more than 10% of the total combined voting power of all classes of the company's outstanding stock, the maximum permitted option term for an ISO is five years.

1.2.9 Special Situations

From time to time, procedural questions may arise in connection with a stock option grant, such as how fractional shares of stock are to be allocated under the vesting schedule for the option. Most companies do not wish to show fractional shares vesting on a vesting date and will either drop or round the fractional amount. If the fraction is dropped, it is merely allocated to a later vesting period until the aggregate amount equals a whole share. If the fraction is rounded, it is usually rounded to the nearest whole share, and, if rounded down, the fractional amount is allocated to a later period until a whole share can be shown.

1.3 Exercising Options

1.3.1 Policies and Procedures

Consistent with the efficient administration of their employee stock option plans, many companies establish formal policies and procedures in connection with the exercise of their employee stock options. Formal guidelines for processing stock option exercises can serve as an effective means for ensuring that all company procedures are properly followed.

A comprehensive stock option plan policy should address:

- When the option may be exercised and the option shares purchased.
- The determination of the exercise date.
- How applicable withholding taxes are to be calculated and collected.
- The different treatment for directors and officers subject to Section 16 of the Securities Exchange Act of 1934 and other trading restrictions. (Section 16 regulates the trading of their own companies' securities by key corporate insiders, such as officers and directors, by requiring such insiders to publicly disclose their transactions in their companies' equity securities and to disgorge to their companies any "short-swing profits" realized from their trading activities in the companies' equity securities. Other trading restrictions, such as Exchange Act Rule 10b-5 and Regulation Blackout Trading Restriction ("BTR"), may also limit the ability of officers and directors to exercise their stock options and sell the underlying option shares.)
- Permissible exercise methods.
- Exercise limits.

A written procedure should address:

- The required documents for processing the exercise.
- The tasks of the plan administrator.
- Transfer agent communications.
- Broker communications (if applicable).
- Inter-departmental communications.

1.3.2   Exercisability

An employee's right to exercise a stock option will be governed by the terms of the grant agreement. Where the stock option is exercisable only as the option vests, the employee will be able to exercise the option only on or after the vesting date. Alternatively, where the stock option is exercisable before vesting, the employee will be able to exercise the option at any time during its term. Generally, the date of exercise will be considered to be the date on which the plan administrator or other designated representative of the company receives both an executed stock option exercise notice and payment of the total option exercise price for the number of option shares being purchased.

1.3.3 Notice of Exercise

To purchase the shares of stock underlying a stock option, the employee must follow the procedures established by the company for exercising the option. Typically, these procedures will be set forth in the employee's grant agreement. At a minimum, these procedures will require that the employee provide written notice to the company stating his or her intention to exercise all or a portion of his or her vested options.

To exercise a stock option, the employee will complete and sign a stock option exercise notice identifying the stock option being exercised and indicating the number of option shares that the employee intends to purchase. The exercise notice may also indicate how the employee intends to pay for the option shares. Most stock option plans require a written exercise notice as a prerequisite to a valid exercise in order to establish the exercise date and document the employee's intent to exercise.

The stock option exercise notice may also contain other information, such as (1) specific representations and/or statements by the employee deemed necessary by the company to ensure compliance with all required federal and/or state securities laws, (2) information relevant to the form of payment that the employee has selected to pay the total required option exercise price for the number of option shares being purchased, (3) specific statements pertaining to the tax withholding obligations of the employee, if any, arising in connection with the exercise, or (4) specific statements regarding any restrictions and/or conditions imposed on the option shares.

Generally, the stock option exercise notice must be submitted to the plan administrator or other designated representative of the company in person, or by registered or certified mail, return receipt requested, before the expiration date of the stock option, accompanied by full payment of the total required option exercise price for the number of option shares being purchased and any other required documents. Where the optionee is not a local employee, alternate procedures may be in place for the delivery of the stock option exercise notice and payment of the option exercise price (such as by facsimile or electronic transmission).

Where the stock option is being exercised by means of a broker's "same-day-sale" exercise (see below), additional documents may have to be executed by the employee in order to complete the transaction.

Many companies have eliminated much of the paperwork associated with stock option exercises by implementing electronic "self-service" exercise programs. Through these programs, employees are able to exercise their stock options via a Web site or an automated telephonic system. Readily available from many securities brokerage firms, these systems eliminate most of the manual data entry associated with option exercises and can also reduce the number of employee inquiries about exercise procedures.

1.3.4 Methods of Payment

An employee stock option plan may provide for a variety of methods for exercising a stock option—that is, for paying the purchase price for the option shares. These payment methods include cash (usually in the form of a check), stock swaps, brokers' "same-day sales," and use of a promissory note. Some plans also permit the delivery of already owned shares of stock or the withholding of option shares from the stock option exercise to satisfy the withholding tax obligation arising from the exercise. Company policy should set out the methods available to the employee and the relevant guidelines for each.

Cash Exercises. The most common form of payment for a stock option exercise is cash. At the time of exercise, the employee is required to remit the total required option exercise price for the option shares being purchased plus any withholding taxes due to the company. Generally, payment will be made in the form of a check made payable to the company. The company should decide whether a bank or cashiers' check is required for payment or whether a personal check is acceptable, whether separate checks are required for the total option exercise price and the taxes due, and the permissible time period for remitting payment.

Stock Swaps. When an employee elects to exercise a stock option by means of a stock swap, he or she is surrendering already owned shares of stock to pay the total required option exercise price for the option shares being purchased. Typically, the surrendered shares are valued at the fair market value of the company's stock on the date of exercise. An employee will be permitted to engage in a stock swap exercise only if the stock option plan expressly authorizes the delivery of already-owned shares of stock as a permissible payment method. The surrendered shares are either held by the company as treasury shares, returned to the plan share reserve for regrant (if permitted under the plan), or retired by the company (thereby reverting to the status of authorized but unissued shares).

Some employee stock option plans permit an optionee, in lieu of actually delivering shares to the company in order to exercise an option, to simply "attest" to owning sufficient shares to pay the total required option exercise price and, thereafter, receive from the company only the number of shares upon exercise that reflect the appreciation in the exercised option. In addition to the administrative benefits of this procedure, the attestation approach may provide additional recordkeeping and tracing advantages.

Officers and directors subject to Section 16 of the Securities Exchange Act of 1934 may, if certain requirements have been satisfied, engage in a stock swap without the transaction giving rise to either a "purchase" or "sale" for purposes of the "short-swing profits" recovery provision of Section 16(b).

For financial reporting purposes, generally the surrender of already-owned shares of stock to pay the total required exercise price for the exercise of an employee stock option will not trigger the recognition of a compensation expense. In the rare case where the optionee has the ability to compel the company to repurchase his or her option shares, a stock swap could give rise to liability accounting treatment under FAS 123(R). Thus, if a stock option plan contains a "put" feature, the company should confirm the accounting consequences of a stock swap exercise before permitting such transactions.

Reload Stock Options. Some employee stock option plans provide for the grant of so-called "reload" stock options in connection with stock swap exercises. Essentially, a reload option feature provides that upon a stock swap exercise, the employee will receive an automatic grant of a new stock option at the then-current fair market value of the company's stock for a number of shares of stock equal to the number of already-owned shares surrendered to the company to complete the stock swap exercise.

Brokers' "Same-Day-Sale" Exercises. A "same-day-sale" exercise is a means by which an employee can finance the exercise of a stock option by immediately selling through a securities brokerage firm that number of option shares from the stock option being exercised necessary to satisfy the payment of the total required option exercise price for the option shares being purchased plus any withholding taxes due to the company.

Generally to effect a "same-day-sale" transaction, an employee will first contact the plan administrator and indicate his or her decision to exercise a vested stock option. At that time, the employee will be advised of the securities brokerage firm or firms used by the company for these transactions and asked to select a broker (if the employee does not already use one of the brokerage firms included on the company's list). The employee will also complete the required forms for a standard stock option exercise (typically, a stock option exercise notice) and the additional forms necessary for a "same-day-sale" exercise (such as a set of irrevocable instructions to the company, a stock transfer power, a Form W-9, and, if a brokerage account needs to be established, a new account form and/or a margin agreement form).

Once the forms have been completed and the plan administrator has confirmed that the employee does, in fact, have sufficient option shares to cover the proposed transaction, the exercise notice and the irrevocable instructions (which may be integrated into a single document) will be immediately transmitted to the securities brokerage firm. The securities brokerage firm will also be instructed as to how many option shares are to be sold (either just enough to cover the total required option exercise price for the transaction and any associated withholding taxes or some greater number, up to all, of the option shares).

Following the sale, the company is notified of the sale price so that the required withholding taxes, if any, can be calculated. This figure is then transmitted to the securities brokerage firm so that it can divide the sales proceeds between the company and the employee.

Generally, within the settlement period (currently three business days), the securities brokerage firm will remit to the company the portion of the sales proceeds necessary to cover the total required option exercise price for the option shares being purchased and any applicable withholding taxes due to the company. This amount is usually paid by check, by wire transfer, or through a deposit into the company's account at the securities brokerage firm.

Typically, the company will not instruct its transfer agent to deliver a share certificate for the "same-day-sale" to the securities brokerage firm until payment of the option exercise price has been made. Upon receipt of the certificate, the transaction will be completed and the balance of the sale proceeds, less brokerage commissions, is remitted to the employee.

A company may make formal arrangements with one or more securities brokerage firms to facilitate "same-day-sale" exercises. Not only do such arrangements simplify the administration of these programs, they also enable the transactions to be completed more expeditiously. Sometimes referred to as "captive broker" programs, the company will keep the securities brokerage firm or firms updated on outstanding stock options and vested shares, thereby enabling the employee to contact the brokerage firm directly when he or she wants to exercise a stock option. To further simplify the administration of these transactions, some companies will establish an "omnibus" account with one or more securities brokerage firms and transfer a block of shares to the account for the purpose of ensuring that sufficient shares are available to deliver upon the settlement of the sale.

For income tax purposes, it is important for a company to satisfy itself as to when the option exercise is deemed to occur in the context of a "same-day-sale" transaction—either the date that the stock option exercise notice is submitted or the date that payment of the total required option exercise price is received. To the extent that these are different dates, the amount of income realized from the exercise, if any, and the applicable withholding taxes may vary. In addition, the determination may result in a difference between the exercise date and the sale date, thereby resulting in variations between the amount of gain reported by the company and by the securities brokerage firm. Companies employ various techniques to ensure that payment of the option exercise price is received or credited for the employee's benefit on the earliest possible date, such as providing in their stock option plans that delivery of the appropriate paperwork for a "same-day-sale" exercise will be an acceptable payment method or by arranging for immediate payment by, or receipt of a short-term "loan" from, a securities brokerage firm. The resolution of this matter for an individual company generally will be based upon the provisions of the company's stock option plan and/or the grant agreement, as well as by any applicable provisions of state corporate law.

Except as discussed below, officers and directors subject to Section 16 of the Securities Exchange Act of 1934 may participate in these "same-day-sale" exercise programs. As affiliates of the company, however, they are subject to certain restrictions not imposed on regular employees. For example, such "same-day-sale" exercise transactions may be restricted to the company's trading "window period." As affiliates, their sales of company stock also must be made in compliance with the conditions of Securities Act Rule 144, the resale exemption from the registration requirements of the Securities Act of 1933 that imposes certain conditions on any sale of securities by a company's officers and directors. In addition, in some circumstances, a "same-day sale exercise" may be viewed as involving either an extension of credit or an arrangement for the extension of credit in the form of a personal loan by the company, which is prohibited under Section 13(k) of the Securities Exchange Act of 1934. This prohibition precludes the directors and executive officers of companies that are subject to the reporting requirements of the Exchange Act from engaging in certain types of "same-day-sale" exercises. Accordingly, a company should consult with its legal counsel before allowing directors and executive officers to engage in a "same-day-sale" exercise of a stock option to ensure its procedure does not violate Section 13(k).

For financial reporting purposes, the implementation of a broker's "same-day-sale" exercise program does not result in the recognition of a compensation expense, because the company receives the full option exercise price for the option shares purchased, the company actually issues the shares, and no payment related to the exercise originates with the company.

Use of a Promissory Note. Some companies permit employees to deliver a promissory note to pay the total required option exercise price for the option shares being purchased. Generally, the promissory note will be a full recourse obligation secured by the option shares being purchased or other property acceptable to the company.

If the use of promissory notes is permitted, such arrangements must provide for the payment of at least the minimum amount of interest that is required under the Code. If the interest rate charged is less than the applicable federal rate, the Internal Revenue Service (IRS) will treat a portion of the amount repaid as imputed interest, which may have significant income tax consequences to the employee and the company. The applicable federal rates are published by the IRS monthly.

In addition, if the stock option is intended to be an incentive stock option, failure to provide for adequate interest for the promissory note may jeopardize the tax status of the option. Consequently, the promissory note must meet the interest requirements of Section 483 of the Code or interest will be imputed, thereby reducing the principal amount of the promissory note. To the extent that this occurs, the amount deemed paid for the option shares will be less than the fair market value of the company's stock on the date of grant. Because less than fair market value will be deemed paid for the shares, incentive stock option treatment will not be available, and the option may be considered to involve a deferral of compensation subject to Section 409A of the Code.

Under current accounting rules, a failure to provide for adequate interest in a promissory note may be viewed, under certain circumstances, as a reduction of the exercise price of the stock option, resulting in "variable" accounting treatment for the transaction. Thus, it will be necessary to confirm the accounting consequences of the use of a promissory note to exercise an option before permitting such transactions.

As previously noted, under Section 13(k) of the Securities Exchange Act of 1934, companies that are subject to the reporting requirements of the Exchange Act are prohibited from extending credit or arranging for the extension of credit in the form of a personal loan to their directors and executive officers. Because this prohibition applies to the delivery of a promissory note to purchase company stock, directors and executive officers may not exercise a stock option through the delivery of a promissory note.

1.3.5 Calculating the Gain on Exercise

Upon the exercise of a nonstatutory stock option, an optionee will recognize ordinary income in an amount equal to the difference between the fair market value of the option shares on the exercise date and the option's exercise price (the option "spread"). In the case of a "same-day-sale" exercise, the fair market value of the option shares should be determined without regard to the optionee's actual sale price or any brokerage commissions paid on the transaction. (Nonetheless, some companies use the sale price as the fair market value amount for purposes of making the ordinary income calculation.) Because the amount realized from the sale of the option shares may (and usually will) differ from the company's fair value calculation, the optionee must account for this discrepancy. Note that this amount should not affect the optionee's recognized income (nor the company's income tax deduction). Instead, it should be treated as a capital gain or loss (depending upon whether the amount realized by the optionee is more or less than his or her adjusted basis in the option shares). In this situation, the amount realized by the optionee should equal the sale price net of any brokerage commission, while the optionee's adjusted basis in the option shares is the sum of the option's exercise price and the ordinary income recognized from the transaction.

The calculation for the exercise of an ISO is more complex. At the outset, the transaction will involve a disqualifying disposition because the ISO holding periods will not have been satisfied. The general rule applicable to NSOs is modified in the case of an ISO. Section 422(c)(2) of the Code provides that if the amount realized from the sale is less than the fair market value of the option shares on the exercise date and the transaction would result in a realized loss by the optionee, the amount of ordinary income is limited to the difference between the amount realized and the optionee's basis in the option shares. In this case, any brokerage commissions incurred in the transaction would not be deducted in determining the amount realized by the optionee.

1.3.6 Withholding Taxes

Upon the exercise of a nonstatutory stock option, a company is obligated to withhold federal income tax from the optionee (if an employee) and, if the optionee is a resident of a state with an income tax, to withhold state income tax as well. In addition, withholding will be required for purposes of the Medicare insurance portion of the Federal Insurance Contributions Act (FICA) and may be required for purposes of the Social Security portion of FICA to the extent that the employee has not already satisfied his or her annual obligation.

Where the optionee is an employee of the company, arrangements must be made to satisfy any withholding tax obligations that arise in connection with the exercise. If the optionee is a local employee, generally any withholding tax payment due should accompany delivery of the stock option exercise notice. If the optionee is not a local employee, generally the date of exercise will be considered to be the date on which an executed stock option exercise notice is received by the company via facsimile or electronic transmission and/or funds representing the total required option exercise price for the number of option shares being purchased are wired to the company. The original exercise notice is then mailed to the company along with the necessary withholding tax payment, if applicable.

Where not addressed in the employee stock option plan or the grant agreement, the company may adopt a formal policy establishing the date on and price at which any applicable income and withholding taxes will be calculated. In accordance with Section 83 of the Code, the applicable taxes will be calculated based on the fair market value of the company's stock on the exercise date. If the amount of withholding taxes due cannot be calculated in advance, the policy usually states the time period within which the withholding tax payment must be received by the company. Frequently, a company will hold the certificate for the option shares purchased until full payment of all amounts due is received.

1.3.7 Trading Shares for Taxes

Some companies allow their employees to pay the withholding taxes due in connection with the exercise of a stock option by electing to have a portion of the option shares withheld from the exercise transaction. The number of option shares withheld to satisfy the withholding tax liability is usually calculated based on the fair market value of the company's stock on the date of exercise. The employee receives only the net shares (after taking account of the withholding) from the exercise of the stock option.

Officers and directors subject to Section 16 of the Securities Exchange Act of 1934 may, if certain requirements have been satisfied, elect to have shares withheld to pay withholding tax obligations without the transaction giving rise to a "sale" for purposes of the "short-swing profits" recovery provision of Section 16(b).

1.3.8 Exercise Restrictions

To control administrative costs, the company may adopt a formal policy establishing a minimum number of option shares that must be exercised at any one time. This may be especially important if the company's vesting schedule contemplates frequent (for example, monthly) vesting dates. For example, company policy may restrict the exercise of fewer than 100 option shares at a time unless the balance of the shares remaining in the grant are fewer than the minimum exercise amount.

1.3.9 Exercise of Unvested Shares

As previously described, some companies permit employees to exercise stock options before the date that the option shares vest. These unvested option shares will be subject to a right of repurchase in favor of the company in the event the employee terminates his or her employment before the vesting date. This right of repurchase expires either all at once or as to incremental portions of the option shares over the vesting period. When an exercise for unvested option shares occurs, typically the shares will be issued in the name of the employee and then held in escrow until they vest. The option shares cannot be sold while they are held in escrow, nor can they be used as collateral for loans. Consequently, the employee will usually execute and deliver to the company a form of joint escrow agreement or escrow instructions when exercising a stock option for unvested shares.

The unvested share repurchase right held by the company will be exercisable only upon the termination of employment of the employee and then only to the extent of any shares of stock previously acquired by the employee that remain unvested on the date of termination. Typically, the grant agreement will specify the rights and obligations of the company and the employee under this repurchase right.

Since a right of repurchase on unvested option shares renders the shares nontransferable and is considered to be a "substantial risk of forfeiture," the employee is normally not subject to taxation in connection with the purchase of the option shares until the shares vest. The employee may elect to close the compensatory element of the purchase and accelerate the time at which gain will be realized (and at which taxes, if any, will be paid) to the date of exercise by making a so-called "Section 83(b) election."

1.3.10 Confirmation of Exercise

After processing the exercise, generally the plan administrator will confirm the transaction by sending a written notice to the employee. In the case of an exercise of an incentive stock option, this notification is required by Section 6039 of the Code. The notification must include the following:

- The name, address, and identification number of the employer company.
- The name, address, and identification number of the employee purchasing the option shares.
- The date of grant.
- The date of exercise.

- The fair market value of the company's stock on the date of exercise.
- The number of option shares exercised.
- The type of stock option exercised.
- The total cost of the shares exercised.

In addition, this notification should be kept on file by the plan administrator, and one copy should be submitted to the accounting department along with the payment received for the total option exercise price. If the exercise of the stock option requires the withholding of income and/or employment taxes, a copy of the notification also should be provided to the payroll department.

1.3.11 Issuance of Shares

The plan administrator must provide instructions to the company's transfer agent for the preparation and issuance of a certificate for the option shares purchased. The instructions should include the number of shares of stock to be issued, the number of certificates to be issued, the correct name in which the shares are to be registered, and appropriate mailing instructions. Generally, the transfer agent's instructions require the signature of an authorized company representative.

In anticipation of the initial exercise of any stock options, the plan administrator should provide the company's transfer agent with a list of the relevant legends to be placed on the certificates for the option shares. Transfer agents or the company's legal counsel are usually able to assist with the drafting of these legends. Legends may be required by applicable federal and/or state securities laws in order to prevent transfers of the option shares that are not in compliance with such laws. In addition, if the option shares are subject to repurchase rights or transferability restrictions set forth in the stock option plan or imposed by the company, the certificates should be appropriately legended to notify potential purchasers of these restrictions. Some companies legend certificates for incentive stock option shares in order to track disqualifying dispositions.

If the exercise is pursuant to a broker's "same-day-sale" program, the plan administrator must also be in communication with the securities brokerage firm handling the transaction. Before the exercise, confirmation must be obtained that the option shares being purchased are vested. Although actual practice will vary between companies, the employee will typically verify exercisability and then either the employee or the plan administrator will contact the securities brokerage firm to arrange for the option shares to be sold. The securities brokerage firm will open an account for the employee if none currently exists. In addition to the stock option exercise notice, the employee must complete the appropriate documents authorizing the securities brokerage firm to sell all or a portion of the option shares.

1.3.12 Collateral Documents

In addition to the grant agreement, the company may provide several other documents to an employee in connection with the grant and/or exercise of a stock option. For purposes of compliance with applicable federal and/or state securities laws, it is customary for the company to provide each employee with a copy of the employee stock option plan or with a document (often referred to as the plan "prospectus") that summarizes the principal terms and conditions of the plan, describes the tax consequences of participation in the plan, and advises the employee where to obtain additional information about the company and the plan.

Other relevant documents may include a form of stock option exercise notice, memoranda describing the company's exercise procedures, investment representation letters or statements (in the event the option shares have not been registered with the Securities and Exchange Commission), escrow instructions (in the event the option may be exercised for unvested shares of stock), a form of promissory note and security agreement, and the appropriate forms for conducting a broker's "same-day-sale" exercise.

Many companies also prepare and distribute fact sheets and/or question and answer memoranda that address many of the common questions asked by employees concerning their stock option grants.

If the company maintains an internal employee Web site, some or all of these documents and information may be posted to the appropriate Web page or pages for optionee access.

1.4 Other Common Situations

1.4.1 Termination of Employment

An employee stock option plan usually addresses the treatment for stock options when an optionee terminates his or her employment or otherwise severs his or her relationship with the company. Typically, the optionee will have a specified period of time following termination in which to exercise his or her stock options to the extent of the option shares that have vested (and have not already been purchased) as of the date of termination. The optionee is not normally entitled to purchase option shares that vest after the termination date. This post-termination exercise period ranges in length from 30 to 90 days, depending upon the terms of the company's stock option plan. In the event that the termination of employment resulted from the death or disability of the optionee, the post-termination exercise period is typically extended to 6 or 12 months. Occasionally, in the event that the termination of employment resulted from the retirement of the optionee, the post-termination exercise period may be extended until the end of the option's full contractual term.

1.4.2   Repurchase of Unvested Shares

If the employee has exercised his or her stock option for unvested shares (which would be possible if the company allows its stock options to be exercised before the date that the option vests) and then terminates employment before these option shares have vested, the unvested shares will typically be subject to repurchase by the company.

Generally, the terms and conditions of the company's unvested share repurchase right will be set forth in the grant agreement. The company must notify the employee in writing within a specified period of time (usually two to three months following termination) of its decision to repurchase some or all of the unvested shares. The decision to repurchase the unvested shares is typically made by the board of directors. The repurchase price will be an amount equal to the original option price paid by the employee for the option shares. This payment will be made in cash or by cancellation of any outstanding indebtedness of the employee to the company. Typically, the company will hold the unvested shares pending vesting. Alternatively, if the option shares have been issued to the employee, payment of the repurchase amount will not take place unless and until the certificate for the unvested shares is delivered to the company.

1.4.3   Restrictions on Transfer

Occasionally, privately held companies impose restrictions on the ability of employees to transfer or dispose of vested option shares following the exercise of a stock option. Typically, the terms and conditions of these restrictions will be set forth in the grant agreement. The restrictions usually terminate when the company's securities become publicly traded.

1.4.4 Leaves of Absence

From time to time, an employee will be permitted to take a leave of absence from his or her position with the company. If the employee holds a stock option granted by the company, the plan administrator will face various questions concerning the status of the option during the leave of absence. For example, the company's stock option plan or the grant agreement may address how vesting will be calculated during the leave of absence. In the absence of an express provision, the company may want to establish a policy regarding whether the employee will receive vesting credit during all or any portion of the leave. Typically, companies will toll the vesting period (that is, suspend vesting) during an approved leave of absence unless vesting credit has been specifically authorized before the commencement of the leave or is required by law. Similarly, the company may want to establish a policy regarding whether the employee will be permitted to exercise his or her stock option while on leave.

For purposes of the "employment" requirement for incentive stock options, the income tax regulations provide that among other things, an employee must at all times during the period beginning with the date of grant of the stock option and ending on the date of exercise (or on the day three months before the date of such exercise) have been an employee of the company granting the option (or a related company). For these purposes, the employment relationship will be treated as continuing intact while the employee is on military, sick leave, or any other bona fide leave of absence if the period of such leave does not exceed three months. A leave of absence in excess of three months will not disrupt the employment relationship so long as the employee's right to reemployment with the company is guaranteed either by statute or by contract.

If the employee's leave of absence exceeds three months, or his or her right to reemployment is not guaranteed either by statute or by contract, the employment relationship will be deemed to have terminated on the first day immediately following the end of the three-month period. Thus, if the employment relationship is considered to have been terminated, the three-month period for preserving ISO status (and preferential tax treatment) will begin running, regardless of the company's determination of the status of the option for contractual purposes (that is, whether or not the post-termination exercise period will be deemed to have commenced). If the option is exercised within three months of the first day immediately following the end of the three-month period, the option will be treated as an incentive stock option. If the option is exercised more than three months after the first day immediately following the end of the three-month period, the option will be treated as a nonqualified stock option for tax purposes.

Although not relevant for income tax purposes, many companies apply the ISO standards regarding employment status to their nonqualified stock options as well. This enables them to determine when an employee's employment is to be considered terminated for purposes of calculating the commencement of the post-termination exercise period.

1.4.5 Capital Adjustments

From time to time, a company may engage in a transaction that changes or affects its capital structure, including its authorized capitalization and its outstanding securities. These transactions include, but are not limited to, stock splits, reverse stock splits, stock dividends, corporate combinations, recapitalizations or reclassifications of securities, and other changes that increase or decrease the number of outstanding securities that are effected without the receipt of consideration by the company.

Generally, an employee stock option plan will expressly provide for adjustments to be made in the number and class of shares of stock subject to the plan, and to the number of shares, option exercise price, and class of shares of stock subject to outstanding stock options, to ensure there is no dilution or enlargement of either the number of shares of stock authorized for issuance under the plan or the individual equity interests of optionees as a result of the transaction. These provisions usually grant the board of directors of the company broad latitude to make the necessary adjustments on an equitable basis.

A stock split occurs on a designated "record date." On that date, all the outstanding shares of record will be adjusted according to the split ratio. Grants and exercises of stock options that occur between the record date and the "payable date" must be adjusted to reflect post-split conditions.

1.4.6 Tax Withholding

Federal and state withholding obligations for income and employment tax purposes will arise at the time of exercise (or at the time of vesting, as the case may be) if the optionee is an employee with regard to the compensation income, or "wages," recognized, if any. Relevant withholding taxes include:

- Federal income.
- Social Security.
- Medicare.
- State income (if applicable).
- State disability or unemployment (if applicable).

For federal income tax purposes, the compensation income recognized upon the exercise (or vesting) of a nonstatutory stock option is treated as a supplemental wage payment. This payment is eligible for withholding one of two ways. First, the compensation income may be aggregated with the employee's regular salary payment for the period, with withholding computed on the total amount. Alternatively, the compensation income is eligible for withholding at the flat rate for supplemental wage payments.

In addition, employment taxes under FICA and the Federal Unemployment Tax Act (FUTA) may be due. FICA is made up of two separate taxes: (1) old age, survivor, and disability insurance (Social Security) and (2) hospital insurance (Medicare). The Social Security component of FICA is collected up to an annual maximum. The Medicare component is collected against the employee's total income. The FICA rates and their applicable ceilings, if any, are subject to change annually. Arrangements should be made with the company's payroll department for notification when any rate changes occur. FICA taxes are imposed on both the employee and the company, while FUTA taxes are levied against the company.

The withholding taxes collected by the company are only an estimate of the employee's ultimate tax liability. It may be necessary for the employee to make additional quarterly tax deposits depending upon his or her personal tax situation (or to remit additional amounts owed when tax returns are filed). The company must furnish an employee (or former employee) exercising a nonqualified stock option with a Form W-2 for the year of exercise (or vesting) reporting the compensation income recognized as "wages." If the optionee is a non-employee, the compensation income is not subject to withholding but must be reported on a Form 1099-MISC for the year of exercise (or vesting).

Most states follow the federal treatment for income tax purposes and may require the withholding of state disability or unemployment taxes. Generally, state taxes are determined on the basis of the employee's state of residence.

1.5 Disposition of Option Stock

1.5.1 Income Tax Issues

Upon a sale or other disposition of nonqualified stock option shares, the optionee generally recognizes a capital gain or loss equal to the difference between the optionee's adjusted tax basis in the option shares and the sale price. However, upon a sale or other disposition of incentive stock option shares, preferential tax treatment is available if certain holding periods are satisfied. These holding periods require that the employee not dispose of the option shares within two years from the date the incentive stock option is granted nor within one year from the date the option shares acquired through the exercise are transferred to the employee. The exact time of transfer may be unclear, but it is generally believed that a transfer takes place no later than when the option shares are recorded in the employee's name in the company's stock records.

If an employee sells or otherwise disposes of the option shares within one year after the date of transfer or within two years after the date of grant, the employee is considered to have made a "disqualifying disposition" of the option shares. Consequently, for the year of the disposition, the employee recognizes compensation income equal to the difference, if any, between the option price and the lesser of the fair market value of the company's stock on the date of exercise and the amount realized from the disposition. Any additional gain recognized as a result of the disposition will be treated as capital gain.

When an employee engages in a disqualifying disposition of ISO shares that were acquired before vesting, the amount of compensation income recognized by the employee will be equal to the difference, if any, between the option price and the fair market value of the company's stock on the date of vesting.

Generally, a "disqualifying disposition" occurs when an employee no longer possesses the legal power to control or further dispose of the option shares. Thus, the transfer of option shares acquired upon the exercise of an incentive stock option into "street name" or into joint tenancy (with a right of survivorship) will not be considered to be a disqualifying disposition. Nor will a pledge of the option shares, a transfer from a decedent to an estate, or a transfer by bequest or inheritance. Finally, transfers of the option shares to certain types of trusts will not be considered disqualifying dispositions. In contrast, a sale or exchange of the option shares, a bona fide inter vivos gift of the option shares, or any other transfer of legal title to the option shares will constitute disqualifying dispositions. Similarly, a foreclosure on pledged option shares in the event of a default will constitute a disqualifying disposition.

Where an employee transfers shares obtained upon exercise of an ISO to his or her non-employee spouse incident to a dissolution of marriage, the transfer is not considered to be a disqualifying disposition. And, under Section 424(c)(4) of the Code, the option shares will retain their ISO status in the hands of the non-employee spouse (including the original holding period). Where the non-employee spouse subsequently disposes of the option shares before the ISO holding periods have been satisfied, the transfer will then constitute a disqualifying disposition. The company should establish a procedure with its transfer agent to track all disqualifying dispositions.

1.5.2 Securities Law Restrictions

Requirements of the federal securities laws may limit the ability of an employee to resell shares of stock acquired upon the exercise of an employee stock option.

In the case of option shares that are acquired under an exemption from the registration requirements of the Securities Act of 1933, such shares are considered to be "restricted securities." Generally, restricted securities must be sold in reliance on the federal securities law resale exemption contained in Securities Act Rule 144.

In the case of option shares that have been registered for resale with the SEC, the shares may be resold by non-affiliates without regard to Securities Act Rule 144 and by affiliates in reliance on Rule 144 (but without regard to the holding period condition). The securities brokerage firm handling the sale may request company approval, generally of company legal counsel, before completing the transaction.

In addition, if the optionee is an officer or director of the company, he or she may be subject to a variety of so-called "insider trading" restrictions that may limit or prevent the sale. Accordingly, a company should always consult with the company's legal counsel before allowing an officer or director to engage in a sale or other disposition of shares, including option shares.

1.6 Conclusion

Administering an employee stock option plan in today's complex regulatory environment can be a challenging proposition. In addition to the tax, securities, and accounting rules that must be observed, a significant number of procedural matters must also be considered. A company adopting a stock option program for its employees will be well-advised to establish formal policies and procedures in order to ensure that all of the applicable legal requirements are satisfied, as well as the administrative aspects of the program. This includes guidelines for disseminating information and materials about awards granted to employees and for processing exercises when optionees elect to convert their awards to stock and, ultimately, to cash. Additional procedures can be implemented for addressing a variety of other common situations that may arise during the term of the plan. If these policies and procedures are implemented and consistently followed, the company can be assured that its employee stock option program will serve its primary objectives and that a high level of employee satisfaction can be achieved.

Federal Securities Law Considerations for Equity Compensation Plans

Eric Orsic and William J. Quinlan, Jr.

Contents

FOR A VARIETY OF REASONS, company stock continues to be one of the more popular forms of compensation. Most public companies maintain some form of stock benefits plan for their directors, officers, and/or key employees. In addition, many public companies are granting stock benefits at multiple levels within the organization, with some offering stock benefits to all full-time employees. Equity compensation plans are not, however, exclusive to public companies. In order to attract and/or retain talented individuals, many privately held entities and foreign issuers with operations in the United States are offering stock benefits to their key employees.

In recent years, the most common practice has been to adopt an omnibus-type equity compensation plan that covers not only stock options but also restricted stock (including restricted stock units and deferred stock units), stock appreciation rights, performance shares, performance units, and cash awards, along with deferred compensation arrangements. This chapter will focus on the securities law aspects of the foregoing benefits payable in stock.

Although equity compensation plans are exempt from the burdensome requirements of the Employee Retirement Income Security Act of 1974 (ERISA), there are still a number of important rules and regulations that apply. In particular, equity compensation plans maintained by "public companies" are subject to the Securities Exchange Act of 1934 (the "1934 Act"), which imposes various reporting requirements and restricts transactions in issuer securities by, among others, designated executive officers, directors, and persons with material non-public information. In addition, all equity compensation plans are potentially subject to the Securities Act of 1933 (the "1933 Act"), which requires registration of offers to sell securities unless a specific exemption from registration is available.

This chapter focuses on compliance with the federal securities laws rather than on enforcement. Suffice it to say that noncompliance can result in serious penalties and liabilities, including fines, forfeiture of profits, treble damages, and federal criminal prosecution, not to mention the adverse publicity and embarrassment to the corporation and the individuals involved. State securities laws must also be considered, but they are beyond the scope of this chapter. In addition, appendix A to this chapter discusses the executive compensation impact of the corporate reform and governance law known as the Sarbanes-Oxley Act of 2002.

This chapter also focuses briefly on the executive compensation rules made effective in 2007.

This chapter does not focus on Section 409A of the Internal Revenue Code of 1986, as amended, and its related IRS regulations, which may have a substantial impact on stock options, restricted stock, and all forms of deferred compensation for public and private companies.

2.1 Impact of the 1934 Act on Equity Compensation Plans

2.1.1 In General

An equity compensation plan maintained by a "public company" must be administered in light of Section 16 of the 1934 Act and the rules promulgated thereunder (the "Section 16 Rules"). The Section 16 Rules essentially consist of two parts. The first part is Section 16(a) and its related rules, which require directors, certain officers, and principal shareholders of "public companies" to report to the Securities and Exchange Commission (SEC) all transactions in the issuer's securities.[1] The second part is Section 16(b) and its related rules, which require such persons

---

1. 1934 Act, § 16(a) and Rules 16a-1 to 16a-13.

to disgorge any "short-swing profits" received from transactions in the issuer's securities.[2]

2.1.2 Definition of "Public Company"

As indicated above, the Section 16 Rules apply only to "public companies."[3] For these purposes, a "public company" includes any corporation whose stock is *listed* on a national securities exchange, including NASDAQ, which became a national securities exchange in August 2006, but excluding a "foreign private issuer" as described below. A "public company" can also include non-listed companies. Specifically, if a U.S. corporation has more than $10 million in assets (see SEC Rule 12g-1) *and* 500 or more shareholders, it will be considered a "public company" subject to the Section 16 Rules, regardless of whether its stock is listed on a national securities exchange or traded over-the-counter.

Becoming a "public company" due to size and the number of shareholders is an important consideration for non-listed companies that maintain equity compensation plans. If a corporation becomes a "public company" under the 500 shareholder/$10 million asset value rule, it must comply with the registration requirements under Section 12(g) of the 1934 Act, as well as the 1934 Act's proxy solicitation, periodic reporting, and short-swing trading provisions. Accordingly, non-listed corporations that grant stock options and other forms of equity compensation need to closely monitor the number of employees to whom shares are issued or sold to ensure that when and if outstanding awards are exercised or shares are otherwise delivered, the corporation will either stay below the 500-shareholder limit or will otherwise be in full compliance with the requirements of the 1934 Act.

2.1.3 Options as Equity Securities

The SEC takes the position that an option (but not a stock appreciation right) is an equity security for purposes of the 500-shareholder test. This means that, absent relief via a no-action letter or an exemption (see below), a private company can find itself subject to the 1934 Act if it grants options to more than 500 employees and/or consultants (and has more than $10 million in assets). At the present time, the SEC staff is not mix-

---

2. 1934 Act, § 16(b) and Rules 16b-1 to 16b-8.
3. 1934 Act, §§ 12(a) and 12(g)(1).

ing equity holders with option holders. For example, this means that a corporation could have 499 equity holders and up to 499 option holders without having to register under the 1934 Act.

Prior No-action Letter Relief. To get around this option problem, the Division of Corporation Finance issued a set of guidelines in its Current Issues and Rulemaking Projects Outline dated March 31, 2001 (an excerpt is included as appendix C to this chapter). The guidelines were not self-executing, which meant that a company with 500 or more holders of stock options had to seek no-action letter relief. One of the most recent no-action letters is AMIS Holdings, Inc. (July 30, 2001). This no-action letter contains an analysis of each of the guidelines required by the Division of Corporation Finance.

Failure to obtain a no-action letter on a *timely* basis resulted in the staff of the SEC refusing to grant a no-action letter request, thus requiring the corporation to register as a public company. To be timely, the no-action letter request must be made within 120 days of the end of the fiscal year in which the 500-option holder limit has been exceeded. This became a very serious problem for companies (with large groups of option holders) that were planning to go public. It resulted in rescission rights when the corporation did go public and missed the 120-day deadline.[4]

Exemption for Compensatory Employee Stock Options. On November 15, 2007, the SEC voted to adopt amendments to Rule 12h-1 of the 1934 Act to provide two exemptions for compensatory employee stock options. The first amendment provides an exemption for private non-reporting issuers from registration under Section 12(g) of the 1934 Act solely for compensatory employee stock options issued under employee stock option plans. Many of the concepts discussed in the Current Issues and Rulemaking Projects Outline mentioned above and in the AMIS Holdings, Inc., no-action letter are embodied in this exemption.

---

4. See, for example, the Google registration statement and prospectus. As a condition to Google's going public, and to remedy various state blue sky violations, the SEC required Google to prepare and distribute a rescission offer prospectus to all of its employees and other holders of stock options. The offer fixed as a rescission price that would be paid to accepting option holders the amount of 25% of the exercise price times the number of options granted. As one can imagine, no option holder accepted the rescission offer made by Google, but this process greatly complicated Google's ability to go public.

The second amendment provides an exemption for issuers that have been required to register under the 1934 Act and are required to file reports under Section 13 or 15(d) of the 1934 Act solely because they did not obtain a timely no-action letter. They are now exempt from the reporting requirements of the 1934 Act as long as they qualify for the new exemption from registration of compensatory stock options under Section 12(g) of the 1934 Act.

These exemptions apply only to an issuer's compensatory employee stock option program and do not extend to any class of securities underlying those options. These amendments became effective on December 7, 2007, upon publication in the Federal Register. The SEC has published the final release on its Web site. See Release No. 34-56887 for the specific requirements of these exemptions.

2.1.4 Foreign Private Issuers

Publicly listed securities of a foreign private issuer, as defined in SEC Rule 3b-4(c), are exempt from Section 16 pursuant to Rule 3a12-3(b) under the 1934 Act.[5] The term "foreign private issuer" is defined in Rule 3b-4(c) to mean any foreign issuer *except* an issuer meeting the following conditions:

1. More than 50% of the outstanding voting securities of such issuer are held of record either directly or through voting trust certificates or depositary receipts by residents of the United States; and

2. Any of the following:

    (a) The majority of the executive officers or directors are United States citizens or residents,

    (b) More than 50% of the assets of the issuer are located in the United States, or

    (c) The business of the issuer is administered principally in the United States.

For these purposes, the term "resident," as applied to security holders, means any person whose address appears on the records of the is-

---

5. The exemption in Rule 3a12-3(b) under the 1934 Act reads as follows:

    Securities registered by a foreign private issuer, as defined in Rule 3b-4, shall be exempt from sections 14(a), 14(b), 14(c), 14(f) and 16 of the Act.

suer, the voting trustee, or the depositary as being located in the United States. Note that there is no exemption for shareholders of foreign private issuers from the reporting obligations under Regulation 13D-G or for liability under Rule 10b-5, as described below.

2.1.5 Definition of "Reporting Persons"

The Section 16 reporting and short-swing profit rules do not apply to all transactions in issuer securities. Rather, only transactions by those individuals who are either "designated executive officers" of the public company[6] or members of its board of directors[7] (collectively "reporting persons") are subject to the information reporting requirements and short-swing trading restrictions contained in Section 16 of the 1934 Act.[8]

"Designated executive officers" for these purposes includes only those officers of the issuing corporation with certain high level, policy-making responsibilities who are designated as such by the corporation's board of directors (or a committee thereunder) and are listed each year in the issuer's Form 10-K (annual report).[9] For purposes of the Section 16 Rules, an "officer" has been judicially defined as "a corporate employee performing important executive duties of such character that he would be likely, in discharging these duties, to obtain confidential information that would aid him if he engaged in personal market transactions."[10] Merely having the title of an officer does not, by itself, cause an individual to become a "designated executive officer" for purposes of the Section 16 Rules. Instead, the determining factor is whether the individual's duties are commensurate with those of a policy-making position.

The term "officer" includes the following positions: president (CEO and COO); principal financial officer; principal accounting officer (or if there is no such accounting officer, the controller); any vice-president in charge of a principal business unit, division, or function; and any other officer or other person who performs a significant policy-making func-

---

6. 1934 Act, § 16(a), Rule 16a-1(f).

7. 1934 Act, § 3(a)(7).

8. The application of the Section 16 Rules to "principal shareholders" who are neither designated executive officers nor directors is beyond the scope of this chapter.

9. Rule 16a-1(f).

10. *Colby v. Klune*, 178 F.2d 872, 873 (2d Cir. 1949).

tion. This can include officers of a parent or subsidiary corporation if they perform a policy-making function for the entity that issues the stock in question.[11] The issuing corporation should notify every director or designated officer who becomes subject to the Section 16 Rules of his or her status as a Section 16 reporting person. The definition of "officer" in Rule 16a-1(f) contains a footnote instruction that has been interpreted to mean that, if the board of directors adopts a resolution naming its Section 16 officers, the list will be presumed exclusive and correct.

2.1.6 Beneficial Ownership

It is important to note that in most circumstances, a reporting person is presumed to be the owner of all securities in which the reporting person has a "pecuniary interest"—that is, the opportunity to profit or share in any profit, either directly or indirectly.[12] This includes securities held by a spouse, children, grandchildren, parent, grandparent, sibling, and other relatives *sharing the same household*, including step-, in-law, and adoptive relationships, and children living away from home while attending college ("household relatives").[13] For example:

> Officer "B" has a daughter who is in college, is financially dependent on "B," and owns Company X stock. "B's" daughter sells her stock in September. "B" must report the daughter's sale to the SEC on "B's" Form 4 within two business days of the sale.

Even if the reporting person and a relative are not sharing the same household, the reporting person will be deemed the beneficial owner of securities if he or she actually controls the purchase and sale of securities owned by the relative or if the relative is a minor child.

A reporting person may also be deemed to be the beneficial owner of any stock held by a trust, corporation, partnership, or other entity over which he or she has a controlling influence.[14] Special rules exist for trusts in which the reporting person acts as trustee and a member of his or her family (even if such person does not reside in the reporting person's household) has a pecuniary interest in the securities held by the trust.[15]

---

11. Rule 16a-1(f).
12. Rule 16a-1(a)(2).
13. Rule 16a-1(a)(2)(ii)(A), Rule 16a-1(e).
14. Rule 16a-1(a)(2)(ii)(B), (E), and (F).
15. See Rule 16a-8.

The potential application of the Section 16 Rules to shares held by household relatives and entities over which the reporting person has a controlling influence needs to be closely monitored to avoid inadvertent violation of the Section 16 Rules. If a question exists as to whether an individual is the beneficial owner of certain stock, a statement similar to the following can be included on the SEC stock ownership forms: "Reporting person expressly disclaims beneficial ownership of these shares. Reporting person cannot profit, directly or indirectly, from transactions in these securities."

2.2 Reporting Requirements Under Section 16(a) of the 1934 Act

Since August 29, 2002, all transactions (with certain limited exceptions) have been required to be reported within two business days of the date of the transaction. (See appendix A to this chapter, which provides more information on the Sarbanes-Oxley Act of 2002.)

Section 16(a) of the 1934 Act and the rules promulgated thereunder require reporting persons to report to the SEC all transactions in the issuer's securities. As described below, reporting persons must file three kinds of SEC stock ownership forms:

- Initially, a statement of beneficial ownership of issuer stock when the person first becomes subject to Section 16 (Form 3);

- Periodic, as-needed, statements of changes in beneficial ownership (Form 4); and

- Annual statements of changes in beneficial ownership, if needed (Form 5).

2.2.1 Form 3

A reporting person must file a statement of beneficial ownership of issuer stock on Form 3 when the person first becomes a director or designated executive officer of the issuer.[16] If the issuer is already a "public company," Form 3 must be filed—meaning received by the SEC—within 10 days after appointment or designation of the individual as a director or designated executive officer. Otherwise, Form 3 must be filed on or before the date the issuer becomes a public company.

---

16. 1934 Act, § 16(a), Rule 16a-3.

2.2.2 Forms 4 and 5

A reporting person is also required to file periodic statements of changes in beneficial ownership of issuer securities on Form 4 or Form 5, as applicable. Form 4 reports must be filed within two business days after the occurrence of the transaction resulting in a change in the reporting person's beneficial ownership (unless Form 4 is being used on a voluntary basis, as described below).[17] This would include changes in direct ownership of issuer securities, as well as changes in beneficial ownership by reason of transactions involving household relatives or entities over which the reporting person has a controlling interest.

Form 5 must be filed by a reporting person within 45 days after the end of the issuer's fiscal year and must report (1) transactions or changes in beneficial stock ownership not required to have been reported earlier on Form 4, and (2) transactions or changes that should have been reported earlier on Form 4 but were not ("delinquent filings").[18] A Form 5 would not be required from a reporting person who had no reportable transactions during the preceding year (Rule 16a-3(f)(2)). Any transaction normally reportable on Form 5 at year-end may be voluntarily reported on an earlier Form 4 filed at any time before the due date of the Form 5.[19] To avoid confusion and the risk of late or non-filing, it is recommended that transactions which are reportable on the year-end Form 5 be nevertheless reported as soon as possible on a voluntary Form 4 using the "V" code.

SEC Staff Same-Day Non-Aggregation Interpretation. For several years, U.S. stock markets have been using a decimal trading system. This means that transactions on the same day may differ by very small fractions. Until recently, many reporting persons have been reporting their same-day transactions on Form 4 using one line with a weighted average price. Unfortunately, in May 2007, the SEC staff issued an interpretation that requires each transaction to be reported on a separate line of the Form 4. (See Q&A 133.08.) For the following reasons, the SEC staff has been urged to reconsider this interpretation. It can lead to a confusing analysis of the transactions and can result in serious preparation errors. It also can make the two-business day reporting requirement very difficult to meet. For example, a recent reporting person had 191 sales transactions on

---

17. Rule 16a-3(a).

18. Rule 16a-3(f)(1)(ii).

19. Rule 16a-3(g)(5).

one day and 221 sales transactions on the next day. In each instance, the sales were made within 50 cents of each other. To comply with the SEC interpretation, the reporting person would have had to file 14 Form 4s because only 30 Table 1 transactions can be reported on a single Form 4. Complying with the two-business day rule would have been almost impossible. Instead the reporting person reported each day's transactions on a single line and used a weighted average price with an explanatory footnote. It is suggested that, in extreme situations when compliance with the two-business day rule would be very difficult, the weighted average price/explanatory note procedure should be used. The footnote should be worded as follows:

"Weighted average from ___ transactions with prices ranging from $_____ to $_____."

2.2.3 Electronic Filing of Section 16 Reports

The SEC has emphasized the importance of timely filing stock ownership forms. Before June 30, 2003, a document was deemed timely filed with the SEC for purposes of Section 16(a) only if it could be established that it was deposited with a delivery service in time for guaranteed delivery on or before the SEC deadline.[20] Effective June 30, 2003, all Section 16 filings must be made electronically. See SEC Release No. 34-47809 (May 7, 2003). In most instances, this filing must be made no later than 10 p.m. Eastern time on the second business day after the date of the transaction. To become fully versed in the electronic filing process, the following steps should be taken:

1. *Determine whether the Section 16 reporting persons already have EDGAR access codes, and if not, apply for them immediately.* A company's Section 16 reporting officers are not likely to have obtained SEC access codes through another source except for the CEO, who may be serving on other boards of directors that have already obtained the access codes. It is important not to apply for a second set of access codes for any reporting person who has already obtained an access code. Obtaining new codes will deactivate previous codes.

   Once the list of persons needing access codes has been obtained, prepare a Form ID for each insider. The Form ID must be filed

---

20. Rule 16a-3(h).

electronically and signed by the actual person unless a power of attorney has been obtained. A notarized copy of the Form ID must be faxed to the SEC at 202-504-2474. Turnaround time is one to two days. The SEC responds in email with the CIK code. One uses the CIK code and the passphrase, which is created during the electronic Form ID process, to electronically generate the remaining access codes.

2. *Determine which electronic filing system will be used.* Many companies are using software-based systems that have to be loaded on a computer or computers on the company's network. Examples of these systems include the Romeo & Dye Section 16 Filer (http://www.section16.net/Filer/) and Equity Edge (https://us.etrade.com/e/t/corporateservices). In addition, the SEC offers an online service, and the major printers are all offering Web-based systems for specific fees. These include:

- Bowne & Co., Inc. (https://www.bownefile16.com/bownefile16/)

- Merrill Corporation (http://www.merrillcorp.com/cps/rde/xchg/SID-53E1EF62-CC66DF3D/merrillcorp/hs.xsl/565_569.htm)

- RR Donnelley (http://www.rrd.com/wwwRRD/Tools/DocumentManagement/NETfiler/NETfiler.asp)

The local computer-based systems and the printers' Web-based systems both allow the continuing storage and retrieval of information about the issuer and the reporting persons and a general body of footnotes. The SEC's online system does not allow for the storage and retrieval of past information. This means that in the SEC's system, you start from scratch each time you use it.

3. *Start doing test filings immediately.* Once a particular system has been selected, the person designated as the Section 16 filing agent for a particular company should begin test filings immediately to work out the bugs contained in all of these systems with respect to the reporting of different types of ownership, the reporting of different classes of stock, and the use of footnotes and exhibits.

2.2.4 Web Site Posting of Section 16 Reports

The SEC has mandated (Rule 16a-3(k)) that on and after June 30, 2003, all Section 16 reports must be posted on the Web sites of public issuers that maintain Web sites (Release No. 34-47809). Failure to comply with these requirements could result in civil penalties under the general remedies provisions of Section 21 of the 1934 Act. The SEC has indicated three alternatives:

1. Direct posting on the issuer's Web site. Most companies have set up separate sections of their Web sites to hold just their Section 16 reports.

2. Linking to a third-party Web site. This can be accomplished as long as it contains all of the forms in segregated fashion and gives free access; for example, www.10KWizard.com.

3. Linking directly to the SEC's Web site. The SEC suggests in footnote 54 to its final release on electronic filings that the issuer can just use a hyperlink to the SEC's Web site dedicated to Section 16 filings. Footnote 54 indicates how that link should be worded and reads as follows:

> For example, an issuer could use a link such as the following where the issuer's Central Index Key (CIK) code is 0000906648: http://www.sec.gov/cgi-bin/browse-edgar?company=&CIK= 0000906648&owner=only&action=getcompany

The instructions to Forms 3, 4, and 5 require that these forms must also be filed with the stock exchange on which the issuer's securities are listed, if any. Now that the forms are required to be filed electronically, they will be deemed filed with the exchanges as well as with NASDAQ (which is now considered a securities exchange) without any additional filings with the exchanges or NASDAQ. This relief comes from SEC staff no-action letters to the exchanges dated July 22, 1998, and a no-action letter issued to NASDAQ dated August 1, 2006.

2.2.5 Transactions Required to Be Reported

Before the Sarbanes-Oxley Act, Forms 3, 4, and 5 were last revised in 1996, and the exemptions to such filings were broadened substantially. Certain stock transactions are now completely exempt from the reporting requirements of Section 16(a). The following will serve as a general guide for reporting transactions in issuer stock that may arise pursuant to a typical equity compensation plan:[21]

---

21. Rule 16a-4.

Transactions Required to Be Reported on Form 4 (Within Two Business Days):

- Grant or exercise of a stock option or stock appreciation right.

- Delivery of stock to issuer to pay for exercise price of an option (i.e., pursuant to a stock-for-stock exercise) or to pay taxes.

- Amendment of a stock option (including the repricing of an outstanding option and the grant of replacement option upon exercise of predecessor option) or stock appreciation right.

- Grant of stock awards in the form of restricted stock, restricted stock units, deferred stock units, certain performance shares, or performance units.

- Withholding of stock by the issuer to satisfy taxes required to be withheld on the exercise of an option or a stock appreciation right, or upon the vesting of a stock award or performance share award.

- Sale of stock acquired pursuant to the exercise of a stock option or stock appreciation right into the open market, including the sale of stock pursuant to a "cashless" option exercise arrangement.[22]

- Sale of stock received in connection with a stock award or a performance share award.

- Purchases and sales.

- Any of the foregoing transactions by a reporting person's spouse or other "household relatives," or by an entity over which the reporting person has a controlling interest.

Transactions Required to Be Reported on Form 4 Within Up to Five Business Days:

- Transactions under a Rule 10b5-1 plan (see appendix A).

- Discretionary transactions as defined in Rule 16b-3(f).

---

22. A "cashless exercise" is an arrangement under which a stock brokerage firm agrees to pay the issuer the funds required for the exercise of a stock option. The broker provides the funds either in the form of a loan to the option holder from a margin account in which the shares acquired are held as collateral or as an advance on the proceeds from the sale of some or all of the shares acquired on the exercise. Most brokers offer this service. See the discussion of cashless exercises in appendix A.

Transactions Required to Be Reported on Year-End Form 5 (But It Is Recommended That These Transactions Be Reported Earlier on a Voluntary Form 4):

- Gifts to anyone, including family members, public charities, and private foundations (Rule 16b-5).

- Transfers of stock or options to family members, or to a family-controlled entity for estate planning purposes (Rule 16b-5).

- Small acquisitions (not exceeding $10,000 in market value), but not from the issuer or an issuer sponsored stock benefit plan (Rule 16a-6).

Transactions That Are Not Required to Be Reported:

- Expiration or cancellation of stock options where no consideration is received by the reporting person (Rule 16a-4(d) and Rule 16b-6(d)).

- Vesting of an outstanding stock option, stock appreciation right, stock award, or certain performance shares.

- Change in beneficial ownership, i.e., from direct to indirect or vice versa (this exemption is strictly construed to require that the person's pecuniary interest does not change; for example, a gift to a minor child is not covered by this exemption even though the reporting person is deemed to have an indirect beneficial interest; such a gift must be reported on a voluntary Form 4 or a mandatory Form 5) (Rule 16a-13).

- Transfer of an option, SAR, stock award (including restricted stock units and deferred stock units), or performance shares pursuant to a domestic relations order, including any order entered pursuant to a divorce decree (Rule 16a-12).

- Dividend reinvestment plans or their equivalents, provided the issuer has a dividend reinvestment plan generally available to all its shareholders (Rule 16a-11).

- Transactions in "tax-conditioned plans" (other than "discretionary transactions"), including routine purchases under the payroll deduction provisions of a 401(k) plan, excess benefit plan, employee stock ownership plan (ESOP), or employee stock purchase plan (Rule 16b-3(c).

- Stock splits, reverse stock splits, and other recapitalizations, including possibly pro-rata distributions from limited partnerships and limited liability companies (Rule 16a-9).
- Dividend reinvestments and other stock activities in a rabbi trust.

Note that while the above-listed events do not have to be reported as transactions on the Section 16 stock ownership forms, the SEC does require that the net result of the transactions (other than transactions in a rabbi trust) be reported in the total ownership column with a footnote explanation at least once a year. Failure to do so does not, however, make the reporting person a delinquent filer.

As a general rule, reporting persons should assume that any transaction in issuer stock must be reported to the SEC, even if the transaction is involuntary on the part of the reporting person or, when combined with another transaction, results in no net change in ownership. Because of the new two–business day reporting requirement, reporting persons should be counseled to contact a designated representative of the issuer regarding any potential transaction involving the issuer's securities, no matter how minor it may seem, before consummating the transaction, to receive assistance in filing any needed SEC forms, as well as information regarding the potential Section 16(b) implications, which are described below. See the discussion in appendix A to this chapter concerning a mandatory pre-clearance policy and appendix B for the suggested form of pre-clearance policy.

Also, a reporting person who has retired, terminated employment, or otherwise ceased to be a reporting person continues to have reporting obligations for a limited period following cessation of "insider" status.[23] Such a person is still required to report opposite-way matchable non-exempt transactions on a Form 4 for six months after the last change in beneficial ownership while he or she was still a Section 16 reporting person. If a reporting person has not had any non-exempt transactions for the six months before his or her termination, then no further reporting obligation continues except for possible Form 5 filing requirements; i.e., a gift made while still employed and deferred to Form 5 reporting will still be required to be filed. See appendix D to this chapter for an explanation of exit strategies and a form of exit memorandum to be given to departing Section 16 reporting persons.

---

23. Rule 16a-2(b).

In addition, opposite-way non-exempt transactions made during the six months following cessation of insider status can be matched (for Section 16(b) purposes) with transactions made while an insider to find short-swing profits owed to the issuer. For example:

"A" will cease to be a director of Company X on October 1. On September 20, "A" sells Company X stock. "A" not only must report this sale on a Form 4 by September 22 (two business days) but also must continue to file Form 4s to report any non-exempt purchases that occur before the next March 20, and any such purchases will be matched with the September 20 sale.

Opposite-way exempt transactions and same-way non-exempt transactions made during the six months following cessation of insider status are not reportable.

2.2.6 Issuer Reporting of Noncompliance

As indicated above, the SEC is serious about compliance with the Section 16(a) reporting requirements. Accordingly, public companies are required to report any noncompliance pursuant to Item 405 of Regulation S-K.[24] This report is set out in the issuer's proxy statement for its annual meeting under an appropriate and discrete caption that reads "Section 16(a) Beneficial Ownership Reporting Compliance." The Section 16 Rules also clarify that the issuer is entitled to rely on the Forms 3, 4, and 5 furnished to it, as well as written representations by a reporting person that no Form 5 is required.[25] Also, the SEC can impose fines for late filings or enjoin the late filer from serving as a director or officer of the issuer and/or other public companies, although the SEC typically employs this additional penalty only in egregious cases.

The Section 16 Rules make it clear that the issuer is obligated to consider the absence of certain forms. Specifically, the absence of a Form 3 filing by a Section 16 reporting person is an indication that disclosure is required. Similarly, the absence of a Form 5 is an indication that disclosure is required, unless the issuer has received a written representation that no Form 5 is required, or the issuer otherwise knows that no such filing is required.[26] A "safe harbor" from disclosure is available for an issuer who receives a written representation from the reporting person

---

24. Item 405(a)(1), Regulation S-K (amended to eliminate the three-day mailing presumption).

25. Item 405(a)(2), Regulation S-K.

26. SEC Release No. 34-37260.

that no Form 5 was required.[27] This representation is usually set out in an officers and directors questionnaire, which the issuer should send out annually.

The SEC has recently amended Item 405 to eliminate the presumption that a Form 4 received by the issuer within three calendar days of the required transaction may be presumed to have been filed with the SEC by the required filing date. Because all Section 16 reports are required to be filed electronically, issuers are able to review the filings on EDGAR and determine whether a report was timely filed.

2.2.7 Reporting Recommendations

In light of the complexity of the Section 16 rules, the following recommendations will help in the administration of stock benefit plans (see appendix A to this chapter for recommendations covering all types of benefit plans):

- Have a mandatory pre-clearance policy for all transactions as to which the timing is within the control of the Section 16 reporting person.

- Establish a cashless exercise policy for Section 16 reporting persons in which the Section 16 reporting person obtains any credit extension from the broker or other third party of his or her choice (and not the issuer) and results in the issuer being paid the exercise price on the day of exercise. See appendix A for more information on this subject.

- Educate all Section 16 reporting persons by a memorandum, which they should read, sign, and return.

- Obtain powers of attorney with multiple attorneys-in-fact from all Section 16 reporting persons.

2.3 Six-Month "Short-Swing" Profit Recapture Under Section 16(b) of the 1934 Act

To deter insiders from profiting on short-term trading in the securities of their company, Section 16(b) of the 1934 Act requires a public company to recover from any such person the "statutory profit" realized by him or her in either a purchase and sale, or a sale and purchase (or any number

---

27. Item 405(b)(2), Regulation S-K.

of these transactions) which take place within a six-month period. It is important to note that the actual possession of inside information regarding the issuer is *not* a precondition to the recovery of short-swing profits under Section 16(b). This recoverable profit is not necessarily based on economic realities, and there have been situations where an individual actually lost money on a transaction but was held accountable for the return of "profits."

In determining whether there has been a purchase and sale within the meaning of Section 16(b), it is not necessary to establish that the same shares were purchased and sold, or sold and purchased, within the six-month period. Instead, all that needs to be established is that issuer stock (or warrants or similar rights to buy or sell issuer stock) was either purchased and sold, or sold and purchased, during a six-month period. The identity of the particular shares is irrelevant for determining Section 16(b) liability.

Like the reporting requirement under Section 16(a), Section 16(b) may apply to transactions made after an individual ceases having reporting-person status. That is, a purchase (or sale) after retirement or termination of employment from the issuer can be matched against any sale (or purchase) effected less than six months earlier at the time the individual was still a reporting person. See appendix D for more information on this subject.

To compute statutory short-swing profits, the highest sale price and lowest purchase price during the six-month period are matched, regardless of whether the sale and purchase involved the same shares. For a series of transactions, the difference between the highest sale price and the lowest purchase price during the period is computed (regardless of the order in which they occur), then the difference between the next highest sale price and the next lowest purchase price, and so forth. These differences are then totaled to determine the "profit realized" in a series of transactions. For example:

Director "D" effects the following 100-share lot transactions of Company X stock within a six-month period:

	Price per Share			
Purchases	$100	$80	$50	$30
Sales	90	70	40	40

Applying the method of calculation used under Section 16(b), the recoverable "profit realized" would be $8,000:

Transaction	*Profit*
Purchase at $30 and sale at $90 × 100 shares	$6,000
Purchase at $50 and sale at $70 × 100 shares	+2,000
	$8,000

For purposes of Section 16(b), it does not matter that Director "D" actually sustained an economic loss of $2,000 during the period:

Total of sale prices	$24,000
Total of purchase prices	– 26,000
Actual loss	($2,000)

As with Section 16(a), the director or officer is considered the beneficial owner of stock held by certain family members for short-swing profit purposes. For example:

> Officer "E" purchased Company X stock in September. His spouse, Mrs. "E," sold some shares of Company X stock in December. Despite the fact that Mrs. "E's" accounts were separate from her husband's, her sale would be matched with his purchase; consequently, Officer "E" is liable for any short-swing profit on the matched transactions.

The recovery for short-swing profits belongs to the issuer and cannot be waived by it. If an issuer fails or refuses to collect or sue a reporting person for short-swing profits within 60 days of demand by a shareholder, the shareholder may bring suit in the issuer's name for recovery. Courts have regularly awarded attorney's fees to the plaintiff's counsel in these actions based upon the amount recovered. As a result, there are "strike lawyers" who carefully review SEC reports for violation of Section 16(b), with the intention of bringing lawsuits against the reporting person and/or the directors of the issuer if the issuer's directors fail to do so after demand. These lawyers receive a percentage of the recovery (up to 30%) as a reward for bringing the action and obtaining a recovery for the issuer. Any unpaid Section 16(b) liability in excess of $120,000 must be shown as an indebtedness of the reporting person to the issuer in the issuer's proxy statement (Item 404(a) of Regulation S-K).

Computation of Six-Month Period. Profits are recoverable under Section 16(b) of the 1934 Act only if the transactions being matched occurred "within any period of less than six months." The computation of this period has been the subject of considerable litigation. For planning purposes we recommend making the computation by looking forward and backward six calendar months plus one day to the first transaction. For example, a purchase on January 1 will not be matched with a sale on July 2, nor will the sale on July 2 be matched with a purchase on the following January 3. This method of computation will avoid any possible litigation. We feel the only reason for using a more aggressive approach is if a particular Section 16 reporting person has bought and sold within a tighter timeframe.

Romeo & Dye's Section 16 Deskbook, which is the standard reference in the field, recommends using a less conservative approach, based on a line of cases beginning with *Stella v. Graham-Paige Motors Corp.:*[28] looking forward and backward six calendar months minus a day (compare our more conservative approach above, which is six months plus a day). Using Romeo and Dye's approach, a purchase on January 1 will not be matched with a sale on June 30 (i.e., January 1 to July 1 minus a day), nor will the sale on June 30 be matched with a purchase on the following December 29 (i.e., June 30 to December 30 minus a day). This topic is thoroughly covered in Part III-F-1 of *Romeo & Dye's Section 16 Deskbook.*

The date of purchase or sale is based on the existence of an irrevocable commitment, not the formalities of stock transfer, such as the delivery of stock certificates or the payment of the purchase price. See Part III-F-2 of *Romeo & Dye's Section 16 Deskbook.*

2.3.1 Section 16(b) Exemptions

Not every transaction in issuer securities is considered a "purchase" or "sale" for purposes of the short-swing trading prohibition. There are several important exclusions and exemptions from Section 16(b) for certain kinds of stock transactions, which are described below. The exclusions are set forth in Rule 16b-3, which is designed to facilitate the receipt of stock-based compensation by reporting persons without incurring liability under Section 16(b).[29]

Under Rule 16b-3, a transaction between the issuer and a reporting person that involves issuer equity securities will be exempt from the short-swing profit rules of Section 16(b) if it satisfies the appropriate conditions set forth in one of four categories: (1) tax-conditioned plans; (2) discretionary transactions; (3) grants, awards, and other acquisitions

---

28. 132 F. Supp. 100 (S.D.N.Y. 1955), *remanded on other grounds,* 232 F.2d 299 (2d Cir.), *cert. denied,* 352 U.S. 831 (1956).

29. 1934 Act, Rule 16b-3.

from the issuer; and (4) dispositions to the issuer.[30] The exemptions for tax-conditioned plans and discretionary transactions (with respect to profit sharing and 401(k) plans) generally are not available for discretionary equity compensation plan transactions[31] and are not described herein. The third and fourth exemptions are the ones that provide the relevant exemptions for equity compensation plan transactions and therefore are discussed below in greater detail.

Grants, Awards, and Other Acquisitions from the Issuer. Any grant or award of issuer stock from the issuer to a reporting person is an exempt transaction under Section 16(b) if it satisfies any one of the three conditions described below. Grant and award transactions are those that provide issuer stock to participants on a basis that does not require either the contribution of assets or the exercise of investment discretion by participants. Examples of grant and award transactions that are not participant-directed include grants of stock options, stock appreciation rights, restricted stock (including restricted stock units and deferred stock units), or performance share awards. A participant-directed transaction, on the other hand, requires the participant to exercise investment discretion as to either the timing of the transaction or the assets into which the investment is made. Examples of participant-directed transactions include the exercise of an option or stock appreciation right or the sale of shares acquired thereunder. Participant-directed dispositions to the issuer are potentially eligible for the "dispositions" exemption described below.

Any transaction involving a grant, award, or other acquisition by a reporting person from the issuer (other than a transaction meeting the definition of a discretionary transaction) will be exempt from Section 16(b) if any one or more of the following conditions are met:

---

30. The Section 16 Rules exempt only transactions between a reporting person and the issuer and not between the issuer and persons who are subject to Section 16 solely because they beneficially own greater than 10% of the issuer's equity securities.

31. This assumes the option plan is not an employee stock purchase plan that satisfies the relevant provisions of Section 423 of the Internal Revenue Code. Under the tax-conditioned plan exemption, certain transactions in issuer securities in connection with an employee stock purchase plan governed by Code Section 423 are exempt without further condition from Section 16(b).

- The issuer's board of directors or a committee of the board comprised of two or more "non-employee directors"[32] approves the acquisition in advance;[33]

- The issuer's shareholders approve the acquisition in advance or ratify it not later than the date of the next annual meeting of shareholders;[34] or

- The insider holds the securities acquired for six months following the date of acquisition.[35]

Thus, exercises of stock options or stock appreciation rights will be exempt from Section 16(b) if approved by the issuer's board of directors, by a committee consisting of two or more non-employee directors, or by the issuer's shareholders.

The SEC has made clear that this approval requirement relates to each specific transaction and is not satisfied by approval of a plan in its entirety, except for plans where the terms and conditions of each transaction are fixed in advance, such as a formula plan.[36] Where the terms of a subsequent transaction are provided at the time a transaction is initially approved, the subsequent transaction does not require further specific approval. For example, the acquisition of common stock that occurs upon the exercise of a stock option or stock appreciation rights is exempt as long as the exercise is pursuant to the express terms provided for in the option as originally approved.[37] Similarly, if an option as originally ap-

---

32. Under Rule 16b-3(b)(3), a "non-employee director" is defined as a director who (1) is not currently an officer or otherwise employed by the issuer, or a parent or subsidiary of the issuer; (2) does not receive compensation directly or indirectly from the issuer, its parent, or subsidiary for services rendered as a consultant or in any capacity other than as a director, except for an amount that does not exceed the dollar amount (currently $120,000) for which disclosure would not be required pursuant to Item 404(a) of Regulation S-K; and (3) does not possess an interest in any other transaction for which disclosure would be required pursuant to Item 404(a) of Regulation S-K (amended as part of the current executive compensation rules).

33. 1934 Act, Rule 16b-3(d)(1).

34. 1934 Act, Rule 16b-3(d)(2).

35. 1934 Act, Rule 16b-3(d)(3).

36. SEC Release No. 34-37260, Part II, D.

37. The disposition of the option that occurs upon exercise would be exempt pursuant to the rule relating to dispositions described below. In the same manner, if the terms of an award of stock options, as approved, provide for

proved specifically provides for the automatic grant of "reload" options, reload grants pursuant to those terms would not require subsequent approval. Conversely, if a reload option was not specifically contemplated at the time of approval of the initial option grant, the replacement grant would require approval in advance of the grant.

Note that if an option, SAR, or stock award does not satisfy one of the approval requirements, it may in any event qualify for an exemption from Section 16(b) under the six-month holding period rule. This rule provides that the acquisition of a security will be exempt from Section 16b-3 if the security is held by the recipient for six months following the acquisition or, in the case of a derivative security, if the underlying security is held for six months after the acquisition of the derivative security.[38] In the case of a stock option, this means that the grant will be an exempt *purchase* of issuer securities if the option (or the underlying issuer stock) is held for at least six months from the date of grant. For example, if an option is granted on May 1, 2005, and the option is exercised on or after November 1, 2005, the exercise of that option will be an exempt purchase that cannot be matched up with any other nonexempt sales. However, if the option is exercised earlier and the underlying stock is sold before November 1 (in this example), the option grant itself can be treated as a nonexempt purchase of issuer stock matchable against the subsequent sale.

Dispositions to the Issuer. In addition to the potential Section 16(b) impact of the grant or exercise of an option, the disposition of shares in connection with an option also must be considered. The issue here is whether or not a disposition of issuer securities in connection with or following the exercise of a stock option will be an exempt or nonexempt sale. In this regard, all dispositions of issuer securities by a reporting person pursuant to open market transactions will be treated as *nonexempt* sales that can potentially be matched against any nonexempt purchases occurring within six months of the sale. As a result, sales of issuer securities into the open market pursuant to a "cashless exercise" arrangement with

---

a stock-for-stock exercise (a "stock swap"), the disposition of company stock in connection with the subsequent stock swap would be exempt without further condition if effected pursuant to those terms. Conversely, if a stock swap was not approved at the time of the initial grant, it would require subsequent approval before exercise.

38. Rule 16b-3(d)(3), Note (3).

a broker or other third party will result in nonexempt sales of issuer securities by a reporting person.

However, dispositions of issuer securities *back to the issuer* will be exempt if approved in advance by the issuer's board of directors, by a committee of the board comprised of two or more non-employee directors, or by the shareholders.[39] Note that these are the same approval requirements described above in connection with grants, awards, and other acquisitions. Unlike the exemptions for "acquisitions," however, the six-month holding period rule does *not* apply to "dispositions" of issuer securities.

Thus, as long as the approval requirements are met, the Section 16(b) Rules will exempt a disposition of issuer stock by a reporting person *back to the issuer* pursuant to (1) the right to have securities withheld, or to deliver securities already owned, either in payment of the exercise price of an option or to satisfy the tax withholding consequences of an option exercise; (2) the expiration, cancellation, or surrender to the issuer of a stock option or stock appreciation right (SAR) in connection with the grant of a replacement or reload option;[40] or (3) the election to receive, and the receipt of, cash in complete or partial settlement of an SAR.[41] Additionally, the Section 16 Rules will give the issuer the flexibility to redeem its equity securities from reporting persons in connection with nonexempt replacement grants and in discrete compensatory situations such as individual buy-backs.

For issuers that intend to provide reporting persons with the ability to engage in share-for-share exercises or the delivery of issuer securities to satisfy tax withholding, it is recommended that these features be included in the original option grant so as to avoid the need for additional approval of the disposition of securities at the time of option exercise. Also, it is important to note that the sale of shares to pay the exercise price of an option under a cashless exercise program will be exempt from Section 16(b) *only* if the issuer is the purchaser, and not if the shares are sold on the open market by a broker or other third party.

---

39. SEC Release No. 34-37260, Part II, E.

40. A "reload option" generally means an option that is granted in replacement of shares purchased upon the exercise of a prior granted option. Reload option programs generally work in tandem with a stock-for-stock exercise feature. If the optionee exercises his or her option by delivering previously owned issuer shares, the issuer may grant a new option replacing the number of shares delivered to exercise the prior option.

41. SEC Release No. 34-37260, Part II, E.

SEC Revisions to Rule 16b-3 and Rule 16b-7.[42] The SEC amended Rules 16b-3 and 16b-7 under the 1934 Act in light of the decision of the U.S. Court of Appeals in *Levy v. Sterling Holding Company, LLC*, 314 F.3d 106 (3d Cir. 2002), cert. denied, 124 S. Ct. 389 (2003). In *Levy*, the court held that the provisions of these rules were not available to exempt from Section 16(b) of the 1934 Act acquisitions of issuer securities in a reclassification undertaken by the issuer before its initial public offering (IPO). The court's position permitted matching of those acquisitions with subsequent sales made within six months of the IPO, thus creating substantial Section 16(b) liability. As indicated above, Rule 16b-3(d) exempts from the application of Section 16(b) any transaction involving a

---

42. Rule 16b-7 exempts from Section 16(b) acquisitions and dispositions in transactions that are mergers, reclassifications, or consolidations that do not involve a significant change in the issuer's business or assets and that comply with an 85% continuing ownership test. The rule is typically relied on where a company reincorporates in a different state or reorganizes its corporate structure. The court in *Levy* held that Rule 16b-7 did not exempt an acquisition pursuant to a reclassification that resulted in an insider owning equity securities (common stock) with different risk characteristics from the securities (preferred stock) extinguished in the transaction and thus involved an increase in the percentage of the insider's common stock ownership where the preferred stock previously had not been convertible into common stock. To eliminate uncertainty generated by the court's ruling that Rule 16b-7 imposed different requirements for reclassifications than for mergers or consolidations, the SEC has revised Rule 16b-7 so that it states "merger, reclassification or consolidation" in each place it previously stated "merger or consolidation." In addition, the SEC has clarified that the exemption provided by Rule 16b-7 applies to any securities transaction that satisfies the conditions of the rule and is not conditioned on the transaction satisfying any other conditions. Revised Rule 16b-7 became effective August 9, 2005, but because it clarifies regulatory conditions that applied to that exemption since it was amended effective May 1, 1991, it is available to any transaction on or after May 1, 1991, that satisfies the regulatory conditions so clarified. The SEC has made clear that a reclassification includes any transaction in which the terms of the entire class or series of securities are changed, or the securities of the entire class or series are replaced with securities of a different class or series of securities of the company, and all holders of the reclassified class or series are entitled to receive the same form and amount of consideration per share. Rule 16b-7 also applies in such transactions where shareholders have the right to receive cash instead of stock by exercising their dissenters' appraisal rights, or the option to surrender their shares for stock or for cash in certain circumstances The SEC has also clarified that a transaction that has the same characteristics and effect as a reclassification, merger, or consolidation, whether domestic or foreign, is exempt without regard to its formal name.

grant, award, or other acquisition from the issuer if specified conditions are satisfied. The court in *Levy* held that the Rule 16b-3(d) exemption was applicable only if the grants, awards, or other acquisitions had some compensation-related aspect. To eliminate the uncertainty created by the court's ruling, the SEC has revised Rule 16b-3(d) to make it clear that any acquisition from the issuer (other than a discretionary transaction), including without limitation an award or grant, *whether or not intended for a compensatory or other particular purpose,* is exempt if any one of the Rule's three existing alternative conditions is satisfied. A similar revision has been made to Rule 16b-3(e) (dispositions to the issuer) since it has the same conditions as Rule 16b-3(d) and operates in the same way. The provisions of revised Rule 16b-3(d) became effective August 9, 2005, but because they clarify regulatory conditions that applied to this exemption since it became effective on August 15, 1996, they are available to any transaction on or after August 15, 1996, that satisfies the regulatory conditions so clarified. See SEC Release 33-8600.

Merger No-Action Letter. In 1999, the SEC issued a no-action letter setting forth how shares acquired by officers and directors of a public company within six months of that company being acquired for cash or stock in a merger can be protected from the short-swing profit recapture under Section 16(b) pursuant to the exemption in Rule 16b-3.[43] This no-action letter has become the standard under which these transactions are being conducted. It relies on the exemption for dispositions to the issuer in Rule 16b-3(e). Language should be put in merger documents to protect the directors and executives of public target companies referencing the procedures in this no-action letter.

Drafting and Other Considerations. Under the Section 16 Rules, it is no longer necessary that an employee benefit plan be in writing or that the plan receive shareholder approval in order to qualify for the Section 16b-3 exemptions. The shareholder approval element of the Section 16 Rules relates to each individual option grant rather than the plan in its entirety and therefore is not needed. As a result, most issuers will rely on the board of directors' or the committee's approval to satisfy an exemption under Section 16(b). However, most issuers have continued to seek shareholder approval of their equity compensation plans to satisfy other requirements, such as requirements of the stock exchanges, NAS-

---

43. See *Skadden, Arps, Slate, Meagher & Flom,* SEC No–Action Letter (April 28, 1999).

DAQ, state corporate law, Internal Revenue Code Section 162(m) (which requires shareholder approval of an option plan to qualify for one of the exemptions to the $1 million deduction limitation for compensation paid by public corporations), or Internal Revenue Code Section 422 (which requires shareholder approval of an equity compensation plan). Effective June 30, 2003, most equity compensation plans are required to be shareholder-approved under stock exchange and NASDAQ rules. See SEC Release 34-48108 (June 30, 2003).

Under Rule 16b-3 before the 1996 amendments, amending a stock option plan required shareholder approval if the amendment would (1) materially increase the benefits accruing to participants under the plan, (2) materially increase the number of securities that could be issued under the plan, or (3) materially modify the requirements for participation in the plan. Following the 1996 amendments, shareholder approval of plan amendments is not required, except for increases in shares to satisfy stock exchange rules, etc., as described above.

Employers with equity compensation plans adopted before the 1996 amendments to the Section 16 Rules may wish to amend their plans to remove some of the restrictions imposed by Rule 16b-3 before the 1996 amendments. For example, provisions requiring disinterested administration, restrictions on transferability of options, or shareholder approval of plan amendments (unless required by other rules or regulations) may be removed. Likewise, to the extent that the plan mandates a six-month holding period, this restriction may be removed, unless the issuer otherwise desires to retain the holding period to ensure the availability of an exemption under the Section 16 Rules without the need for shareholder, director, or committee approval. Note, however, that effective June 30, 2003, most of these changes require shareholder approval under NASDAQ and stock exchange rules.

Transaction Review and Assistance. Because of the complexities involved in reporting under Section 16(a) and the danger of short-swing recapture under Section 16(b), most companies have developed programs to assist directors and officers in complying with these federal statutes. The compliance program usually consists of the following:

- All directors and designated officers must contact the issuer's designated compliance officer before they, a family member, or a trust or other entity which they control engage in any transactions in company stock, including gifts, purchases, sales, etc.

- The designated compliance officer usually prepares the Section 16 reports and files them with the SEC.

- All directors and designated officers are requested to execute a power of attorney enabling the designated compliance officer to sign and file the necessary forms with the SEC.

- Brokers representing directors and designated officers are informed of the company's policies concerning insider trading and Section 16 reporting.

See the model pre-clearance policy included as appendix B to this chapter.

2.4 Trading While in Possession of Inside Information

As a general rule, any person with material non-public information about the issuer is obligated under Rule 10b-5 under the 1934 Act to refrain from purchasing or selling common stock until such information has been released into the marketplace.[44] Although stock options or stock appreciation rights may be exercised at any time even if the holder has material non-public information about the issuer, such person is obligated under Rule 10b-5 to refrain from selling common stock acquired upon exercise of an option or stock appreciation right until the material non-public information has been released into the marketplace.

To be found liable for insider trading, the reporting person must have benefited from material, non-public information in connection with a purchase or sale of a security. (Using material, non-public information to refrain from a purchase or sale does not violate Rule 10b-5.) Information is considered "material" for these purposes if there is a substantial likelihood that a reasonable investor would consider it important in arriving at a decision to buy, sell, or hold stock of the issuer. Examples of inside information that might be deemed material include:

---

44. Also, the Insider Trading and Securities Fraud Enforcement Act provides civil penalties for insider trading in the amount of the greater of $1 million or three times the profit gained or loss avoided. It also prescribes criminal penalties of a maximum 10-year jail term and a maximum fine of $1 million for individuals.

- Actual or projected sales or earnings (including changes of previously announced estimates).
- Actual or projected significant capital expenditures.
- Actual or projected significant borrowings.
- Public or private sale of a significant amount of additional securities of the company, or major financings or refinancings.
- Non-business matters affecting the market for company securities (such as upcoming research, brokerage firm recommendations, or the intention of parties to buy or sell an abnormal amount of securities).
- A proposed merger, acquisition, joint venture, or disposition of stocks or assets, or a tender offer for another company's securities.
- Any action or event that could have a significant effect on annual sales or earnings.
- Any action or event that may result in a special or extraordinary charge against earnings or capital, or significant changes in asset values or lines of business.
- A significant change in capital investment plans.
- Major new products, discoveries, or services.
- A call of securities for redemption or a program to repurchase company shares.
- A change in control or significant management changes.
- Significant litigation and changes in pending litigation.
- Significant changes in operating or financial circumstances.
- Significant labor disputes or other pay-related issues.
- Significant actions by regulatory bodies.
- Prohibited information on other companies learned through special business relationships with them.
- Dividend increases or decreases.
- Rating agency upgrades or downgrades.

The foregoing list is for illustration only and is not exhaustive; other types of information may be material at particular times, depending upon all the circumstances.

Insider Trading Policies. The most dangerous time to engage in a purchase or sale of issuer stock is shortly in advance of the public release by the issuer of important financial information, such as quarterly or year-end results, or other important news. Many companies impose blackouts on their officers and directors beginning 15 days before the end of the quarter or fiscal year and ending 2 or 3 days after the releases of earnings. The safest time to engage in purchases or sales is the period—commonly referred to as a window period—shortly following the release and publication of such information. However, even engaging in transactions during a window period presumes that the person is not aware of any other material information which has not been made public. Even after such information has been released, it is important to be sure that sufficient time has elapsed to enable the information to be disseminated to and considered by investors.

Stock Transactions During Blackout Periods. Insider trading policies generally prohibit cashless exercises of stock options (involving open market sales through a broker or other third party) while in possession of material non-public information, but they do not prohibit stock-for-stock exercises or share withholding to pay taxes where the issuer is the purchaser. These transactions are with the issuer, which is the ultimate insider and is presumed to have full knowledge. If the issuer is holding back on "good news," these transactions will be at a bargain price to the issuer and will not create insider trading liability as long as the person exercising the option has full knowledge of the "good news." If the issuer is holding back on "bad news," the person exercising the option by the delivery of previously owned shares is getting the benefit of too high a price for those shares, but once again this should not create insider trading liability. At worst, it creates a claim of corporate waste by the shareholders if they become aware of the transaction. This claim should be defended against on the basis of the "business judgment rule" that it was in the best interest of the company to permit the transaction. Given the shareholder and SEC activity in the area of option exercises, the authors now believe the safer practice would be to *prohibit* stock-for-stock exercises and share withholding to pay taxes during the company's traditional black-out periods. See further discussion in the following paragraphs.

In a 2005 SEC investigation involving Analog Devices, Inc. (NYSE: ADI), the SEC appeared to be concerned about a company granting stock options to its directors and executive officers immediately before the announcement of good news. In connection with the settlement, ADI consented to a cease-and-desist order under Section 10(b) of the Securities Exchange Act and Rule 10b-5 thereunder, paid a civil money penalty of $3 million, and repriced options granted to the CEO and other directors in certain years. Options granted to all other employees were excluded from the repricing. The CEO consented to a cease-and-desist order under Sections 17(a)(2) and (3) of the Securities Act, paid a civil money penalty of $1 million, and made a disgorgement payment with respect to options granted in certain years.

Taking this SEC concern to the next level could lead one to conclude that the SEC would be equally concerned with a company permitting the delivery of previously owned shares to pay the exercise price of a stock option or related taxes at a time when the company was in a blackout involving the nondisclosure of material adverse information. In light of the SEC's activity in this area, it may be sensible for a public company's insider trading policy to include the delivery of shares to pay the exercise price or related taxes.

2.4.1 Backdating of Stock Option Grants

On an almost daily basis, corporations are announcing their involvement in investigations concerning the timing of stock option grants made to senior executives. These investigations—which are being separately pursued by the SEC and the U.S. Department of Justice (DOJ)—have prompted financial restatements by some corporations and in some instances have led to the resignations of senior corporate officials.

The issue catalyzing these investigations is whether corporations used stock option grants to improperly enrich their senior executives. These investigations focus on two main issues:

- Whether options were "backdated," or retroactively granted on a date when the stock price was low in order to build in a profit for the executives

- Whether the options were "spring-loaded," or granted immediately before corporate announcements that were likely to increase the price of the shares

The options backdating investigations raise both civil and criminal issues for corporations and their executives. The SEC is investigating whether companies backdated options to provide undisclosed compensation to senior executives and whether the failure to disclose this practice constituted securities fraud. Thus, these recent investigations focus on how companies report and disclose backdated options for financial and tax reporting purposes.

Similarly, the DOJ is also looking at these cases from a criminal standpoint, i.e., was there fraud? Were documents altered or misdated as a part of the fraud? Finally, were shareholders told the truth about the option grants and the compensation of corporate officials? The corporations and executives involved in improperly backdating options may face securities, mail, and wire fraud charges as well as tax charges. Private civil litigation involving these same issues also has been filed against some companies.

Because of the potential civil and criminal liability that companies and their officers may face, corporations suspecting they may have problems relating to the backdating of options need to evaluate a number of possible compliance issues and should consult counsel. In some instances, corporations acting through special committees of the board of directors may want to seek independent counsel to investigate such problems.

It should be noted that options backdating can occur without any intentional wrongdoing merely due to failures in corporate procedures. Even though such inadvertent errors are uncommon, the consequences can be serious.

The current executive compensation rules discussed below address this issue of option backdating in a disclosure manner. If the options are not granted at the "closing market price" (last sales price), an extra column must be added in the proxy statement in the table disclosing option grants showing the difference between the grant price and the closing market price. Many omnibus plans have a definition of fair market value related to the average of the high and low prices on either the date of grant or the date preceding the date of grant. This definition will trigger the disclosure discussed above. Many public companies are either amending their plans or adopting compensation committee resolutions providing that options will only be granted at the closing market price (last sales price) on the date of grant. This concept of last sales price is also applicable to any use of fair market value for equity compensation plans; i.e., for the delivery of previously owned shares to pay the exercise price or for share withholding to pay taxes.

The SEC's website (sec.gov) contains a link entitled "Stock Options Backdating" (on the left-hand side of the SEC home page at the time of this writing) which presents considerable information on this subject, including enforcement actions, Commission speeches, Commission Staff speeches, and listing of complaints brought by the SEC.

2.5   1933 Act Registration Requirements; Resales by Plan Participants

The 1933 Act makes it unlawful for any person to sell or to offer to sell any security unless an effective registration statement has been filed and declared effective with respect to such security or the offer (sale) is pursuant to an available exemption from registration.[45] There are a number of exemptions from the registration rules listed below that may be available for stock issued pursuant to an employer-sponsored equity compensation plan. Failure to comply with the registration requirements may give the purchaser of securities a rescission right.[46] In order to allow for marketability of shares acquired in connection with an equity compensation plan, it is important to make sure the shares have been properly registered or an exemption from registration is available.

2.5.1   Registration Requirements

Section 5 of the 1933 Act provides that it is unlawful for any person, directly or indirectly, to use any form of interstate transportation or communication or the mails to offer a security for sale unless a registration statement has been filed with respect to such security or to sell, carry, or deliver for sale any security unless a registration statement is in effect for such security.[47] Thus, in implementing an equity-based compensation arrangement, an employer must consider whether the arrangement involves the issuance of a security and, if so, whether the security to be issued under such plan should be registered pursuant to the provisions of the 1933 Act, or whether one or more exemptions from registration may be available.

Even if an exemption from registration is applicable, the employer should also consider whether participants in the plan are, without violation of federal securities laws, free to sell securities received under such a plan. The latter consideration, of course, relates to the value of the plan benefits to employees as an incentive compensation device.

---

45. 1933 Act, § 5.

46. 1933 Act, § 12.

47. 1933 Act, § 5(a)(1).

Registration on Form S-8. If an issuer is subject to the reporting requirements of the 1934 Act—that is, the issuer is a "public company" (including, in this instance, a foreign private issuer)—registration of stock to be issued to officers, directors, and employees under any employee benefit plan of the employer can be accomplished very simply by filing Form S-8 with the SEC.[48] The Form S-8 consists of a prospectus and a registration statement. This registration statement registers a fixed number of shares for use with respect to the benefit plan. When those shares are used up, a new registration statement should be filed. The registration statement incorporates by reference the employer's current and future 1934 Act reports, including certain information incorporated into such reports to satisfy certain Form S-8 updating requirements. The prospectus is not filed with the SEC. Thus, the registration statement can remain "alive" for a number of years (until the registered shares are used up) without any need to rewrite and redistribute the prospectus. Most changes to the information in the prospectus can be made by means of a prospectus supplement or appendix. Not only does registering the stock on Form S-8 satisfy the employer's requirements under Section 5 of the 1933 Act, it also permits all plan participants, except "affiliates," to sell stock received under the registered plan freely and immediately. It also preempts filing requirements in most states.

- *Sales by Affiliates.* As a result of their control relationship with the employer, affiliates[49] may be deemed to be acting as the corporate issuer when they sell the issuer's stock. Thus, even though stock issued pursuant to an equity compensation plan may be registered on Form S-8, an affiliate may not freely sell such stock unless an exemption applies or unless the affiliate's sale itself is registered.[50] In most cases, resales by affiliates are made pursuant to the exemption from registration provided by SEC Rule 144.[51] If the shares being sold by the affiliate have been registered under the 1933 Act (on Form S-8, for example), the six-month holding period requirement (previously

---

48. SEC Release No. 33-6188, Part VI, A.

49. An "affiliate" is defined as any person in control or sharing control of the issuer. All directors, the CEO, CFO, and general counsel are presumed to be affiliates. Other vice presidents are presumed *not* to be affiliates. This is a question of fact to be determined by each company and its counsel.

50. SEC Release No. 33-6188, Part VI, A.

51. For a more detailed discussion of Rule 144, see "1933 Act Registration Requirements; Resales by Plan Participants—Sales Under Rule 144" below.

one year) of Rule 144 does not apply. However, the other conditions of Rule 144 continue to apply.

As an alternative to Rule 144, an affiliate's shares can be registered for resale, either by means of a separate registration statement or by means of a resale prospectus filed together with the plan's registration statement on Form S-8. A resale prospectus filed with Form S-8 may under certain circumstances be prepared in accordance with the requirements of Form S-3, even though the issuer is not otherwise eligible to use that abbreviated form. Most companies do not use this resale prospectus because of the negative impact it has on the trading market for the stock: the public shareholders could construe it as a vote of no confidence by the company's affiliates.

Finally, an affiliate may be able to sell stock received under a stock plan in a privately negotiated transaction. However, the various considerations that apply to such sales under the securities laws are complex, and careful consultation with counsel is recommended before any such transaction is undertaken.

Issuance of Stock Without Registration. In certain instances, stock can be issued pursuant to an equity compensation plan without registration of the stock or the plan. However, under most of the available exemptions from registration, the participant will receive stock that is not freely tradable. Some of the exemptions from registration do not require the employer to provide specified information; nevertheless, sales under any of these exemptions will remain subject to the antifraud provisions of the 1933 and 1934 Acts. Several of the commonly used exemptions from registration for equity compensation plans are briefly described below.

- *Non-public Offering.* Section 4(2) of the 1933 Act provides an exemption for a "private placement" of securities, which is an offering of stock to a limited number of investors who have access to the same information normally provided in a public offering *and* who are sophisticated enough both to assess and bear the risks of investing in the issuer's securities. No specific information is required to be disclosed to purchasers, but their access to information about the employer is generally considered to be an element of the exemption. This exemption may be available for the issuance of stock to the employer's top executives, but it is less likely to be available for a broad-based stock compensation program.

- *Regulation D Offerings.* Regulation D contains three alternative exemptions from registration under Section 3(b) of the 1933 Act, set forth as Rules 504, 505, and 506.[52] All of the Regulation D exemptions require the filing of a relatively simple form with the SEC. Rule 505 provides an exemption to offerings of up to $5 million in any 12-month period to as many as 35 nonaccredited investors. Note that the $5 million limit during any such 12-month period is reduced by the amount of any other offerings exempt under Section 3(b) of the 1933 Act.

  Rule 504 exempts an offering of up to $1 million of stock in any 12-month period, again reduced by the amount of any other offerings exempt under Section 3(b) of the 1933 Act. The Rule 504 exemption does *not* require that offerees be sophisticated or knowledgeable about the issuer or that specific information about the issuer be disclosed. However, the dollar limitation of Rule 504 can be a significant problem in the case of a stock option plan because the offering is deemed to be continuing for the entire period during which the options are exercisable.

  The final Regulation D exemption from registration is found in Rule 506. Rule 506 does not limit the size of the offering but instead limits the number of purchasers and requires that purchasers, either alone or with a financial advisor, be capable of evaluating the investment. Under both Rule 505 and Rule 506, specific disclosures are required unless the offering is made exclusively to "accredited investors" (which term includes executive officers, directors, and as well as individuals meeting specified income or net worth tests).

- *Rule 701.* Rule 701 (as described in greater detail below) can also exempt sales under compensatory benefit plans if certain conditions are met.[53] This exemption is non-exclusive and can be used in conjunction with Regulation D and other exemptions. In the authors' view, an exemption under Rule 701 is preferable to Regulation D, and in many cases an exemption under Regulation D is a fallback to qualifying under Rule 701.

2.5.2   Rule 701

For certain compensatory issuances of stock or stock options to employees and other service providers, Rule 701 provides an exemption from the

---

52. 1933 Act, Rules 504-506.
53. 1933 Act, Rule 701.

registration requirements of the 1933 Act for offers and sales of securities. The primary features of Rule 701 are as follows:

- The purpose of the issuance must be compensation. If the purpose of the plan is to circumvent registration requirements and is not for compensation purposes, then the exemption is not available.

- Rule 701 is an exemption from federal securities laws and does not provide an exemption from applicable state securities laws. Many states, however, have adopted equivalent exemptions that either specifically provide for issuances made pursuant to Rule 701 or generally exempt issuances that are made for compensatory purposes.

- The issuer cannot be a reporting company under Section 13 or 15(d) of the 1934 Act nor an investment company required to be registered under the Investment Company Act of 1940.[54]

- The participants may be employees, directors, general partners, trustees (if the issuer is a business trust), officers, or consultants and advisors, and their family members who acquire such securities through gifts or domestic relations orders.[55] Further limitations on the participants are detailed below.

- Limitations are imposed on the sales price or amount of securities that can be issued pursuant to Rule 701. Basically, the limitation is that during any 12-month period the aggregate sales price or amount of securities sold in reliance on Rule 701 cannot exceed the greatest of (1) $1 million, (2) 15% of the total assets of the issuer, or (3) 15% of the outstanding amount of the class of securities being offered and sold in reliance on Rule 701. Further details are provided below.

- Although this is an issuer-only exemption, Rule 701 also provides special rules for resale after the company has gone public. Further resale details are provided below.

---

54. A privately held subsidiary of publicly held parent may rely on Rule 701, and may issue securities to its publicly held parent or other majority-owned subsidiaries of its parent. *American Bar Association*, SEC No-Action Letter [1999–2000 Transfer Binder] Fed. Sec. L. Rep. (CCH) ¶ 77,604 at 76,132 (Aug. 3, 1999).

55. Former employees, directors, general partners, trustees, officers, or consultants and advisors can participate only if they were employed by or provided services to the issuer at the time the securities were offered.

- No SEC notice is necessary for an issuance pursuant to Rule 701. Notice requirements, however, exist under some state securities regulations.

- The issuance must be made pursuant to a written compensation contract or written compensatory plan.[56]

- Disclosures must be provided. The issuer must deliver to investors a copy of the benefit plan or contract. If the aggregate sales price or amount of securities sold exceeds $5 million in a consecutive 12-month period, then certain other disclosures (including U.S. GAAP financial statements of the issuer) must be made within a reasonable period before the date of sale, as detailed below.

- Rule 701 transactions are not integrated with other exempt transactions.[57]

- Rule 701 is not exclusive, so that other exemptions may be claimed.

Participants. As noted above, the participants may be employees, directors, general partners, trustees (if the issuer is a business trust), officers, or consultants and advisors, and their family members who acquire such securities through gifts or domestic relations orders. In a 1999 amendment of Rule 701, the SEC significantly restricted the definition of "consultants and advisors" who may participate in a Rule 701 issuance and harmonized the Rule 701 interpretation of the phrase with the Form S-8 interpretation.[58] Consultants and advisors must be natural persons and provide bona fide services to the issuer, its parents, or their majority-owned subsidiaries.

In addition to the above basic requirements to be a consultant or advisor, securities promoters may not participate under the exemption because they do not qualify as consultants or advisors. This exclusion covers people whose services are inherently capital-raising or promotional, such as brokers, dealers, those who find investors, those who provide shareholder communications services, and those who arrange

---

56. A compensatory benefit plan is defined as any purchase, savings, option, bonus, stock appreciation, profit sharing, thrift, incentive, deferred compensation, pension, or similar plan.

57. A general solicitation in connection with a Rule 701 transaction, however, may cause an integration problem with respect to exemptions that do not permit general solicitation.

58. SEC Release No. 33-7646 (April 7, 1999).

for mergers or take the company private. Business advisors whose activities are not inherently capital-raising or promotional would be allowed to participate in an offering under Rule 701.

Independent agents, franchisees, and salespersons that do not have an employment relationship with the issuer are also not within the scope of "consultant or advisor." A person in a *de facto* employment relationship with the issuer, however, such as a non-employee providing services that traditionally are performed by an employee, with compensation paid for those services being the primary source of the person's earned income, would qualify as an eligible person under the exemption. Other persons displaying significant characteristics of "employment," such as the professional advisor providing bookkeeping services, computer programming advice, or other valuable professional services may qualify as eligible consultants or advisors, depending upon the particular facts and circumstances.

The term "employee" specifically includes insurance agents who are exclusive agents of the issuer, its subsidiaries or parents, or derive more than 50% of their annual income from those entities.

Limitations on Issuances. During any 12-month period the aggregate sales price or amount of securities sold in reliance on Rule 701 cannot exceed the greatest of (1) $1 million, (2) 15% of the total assets of the issuer (or of the issuer's parent if the issuer is a wholly owned subsidiary and the parent fully and unconditionally guarantees the obligations of the issuer), or (3) 15% of the outstanding amount of the class of securities being offered and sold in reliance on Rule 701. Both the total assets and outstanding amount of securities are measured at the issuer's most recent annual balance sheet date, if it is no older than its last fiscal year end.

The aggregate sales price means the sum of all cash, property, notes, cancellation of debt, or other consideration received or to be received by the issuer for the sale of the securities. Non-cash consideration must be valued by reference to bona fide sales of the consideration made within a reasonable time or, in the absence of such sales, on the fair value as determined by an accepted standard. The value of services exchanged for securities issued must be measured by reference to the value of the securities issued. Thus, compensatory arrangements for consultant and employee services must be valued, and they cannot be valued at "zero" or as a gift. Options must be valued based on the exercise price of the option, and if options are subsequently repriced, then a recalculation of the aggregate sales price under Rule 701 must be made. The aggregate sales price of options is determined upon the grant of the options, regardless of when the options become exercisable or are exercised. Deferred compensation and similar plans are measured as of the date an irrevocable election to defer compensation is made. The aggregate sale price of other securities not mentioned above is determined on the date of sale.

The total assets of the issuer for the 15%-of-total-assets test are determined by using the calculation of assets on the balance sheet of the issuer. While not specifically mandated by the SEC, in applying for an exemption under Rule 701, companies use the assets total from their balance sheets.

The amount of outstanding securities for the 15% of the outstanding class of securities test is calculated by including all currently exercisable or convertible options, warrants, rights, or other securities. This amount does not include options, warrants, or rights that are not presently exercisable, and it also does not include presently non-convertible securities.[59] "When these securities become exercisable or convertible, subsequent calculations may consider such securities." The amount of outstanding securities does not include securities issuable pursuant to Rule 701. That is, the amount of outstanding securities does not include exercisable options, warrants, or rights issued pursuant to Rule 701 that have not yet been exercised.

In relation to the 15%-of-outstanding-class-of-securities test, for the purposes of determining the number of outstanding shares of a class, separate classes of common stock may be considered as a single class if the rights of such separate classes are nearly identical.[60]

Resale Limitations. Securities issued under Rule 701 are "restricted securities" as defined in Rule 144. Resales of securities issued pursuant to Rule 701 must be in compliance with the registration requirements of the 1933 Act or an exemption from those requirements. Ninety days after the issuer becomes subject to the reporting requirements of Section 13 or 15(d) of the 1934 Act, securities issued under Rule 701 may be resold by persons other than affiliates of the issuer, subject to certain limitations, and by affiliates subject to further limitations.[61]

---

59. *American Bar Association Subcommittee on Employee Benefits and Executive Compensation*, SEC No-Action Letter, LivEDGAR (September 6, 1988).

60. *Osler Health, Inc.*, SEC No-Action Letter (February 11, 1998).

61. See Rule 701(g).

Disclosures. If the aggregate sales price or amount of securities sold exceeds $5 million in a consecutive 12-month period, then certain other disclosures must be made within a reasonable period before the date of sale, which are in addition to the disclosure of the written benefit plan or contract. These additional disclosures include (1) if the plan is subject to ERISA, a copy of the summary plan description required by ERISA, or, if the plan is not subject to ERISA, a summary of the material terms of the plan; (2) information about the risks associated with investment in the securities sold pursuant to the compensatory benefit plan or compensation contract; and (3) U.S. GAAP financial statements as of a date no more than 180 days before the sale of securities in reliance on Rule 701. If the issuer relies on its parent's total assets to determine the amount of securities that may be sold, the parent's financial statements, which must meet certain standards if the parent is a reporting company under Section 13 or 15(d) of the 1934 Act, must be delivered. If the sale involves a stock option or other derivative security, the issuer must deliver disclosures a reasonable period of time before the date of exercise or conversion.

2.5.3 Sales Under Rule 144

U.S. securities laws are based on the premise that every person who wants to sell a security must establish an exemption from applicable federal and state securities law registration requirements or must comply with such registration requirements. When a normal investor wishes to sell IBM or General Motors securities, he or she can rely on the exemption in Section 4(1) of the 1933 Act, but what if the selling shareholder is an affiliate of the issuer or has acquired the securities from the issuer or an affiliate of the issuer in a transaction not registered under the 1933 Act? To answer this question, one must understand Rule 144 promulgated under the 1933 Act. It covers sales of unregistered securities ("restricted stock") by non-affiliates and sales of all securities by affiliates of the issuer.

Under the 1933 Act, an "affiliate" of the issuer (which includes all directors and certain executive officers) may not sell issuer securities unless the sale is covered by a registration statement or falls within an exemption from the registration requirements of the 1933 Act. The exemption most frequently used by directors and officers is SEC Rule 144.[62]

---

62. 1933 Act, Rule 144.

Rule 144 serves as a safe harbor, allowing directors and officers to sell securities without complying with the SEC's registration requirements, provided that certain specific conditions are met.

For purposes of Rule 144, "restricted stock" is stock acquired from the issuer or an affiliate of the issuer in a transaction *not* involving a public offering. Unless shares of common stock issued upon exercise of stock options have been registered under the 1933 Act on a Form S-8, such stock will be considered restricted stock. No shares of restricted stock may be sold unless either the sale of such stock is registered with the SEC or the sale is exempt from the registration requirements, as in the case of a sale that falls within the provisions of Rule 144. Rule 144 is not the only exemption available. Private sales in particular may be eligible for other exemptions. Also, sales to large institutional buyers may be permitted under Rule 144A. However, Rule 144 provides essentially the only way to sell restricted shares in the public market.

In general, "affiliates" are persons in control of the issuer. The term "affiliate" includes *all* directors and certain key executive officers of the issuer. In 1997 the SEC proposed a bright-line test for the definition of affiliate that would indicate that a person would not be deemed to be an affiliate if the person is not (1) a 10% owner, (2) a Section 16 reporting person, or (3) a director of the issuer. While this proposal has not yet been enacted, it is indicative of what the SEC is thinking.[63]

Affiliates usually sell issuer securities under SEC Rule 144. Generally speaking, a Rule 144 transaction is an unsolicited broker's transaction on a stock exchange (including NASDAQ). Rule 144 requires that the issuer be current in its filings with the SEC, and it limits the amount to be sold in any three-month period. A Rule 144 transaction also requires the advance filing of SEC Form 144.

As indicated above, a designated executive officer or director of the issuer is considered an "affiliate" of the issuer. All issuer stock held by such affiliates is "control stock," which generally can be sold only (1) pursuant to a 1933 Act registration statement (as a "selling shareholder"), (2) pursuant to the private placement exemption, or (3) pursuant to Rule 144. If an affiliate received the stock from the issuer or another affiliate in a non-registered transaction, it is also "restricted stock." Stock received through the exercise of a registered stock option is not restricted stock. Such shares are, however, considered "control" stock.

---

63. SEC Release No. 33-7391 (February 20, 1997) (10% ownership creates a rebuttable presumption of affiliate status).

Control stock includes all issuer stock owned by an affiliate, regardless of how the stock was acquired. This includes stock purchased in the open market or received under a registered or unregistered employee stock option plan. Under Rule 144, stock held by any household relative of an affiliate, as well as any stock held by a corporation or trust in which an affiliate has a 10% ownership or beneficial interest, is attributable to the affiliate, and the holder of such stock must also comply with Rule 144 in connection with its sale. Stock received by others by gift or bona fide pledge from an affiliate or a household relative retains its restrictions and must be sold under Rule 144 by the donee or pledgee, except that all Rule 144 restrictions lapse in the hands of the donee or pledgee once the holding period has passed since the date of acquisition of the stock by the donor.

Rule 144 essentially does two things. First, it sets forth the circumstances under which restricted stock may be sold, and second, it sets forth the circumstances under which affiliates may sell *any* shares of common stock (restricted or unrestricted). Persons who own restricted stock but are not affiliates of the issuer and who have not been affiliates during the three months preceding a sale may freely sell restricted stock under Rule 144 so long as they have held the stock for the requisite holding period. (The holding period is determined using the rules described below.) Unlike sales by affiliates and sales of restricted stock held for less than the requisite holding period, these sales may be made *without* complying with the other requirements of Rule 144 described below, and the shares need not bear a restrictive legend.

On November 15, 2007, the SEC voted to approve amendments to Rule 144 that:

- shorten the holding period for restricted securities of reporting companies to six months;

- simplify Rule 144 compliance for non-affiliates by allowing non-affiliates of reporting companies to freely resell restricted securities after satisfying a six-month holding period (subject only to the Rule 144(c) public information requirement until the securities have been held for one year) and by allowing non-affiliates of non-reporting companies to freely resell restricted securities after satisfying a 12-month holding period;

- for affiliates' sales, revise the manner of sale requirements for equity securities and eliminate them for debt securities and relax the volume limitations for debt securities;

- for affiliates' sales, raise the thresholds that trigger Form 144 filing requirements from 500 shares or $10,000 to 5,000 shares or $50,000;

- simplify and streamline the Preliminary Note to and other parts of Rule 144; and

- codify certain staff interpretations relating to Rule 144.

These amendments will be effective on February 15, 2008. The actual language of the amendments as approved by the SEC is available on the SEC's Web site (sec.gov). See Release No. 33-8869. Once effective, the new rules will apply retroactively to any situation in which the new rules will be of benefit; i.e., the reduced holding period and the favorable treatment to non-affiliates. The analysis that follows and the summary of Rule 144 in Appendix D-3, D-4, and D-5 all assume that the new rules are in effect.

Restricted stock and any stock held by affiliates may be sold under Rule 144 pursuant to the following requirements:

Availability of Current Public Information. The issuer must have been subject to the reporting requirements of Section 13 of the 1934 Act for a period of at least three months and must have filed the SEC reports required of it for at least 12 months before the sale of securities (or for such shorter period as the issuer was required to file such reports).[64] Potential sellers are entitled to rely on a statement made on the facing sheet of the most recent Form 10-Q or Form 10-K to the effect that required reports have been filed, or upon a written statement from the issuer that all reporting requirements have been met, unless they know or have reason to know that the issuer has not complied with such requirements.

This requirement applies only to affiliates and non-affiliates who have held the stock for less than one year.

Holding Period for Restricted Securities. Restricted stock must have been "beneficially owned" for at least six months.[65] (Affiliates selling unrestricted shares are not subject to this requirement.) To be beneficially owned, restricted stock that was purchased (rather than obtained, e.g., by gift) must have been fully paid for. Securities received in certain stock splits, stock dividends, recapitalizations, and conversions are deemed to have been acquired when the underlying securities were acquired, but

---

64. 1933 Act, Rule 144(c)(1).
65. 1933 Act, Rule 144(d)(1).

securities received upon exercise of warrants are generally deemed to be acquired when the warrants were exercised and the exercise price paid. Securities being sold by a bona fide pledgee, donee, trust, or estate will in certain circumstances be deemed to have been held from the dates of acquisition by the pledgor, donor, settlor, or decedent, as the case may be. Each shareholder's shares must be analyzed separately in order to determine when they become eligible for sale under Rule 144.

Quantity. Rule 144 also places an upper limit on the amount of securities that may be sold by a single shareholder in any three-month period.[66] The maximum number of shares that may be sold is limited to the greater of (1) 1% of the total number of shares outstanding as last reported or (2) the average weekly reported volume of trading in the issuer's common stock during the four calendar weeks preceding notice of the sale. Sales of this amount may be made in successive three-month periods. For an affiliate these limitations apply to total sales of *both* restricted securities and unrestricted securities. For non-affiliates, the volume limitations apply only to sales of restricted securities made during the first six months after such securities were acquired.

In determining amounts that may be sold by a shareholder (affiliate or non-affiliate), sales by the following are deemed made by the shareholder:[67] (1) relatives living in the same home, (2) trusts or estates in which the shareholder or such relatives collectively have 10% or more of the beneficial interest or act as trustee or executor, and (3) corporations and other organizations in which the shareholder or such relatives collectively own 10% or more of any class of equity securities. In addition, in determining amounts that may be sold by a bona fide pledgee, donee, estate, or trust, sales by the pledgor, donor, decedent, or settlor during the same three-month period must be included if the securities being sold were acquired by the pledgee, donee, estate, or trust within one year (previously two years) before the date of the intended sale. Persons agreeing to act in concert for the purpose of selling stock in the issuer must aggregate their sales in determining whether or not the quantity limitations are met. Stock sold pursuant to a registration statement or another exemption is not aggregated.

Manner of Sale. Sales can be made only in "brokers' transactions," i.e., transactions in which the broker merely executes an order to sell without

---

66. 1933 Act, Rule 144(e).
67. 1933 Act, Rule 144(a)(2).

compensation exceeding normal brokers' commissions.[68] The seller may not solicit orders for the stock or make payments to any person other than the broker. The broker may not solicit or arrange for the solicitation of orders to buy in connection with the transaction. In addition, the broker must satisfy himself or herself after reasonable inquiry that the sale is being made pursuant to the provisions of Rule 144. This requirement only applies to affiliates.

Notice. Notices of intended sales must be filed with the SEC, except for transactions that do not exceed 5,000 shares or $50,000 in proceeds during any three-month period (previously 500 shares or $10,000).[69] Three copies of a notice on Form 144 must be transmitted to the SEC concurrently with the placing of an order with a broker to execute a sale under Rule 144. This requirement applies only to affiliates.

Departing Director or Executive Officer. A departing director or executive officer should be guided by Section 16, insider trading, and Rule 144 considerations, as more fully explained in appendix D, which contains a memorandum on exit strategies, a sample exit memorandum, and a Rule 144 summary. As to Rule 144, control stock can be sold immediately subject to insider trading considerations (Rule 10b-5). As to restricted stock, a departing director or executive officer who is considered an affiliate (the CEO, COO, and CFO are presumed to be affiliates) needs to sell under the conditions of Rule 144 for three months and then can use Rule 144(k) as to restricted stock held for one year. Rule 144(k) permits the sale of restricted stock without compliance with any of the other conditions of Rule 144 as long as the stock has been held for one year and the seller has not been an affiliate for three months. If the restricted stock has been held for less than one year but more than six months, some Rule 144 conditions must be satisfied. If the restricted stock has been held for less than six months, no sales may be made. (These rules apply to any holder of restricted stock.)

As a general rule, it is suggested that the departing director or executive officer comply with the issuer's insider trading policy for three months after departure to allow his or her insider knowledge to go stale. The 90-day period is based on analogy to the three-month period in Rule 144(k).

---

68. 1933 Act, Rule 144(f).

69. 1933 Act, Rule 144(h).

2.5.4 Sales Under Regulation S

Regulation S is technically not an exemption from registration under the 1933 Act, but rather a clarification of the territorial approach to the registration requirements of Section 5 of the 1933 Act. The SEC adopted Regulation S in 1990 to clarify when offers and sales will be deemed to take place outside the United States and, therefore, not be subject to the registration requirements of the 1933 Act.

Rule 904 provides a safe harbor for determining when resales by any person other than the issuer, a distributor, or any of their respective affiliates (except any officer or director who is an affiliate solely by virtue of holding such position) will be deemed to occur outside the United States. To fall within the Rule 904 safe harbor, the offer or sale must take place in an "offshore transaction," and "no directed selling efforts" may be made in the United States. Special additional conditions apply to resales by dealers, persons receiving selling commissions, and certain affiliates (any officer or director of the issuer who is an affiliate of the issuer solely by virtue of holding such position). Each one of these terms is defined in Rule 902. An accurate summary of them would be almost as long as the regulation itself.

This exemption is useful for U.S. issuers with employees outside the United States and for foreign private issuers with employees in the United States. If the foreign private issuer is registered under the 1934 Act, then Form S-8 is available, and there is no need to look to Regulation S; however, if the foreign private issuer is not registered under the 1934 Act, then it will need to use Rule 701 or Regulation D to make offers and sales to its U.S. employees. Those exemptions will result in the purchase of restricted securities that cannot be sold in the United States without further exemptions. In addition, there is probably no trading market in the United States for such securities. To cover that situation, Rule 904 of Regulation S will allow for sales outside the United States without having to comply with any other U.S. exemptions. For further discussion of Regulation S, see SEC Release No. 33-7505.

2.6 2007 Executive Compensation Disclosure Rules

While the scope of this chapter does not allow for a detailed analysis of the new executive compensation disclosure rules, it is necessary to mention them briefly. They are set forth in a 436-page SEC Release (No.

33-8732A) (August 29, 2006). The rules became effective on November 7, 2006, and require significantly greater quantitative and qualitative disclosure of executive compensation by U.S. public companies. Companies generally must comply with the rule changes in annual reports on Form 10-K for fiscal years ending on or after December 15, 2006; registration statements and proxy and information statements for filings made after December 15, 2006; and Form 8-Ks where the trigger event occurs on or after November 7, 2006.

The gathering of the data, assembly, and presentation of the information and the legal and financial analyses needed will require substantial legal, finance, tax, human resources, benefits, actuarial, and accounting input. Companies should start to prepare for the upcoming proxy statement immediately. Commencing preparation of the proxy statement information early will ensure disclosure and timing issues are identified, and circulation of draft disclosures will timely inform management and board members as to the sweeping nature of the rules changes and possibly avoid, in the words of a senior SEC official, "unpleasant surprises."

With respect to equity compensation plans, the rule provides for expanded disclosure regarding stock option grants and grant policies, including any arrangement to time the grant of options in relation to the release of material non-public information. It also requires the Summary Compensation Table to include the grant date FAS 123(R) fair value of equity awards, year-to-year changes in accumulated pension benefits, above-market annual earnings on nonqualified deferred compensation, and every other element of annual compensation (except the value of a minor amount of perquisites and other personal benefits permitted to be excluded).

The new rules also require additional tables and narrative disclosure regarding pension and other retirement benefits, deferred compensation, severance, and change of control payments, all of which could involve equity compensation plans.

The current executive compensation rules also include a number of changes to the Section 16 rules. They eliminated the need to disclose Section 16(b) indebtedness under S-K Item 404(c) and made some changes with respect to the definition of "non-employee director" in Rule 16b-3. These changes were necessary because of the changes that were made in the related party disclosure items in Regulation S-K. Rule 16b-3 also contains a new note (no. 4) to this definition clarifying the determination of non-employee director status and providing for a good-faith analysis of the director's status without a retroactive application if the analysis proves incorrect.

Finally, the new rules require a new table specifying and totaling directors' compensation, including equity compensation awards.

A more detailed analysis of this rule may be found in a memorandum dated September 25, 2006, prepared by McDermott Will & Emery LLP, at http://www.mwe.com/info/news/SECexeccomprules.pdf.

2.6.1 Form 8-K Reporting Requirements and Corporate Governance Shareholder Approval Rules

On April 11, 2002, the SEC proposed rules regarding insider transactions that, if adopted, would have required public companies to file current reports on Form 8-K that describe directors' and executive officers' transactions in company equity securities, directors' and executive officers' Rule 10b5-1 arrangements for the purchase and sale of company equity securities, and loans of money to a director or an executive officer made or guaranteed by the company or an affiliate of the company.[70] On August 23, 2004, the SEC adopted its final changes to Form 8-K (Release No. 33-8400), and none of the foregoing matters were expressly included in the new reporting requirements under Form 8-K. If, however, a material amendment is made to a stock incentive plan or an award document, or if a new benefit plan is adopted by the board of directors (with or without shareholder approval), it must be reported on Form 8-K within four business days under Item 1.01 as a material definitive agreement.

Item 1.01 of Form 8-K has been broadly interpreted to require disclosure of grants of options or awards of stock or other stock benefits to executive officers and directors unless the forms of these award documents are already on file with the SEC (usually in the exhibits section of the Form 10-K or Form 10-Q).

Effective November 7, 2006, Form 8-K has been amended as part of a comprehensive amendment to the executive compensation disclosure rules discussed above (see SEC Release No. 33-8732A). This release amended Form 8-K to move the reporting requirements with respect to executive compensation matters from Item 1.01 to Items 5.02(e) and (f). It also clarified the persons for whom information should be reported—namely, the principal executive officers (CEO and CFO) and the named executive officers from the company's last filed proxy statement. The remainder of current executive officers are no longer covered by this disclosure requirement. Also, compensation for existing directors need not be disclosed, but information about compensation to newly appointed

---

70. SEC Release No. 33-8090 (April 12, 2002).

directors is required to be disclosed. The new item also establishes a materiality test for grants or awards and for material amendments or modifications to those awards. This is a substantial departure from the earlier positions taken with respect to this disclosure.

It should also be noted that effective June 30, 2003, the New York Stock Exchange, American Stock Exchange, and NASDAQ all adopted very broad rules requiring shareholder approval of all stock-based employee benefit plans and material amendments thereto, with very limited exceptions. Further discussion is beyond the scope of this chapter. Finally, the SEC now requires that an elaborate "Equity Compensation Plan Information" table be included in the corporation's proxy statement or Form 10-K (see S-K Item 201(d)).

2.7   Conclusion

As reflected by the above discussion, the federal securities laws issues attributable to an equity compensation plan are numerous and complex. Many times, compliance problems are attributable to a failure by the issuing corporation to either (1) adequately communicate the various securities law reporting and trading restrictions governing the purchase and sale of employer securities by its directors and officers or (2) provide sufficient support to enable such persons to comply with these rules. Companies offering stock options and other equity compensation, particularly public companies, are well advised to provide directors and officers with a summary description of the relevant securities laws and to establish a program for assisting directors and officers in complying with these laws. Along these lines, many companies establish (1) a "code of business conduct" prohibiting insider trading by their employees and establishing "blackout" periods during which company stock may not be traded by officers, directors, and other reporting persons possessing material information about the company and (2) a preclearance policy.

To avoid noncompliance problems, broad assistance should be provided to directors and officers to make sure they understand and comply with trading and reporting restrictions.

APPENDIX A

The Sarbanes-Oxley Act of 2002: Impact on Executive Compensation Plans

On July 30, 2002, President Bush signed into law the Sarbanes-Oxley Act of 2002 (the "2002 Act"), which makes far-reaching changes in federal regulation applicable to corporate America and its executives, auditors and advisers. In addition to corporate governance and accounting reforms, the 2002 Act makes several changes that immediately affect many executive compensation arrangements (including stock benefit plans) and their administration. Directors, executives, Section 16 compliance officers and human resources administrators will want to consider closely the following provisions under the 2002 Act:

- Prohibition on personal loans to directors and executive officers
- Accelerated Section 16 filing deadlines
- Restrictions on stock transactions during retirement plan blackout periods
- Forfeiture of executive pay due to accounting restatements
- Freeze on extraordinary payments to directors and officers

Prohibition on Personal Loans to Directors and Executive Officers

Section 402 of the 2002 Act amends Section 13 of the 1934 Act to prohibit publicly held U.S. and non-U.S. companies from making or extending personal loans to directors and executive officers. Section 402 became effective on July 30, 2002, subject to grandfathering provisions and certain limited exceptions.

General Loan Prohibition Under Section 402. Section 402 states that "[i]t shall be unlawful for any issuer (as defined in Section 2 of the Sarbanes-Oxley Act of 2002), directly or indirectly, including through any subsidiary, to extend or maintain credit, to arrange for the extension of credit, or to renew an extension of credit, in the form of a personal loan to or for any director or executive officer (or equivalent thereof) of that issuer." Unless grandfathering treatment or an exception applies, effective July 30, 2002, issuers are prohibited from extending a personal loan in any manner to a director or executive officer.

Directors and Executive Officers. The term "director" is defined in Section 3(a)(7) of the 1934 Act as "any director of a corporation or any person performing similar functions with respect to any organization, whether incorporated or unincorporated." There are real questions about advisory, emeritus, or honorary directors, and the SEC interpretations under Section 16 of the 1934 Act may be relevant to this issue. The SEC has indicated in various releases that it believes that advisory and emeritus directors generally should be treated as directors for Section 16 purposes, but that honorary directors should not be so treated.

As noted above, the provisions of Section 402 of the 2002 Act are implemented as an amendment to the 1934 Act. Accordingly, unless and until the SEC adopts a different definition, the term "executive officer" under Section 402 should be interpreted in a manner consistent with existing SEC rules. 1934 Act Rule 3b-7 defines an "executive officer" (for purposes of, among others, proxy, 10-K, and other 1934 Act disclosures) as the "president, any vice president of the registrant in charge of a principal business unit, division or function (such as sales, administration or finance), any other officer who performs a policy making function or any other person who performs similar policy making functions for the registrant." Executive officers of subsidiaries may be deemed executive officers of a publicly held company if they perform policy-making functions for the publicly held company.

Grandfather Protection. A limited grandfather provision provides some relief but raises many questions. Section 402 exempts loans maintained before July 30, 2002, "provided that there is no material modification to any term of any such extension of credit or any renewal of any such extension of credit" on or after July 30, 2002. A material modification of any term results in loss of grandfather treatment. Any action that might be considered to be a change to the terms of a loan should be carefully considered, given that Section 402 may be violated even if the change is minor and does not affect the overall financing arrangement.

Identifying Transactions Potentially Subject to Section 402. The ambiguity as to what is a "personal loan" and the breadth of what may be considered an arrangement for "extension of credit" suggest that publicly held companies should immediately identify all transactions potentially subject to Section 402. Common arrangements that may be viewed to involve an extension of credit are split-dollar life insurance and cashless stock option exercises. The following is a partial list of other transactions with directors and executives officers that may be treated as an extension of credit:

- Loans to purchase stock, a personal residence, or other property
- Loans to meet margin calls upon a decline in the price of the company's stock
- Loans for relocation to a different geographic area
- Routine advances for business purposes (such as reimbursement accounts and travel expense allowances), particularly if repaid over long period of time
- Personal use of company credit cards
- Indemnification payments made under company bylaws or an employment agreement before a determination of entitlement to such payment
- Use of company funds to meet an executive's payroll tax obligations for nonqualified deferred compensation benefits
- Signing bonuses subject to repayment on early termination of employment

Cashless Stock Option Exercises Under Section 402. A common executive compensation practice that has been affected by Section 402 is the cashless exercise of stock options facilitated through a broker. In a cashless exercise, the option holder instructs a brokerage firm to sell a sufficient number of the shares being acquired by the option exercise to satisfy the option price and any applicable withholding taxes. The broker sells the shares and remits the exercise price and any taxes required to be withheld to the company, with any balance remitted to the option holder. The company delivers the requisite number of shares to the broker and the balance to the option holder.

There are two common methods to execute a cashless exercise of a stock option. A broker may sell the shares on the date of receipt of exercise instructions and remit the exercise price and withholding taxes to the company a few days later, on the date of the settlement of the sale of those shares. Alternatively, a broker may sell the shares on the date of receipt of the instructions and remit the exercise price and withholding taxes immediately to the company, treating the amount as a margin loan to the option holder. Other variations on this practice also exist.

Any of these cashless exercise methods may be viewed as resulting in an "extension of credit" under Section 402. A broker-assisted direct sale involves the company making stock or cash available to the option holder for the exercise, albeit only for a very short period of time. While a margin loan from a broker does not involve the use of the company funds, it may also be subject to Section 402 to the extent that the company is viewed as having "arranged" this financing by establishing the cashless exercise program with the brokerage firm. None of these methods would seem to be the type of loan targeted by the Congress under the 2002 Act. It was hoped that the SEC would issue guidance to clarify the impact of Section 402 on cashless exercise programs, but the SEC has not done so to date. The margin loan method discussed above has become an acceptable practice to avoid Section 402 problems.

Accelerated Section 16 Filing Deadlines

Section 403 of the 2002 Act amended Section 16(a) of the 1934 Act to require Section 16 reporting persons (directors, 10% or more shareholders, and certain executive officers) to report changes in beneficial ownership of issuer securities within two business days. The two-day filing requirement became effective August 29, 2002, under amended Section 16 rules adopted by the SEC on August 27, 2002 (SEC Release No. 34-46421).

The 2002 Act also requires the SEC to adopt rules requiring that Section 16(a) reports be filed electronically (rather than in paper form) no later than July 30, 2003. These rules went into effect on June 30, 2003. To file electronically, SEC rules require each Section 16 reporting person to apply for and obtain his or her own access codes to the SEC's Electronic Data Gathering, Analysis and Retrieval System (EDGAR).

Foreign Private Issuers

Currently, foreign private issuers with securities registered under the Exchange Act are not subject to any aspect of Section 16. The SEC has indicated that it does not intend to change the exemption for foreign private issuers.

SEC Rulemaking

Highlights of the revised Section 16 reporting rules are follows:

- All transactions occurring on or after August 29, 2002, must be reported on a Form 4 received by the SEC no later than 10 p.m. Eastern time on the second business day following the transaction date. These include:

  — Option grants and exercises

  — Stock awards, performance share awards, and SARs

  — Option repricings, cancellations, regrants, and amendments

  — Dispositions to the issuer, including stock swaps and share withholding to pay taxes

  — Open market purchases and sales

- All of the previously permitted reporting deferrals for transactions between the issuer and Section 16 reporting persons set forth in Rule 16b-3 are subject to two-business day reporting on Form 4 except for the following:

  — Routine purchases under the payroll deduction provisions of a 401(k) plan (including an excess benefit plan), employee stock purchase plan, or employee stock ownership plan (ESOP), which transactions remain exempt from reporting (but must be included in the "shares beneficially owned" column) with a footnote explanation.

  — "Discretionary transactions" under 401(k) and other employee benefit plans and certain transactions made pursuant to so-called Rule 10b5-1 plans, which transactions must be reported on a Form 4 under a special "deemed execution" rule discussed below, which can allow up to five-business day reporting.

- All of the exemptions contained in the Section 16(a) rules remain in effect and may either be voluntarily reported on a Form 4 at any time up to the due date of the Form 5 or reported on a Form 5 within 45 days of the end of the issuer's fiscal year. These include:

  — Gifts

  — Small acquisitions, but not from the issuer or an employee benefit plan sponsored by the issuer

  — Stock splits and stock dividends

  — Pro-rata distributions

  — Transfers under domestic relations orders

— Changes in form of beneficial ownership

— Regular dividend reinvestment plan contributions

— Expiration of options without consideration

Note that the first two situations above require transaction reporting, but the last six situations need not be reported as transactions but should only be identified in the "shares beneficially owned" column with a footnote explanation.

- The SEC has adopted special limited deferred reporting rules (up to five business days depending upon circumstances) for the following transactions:

  — Transactions pursuant to a contract, instruction, or written plan for the purchase or sale of issuer equity securities that satisfies the affirmative defense conditions of Rule 10b5-1(c) where the Section 16 reporting person does not select the date(s) of execution (such as the first date of each month).

  — Discretionary transactions where the Section 16 reporting person does not select the date(s) of execution.

  — Deferred compensation plan investments in a company stock fund, but only if they fall within the scope of a Rule 10b5-1 plan.

  — Transactions that occur over more than one day, but only if they fall within the scope of a Rule 10b5-1 plan.

These transactions are subject to reporting on Form 4 within two business days of the "deemed execution" date of the transaction. The deemed execution date of the transaction will be the earlier of (1) the date on which the executing broker, dealer, or plan administrator notifies the Section 16 reporting person of the execution of the transaction, and (2) the third business day following the trade date. (The SEC noted in its release adopting the new rules that a trade confirmation sent through the mail could take several days to arrive and the SEC would, therefore, usually expect brokers, dealers and plan administrators to provide the information needed for Section 16(a) reporting purposes to the Section 16 reporting person either electronically or by telephone.)

- The rules with respect to the timing of the filing of Form 3 (initial statement of beneficial ownership) have not changed. For a company that is already public, the Form 3 must be filed within 10 days of the person becoming a Section 16 reporting person. For companies going public, the Form 3 must be filed before the company goes public. The SEC noted that a transaction might be required to be filed on Form 4 before the due date of Form 3. In this situation, the SEC encouraged the filing of both the Form 3 and the Form 4 by the due date of the Form 4.

Recommendations

The following recommendations should be considered in order to comply with the revised Section 16 rules:

- Have a mandatory pre-clearance policy for all transactions as to which the timing is within the control of the Section 16 reporting person. Appendix B provides a suggested form of such pre-clearance policy.

- For transactions as to which timing is outside the control of the Section 16 reporting person, require brokerage firms conducting transactions for the Section 16 reporting person to provide promptly upon trade execution, and certainly by the third business day, the information needed for Section 16(a) reporting purposes to the Section 16 reporting person either electronically or by telephone.

- Review and update the procedures for discretionary transactions under benefit plans to ensure that the Section 16 reporting person receives timely notification (no later than three business days) of execution of the transaction from the plan administrator.

- Educate all Section 16 reporting persons by a memorandum that they should read, sign, and return.

- Establish a cashless exercise policy for Section 16 reporting persons in which the Section 16 reporting person obtains any credit extension from the broker or other third party of his or her choice and (not the issuer) and results in the issuer being paid the exercise price on the day of exercise.

- Obtain powers of attorney with multiple attorneys-in-fact from all Section 16 reporting persons.

- Apply for EDGAR access codes for all Section 16 reporting persons. Section 16 reporting persons can obtain a Form ID for obtaining EDGAR access codes from the SEC at http://www.sec.gov/about/forms/formid.pdf.

Forfeiture of Compensation and Stock Sale Profits by CEOs and CFOs upon Restatements Due to Misconduct

Section 304 of the 2002 Act requires forfeiture of certain bonuses and profits realized by the CEO and CFO of a company that is required to prepare an accounting restatement due to the company's "material noncompliance, as a result of misconduct, with any financial reporting requirement under the securities laws." Specifically, the CEO and CFO must reimburse to the company any bonus or other incentive- or equity-based compensation received, and any profit realized from the sale of the company's stock sold, during a specified recapture period. Reimbursement is required whether or not the CEO or CFO engaged in or knew of the misconduct. The "recapture period" is the 12-month period following "the first public issuance or filing with the SEC (whichever first occurs) of the financial document embodying such financial reporting requirement."

It is unclear how one determines when targeted compensation is "received" for purposes of Section 304. The application of Section 304 of the 2002 Act to common executive compensation arrangements will be difficult to apply in practice. For example, is equity-based compensation "received" upon the grant or exercise of a stock option, or both? Is restricted stock "received" upon grant or vesting? Are performance-based nonqualified deferred compensation benefits "received" in the year earned or in the year of actual receipt? Do constructive principles similar to those under the tax laws apply? These and other types of interpretative questions will require regulatory guidance or legislative clarification.

This provision applies to both U.S. and non-U.S. companies. The SEC may exercise its authority to exempt non-U.S. companies.

Insider Trades During Pension Fund Blackout Periods

Section 306(a) of the 2002 Act makes it unlawful for any director or executive officer of an issuer of any equity security (other than an exempted security), directly or indirectly, to purchase, sell, or otherwise acquire or transfer any equity security of the issuer (other than an exempted security) during any pension plan blackout period with respect to such equity security, if the director or executive officer acquires the equity security in connection with his or her service or employment as a director or executive officer. This provision equalizes the treatment of corporate executives and rank-and-file employees with respect to their ability to engage in transactions involving issuer equity securities during a pension plan blackout period if the securities were acquired in connection with their service to, or employment with, the issuer.

Regulation BTR, originally adopted to clarify the scope and operation of Section 306(a) of the 2002 Act and to prevent evasion of the statutory trading restriction, defines terms used in Section 306(a), including the term "acquired in connection with service or employment as a director or executive officer." Under this definition as originally adopted, one of the specified methods by which a director or executive officer directly or indirectly acquires equity securities in connection with such service is an acquisition "at a time when he or she was a director or executive officer, as a result of any transaction or business relationship described in paragraph (a) or (b) of Item 404 of Regulation S-K." To conform this provision of Regulation BTR to the Item 404 amendments in the current executive compensation rules, the SEC has amended Rule 100(a)(2) of Regulation BTR so that it references only transactions described in paragraph (a) of Item 404.

Freeze on Extraordinary Payments to Directors and Officers

Section 1103 of the 2002 Act allows the SEC, during an investigation of an issuer or its directors, officers, partners, controlling persons, or other employees, to seek a temporary order in federal court requiring the issuer to escrow "extraordinary payments" to such person for 45 to three months (or, if such person is charged with a violation of the securities laws, until conclusion of the proceedings). There is no definition of "extraordinary payments" other than to indicate that it includes compensation. "Extraordinary payments" might include bonuses, stock option exercises, payments under a nonqualified deferred compensation plan, and severance pay.

This provision applies to both U.S. and non-U.S. companies. The SEC may exercise its authority to exempt non-U.S. companies.

APPENDIX B
Section 16 Mandatory Pre-clearance Policy

(As Authorized by the Board of Directors of the Company)

To: Section 16 Insiders (all directors and executive officers)

The Sarbanes-Oxley Act of 2002 amended Section 16(a) of the Securities Exchange Act of 1934 to accelerate the reporting by Section 16 Insiders of all transactions involving the Company's stock. Effective August 29, 2002, Section 16 Insiders are required to report changes in beneficial ownership involving the Company's stock within two business days of the transaction. Failure to file on a timely basis will result in the person being named as a delinquent filer in the Company's proxy statement. Repeated failure to file on a timely basis can result in civil actions against the individual by the SEC, which has the power to seek fines for delinquent filings and bring injunctive actions against delinquent filers. Under the Securities Enforcement Remedies and Penny Stock Reform Act of 1990, the SEC is also empowered to seek removal of an officer or director from office and to ban such persons from future service as an officer or director of a public company. The SEC has used these remedies in extreme situations.

The Board of Directors believes that the only way to assure timely compliance is to impose a mandatory pre-clearance policy for all transactions by Section 16 Insiders and members of their immediate family involving the Company's stock. Transactions covered by this policy include, without limitation, stock option grants and option exercises, stock awards and stock equivalent awards, purchases and sales publicly or privately, gifts, and transfers in or out of trusts or limited partnerships or any other estate planning devices.

Accordingly, all Section 16 Insiders and members of their immediate family may not engage in any transactions involving the Company's stock without first notifying the Vice President-Chief Financial Officer *and* the [Vice President-General Counsel and Secretary]. This notice must be given in writing to the designated persons at least three business days before the proposed transaction. Failure to comply with this Policy will result at a minimum in embarrassment to the Company and the Section 16 Insider. It also can expose the Section 16 Insider to the civil actions and penalties discussed above.

If you have any questions about the pre-clearance policy, please contact the [Vice President-General Counsel and Secretary].

APPENDIX C

Excerpts from *Current Issues and Rulemaking Projects Outline* Dated March 31, 2001

Section 12 Registration Relief Involving Employee Stock Option Plans

Companies have granted stock options to broad based groups of employees under stock option plans in anticipation of going public within a short time after the stock option grants. These stock options are granted under stock option plans established for compensatory purposes. Many companies are now finding that they have granted stock options to 500 or more employees and their plans to go public have been delayed.

Under Section 12(g) of the Exchange Act, an issuer with 500 holders of record of a class of equity security and assets in excess of $10 million at the end of its most recently ended fiscal year must register the class of equity security, unless it has an exemption from registration. Stock options are a separate equity security under the Exchange Act. Accordingly, an issuer with 500 or more option holders and more than $10 million in assets is required to register that class under the Exchange Act, absent an exemption. The exemption from registration under Section 12(g) contained in Rule 12h-1(a) for "[a]ny interest or participation in an employee stock bonus, stock purchase, profit sharing, pension, retirement, incentive, thrift, savings or similar plan which is not transferable by the holder except in the event of death or mental incompetency, or any security issued solely to fund such plans" does not apply to stock options.

Beginning in 1991, the Commission by order, and subsequently the staff by no action letter, exempted or relieved issuers with 500 or more stock option holders from having to register their stock options under the Exchange Act when specified conditions were present. For the conditions necessary to receive relief under these letters and orders see, for example, the no action letter to Mitchell International Holdings, Inc. (available December 27, 2000).

Due to current market conditions, which are delaying the plans of many companies to go public, we are revising the conditions necessary to receive relief from registering their employee stock options under Section 12(g). As in the past, any relief granted by the staff would apply only to the stock options. Once a company has 500 holders of record of any other class of equity securities (*e.g.*, common stock outstanding as a result of stock issuances, including option exercises), it would be required to register that class. The modified conditions would need to be present only when the company is relying on the relief.

We will consider granting relief in situations where the conditions of our prior no action letters noted above are met with the following modifications:

- The options may be immediately exercisable.

- Former employees may retain their vested options.

- As with the current conditions, the options must remain non-transferable in most cases. However, we will permit the options to transfer on death or disability of the option holder. The stock received on exercise of the options may not be transferable, except back to the company or in the event of death or disability.

- Consultants may participate in the option plan if they would be able to participate under Rule 701. We encourage you to review the adopting releases effecting the recent changes to Rule 701 and Form S-8 to understand the categories of consulting services that fall within this group. Releases 33-7645 and 33-7646.

We will premise any changes in our current position on option holders receiving essentially the same Exchange Act registration statement, annual report and quarterly report information they would have received had the company registered the class of securities under Section 12, including audited annual financial statements and unaudited quarterly financial information, each prepared in accordance with GAAP.

April 30, 2001 is the filing date for registration statements of issuers that met the Section 12(g) registration requirement as of December 31, 2000. We will consider extending that filing date to July 30, 2001 for any issuer that has submitted a no-action request to us by April 30, 2001. Any questions may be directed to Amy Starr in the Office of the Chief Counsel, (202) 942-2900.

APPENDIX D-1

Memorandum to Company Regarding Continuing Reporting Obligations with Respect to a Departing Officer or Director of the Company

MEMORANDUM

Confidential
Attorney-Client Privilege

Date:

To:

cc:

From:

Re: Continuing Reporting Obligations Applicable to a Departing Executive Officer or Director of the Company

This Memorandum discusses the continuing reporting obligations and transaction restrictions after an executive officer or director of the company ("Section 16 Reporting Person") ceases to be a Section 16 Reporting Person by resigning as an executive officer or director of the company.

Attached is a sample memorandum for departing Section 16 Reporting Persons [appendix D-2]. This memorandum can be used to cover Section 16 reporting obligations as well as insider trading restrictions under Rule 10b-5.

Section 16 Reporting Obligations

A Section 16 Reporting Person has an obligation to file Section 16 reports (Form 4s) for six months after that person's status as a Section 16 Reporting Person is terminated, but only with respect to non-exempt transactions that are matchable with non-exempt transactions that occurred while the person was a Section 16 Reporting Person. For example, if a Section 16 Reporting Person had an open market purchase three months prior to his or her termination of Section 16 reporting status, that person would have to report all open market sales for the three months following his or her termination, and the purchases and sales would be matchable for Section 16(b) purposes.

Option exercises, vesting of restricted stock, and gifts are all examples of exempt transactions that would not have to be reported. To carry this example further, if the option exercise was done by the delivery to the company of previously owned company shares, that transaction would likewise be exempt and not reportable. The same would be true if shares were delivered to the company to pay taxes. If, however, the departing Section 16 Reporting Person uses a cashless exercise method (sale of stock by a broker to pay the exercise price), the sale is not exempt and must be reported and potentially matched if there were opposite-way purchases within the same six-month period while the person was a Section 16 Reporting Person. Finally, we understand that the company's 401(k) plan has a company stock fund. The transfer out of that fund after termination of Section 16 reporting status is reportable only if there has been a transfer into the stock fund within six months while the person had Section 16 reporting obligations. This is considered a "discretionary transaction" and involves very arcane concepts. As a general rule, a departed Section 16 Reporting Person should pre-clear all discretionary transactions with your office before they are entered into.

In addition, if the Section 16 Reporting Person has had a transaction while he or she was a Section 16 Reporting Person that was deferred until the Form 5 was due (such as a gift), that transaction should be reported either on a voluntary Form 4 or a mandatory Form 5 within 45 days of the end of the company's fiscal year. We recommend reporting it on a voluntary Form 4 to get it out of the way. We understand that is the company's present policy.

Rule 10b-5 Insider Trading Restrictions

In addition to Section 16, the departing Section 16 Reporting Person has to be guided by the company's insider trading policy for some period of time after cessation of Section 16 reporting status to allow his or her knowledge about the company with respect to non-public material information to go stale. As a guideline, we recommend that the former Section 16 Reporting Person follow the company's insider trading policies for at least three months after termination of Section 16 reporting status. After that, it is highly likely that the Section 16 Reporting Person's knowledge would be stale. Note that the departing Section 16 Reporting Person can remain employed beyond the date of his or her termination of Section 16 reporting status. As long as the former Section 16 Reporting Person is not performing activities that would cause him or her to continue to be a Section 16 Reporting Person, the three-month period should run from his or her termination of Section 16 reporting status.

Rule 144

It is our understanding that no person at the company has restricted securities within the meaning of SEC Rule 144. By "restricted" we mean securities that have been obtained from the issuer not in a registered public offering. If you wish more information on restricted securities and control securities, involving Rule 144, we will be glad to give you a more detailed analysis. Attached for your reference is a brief outline of Rule 144 requirements [appendix D-3].

Proxy Statement Disclosure

SK Item 405 would still apply to the departing Section 16 Reporting Person and would require disclosure in the proxy statement of any delinquencies in that person's filings.

Any special compensation arrangements for a departing Section 16 Reporting Person may have to be disclosed in the company's proxy statement for the ensuing year, depending on whether that person fits the definition of "named executive officer" in SK Item 402. Usually, there is no disclosure with respect to a departing director who is not named in the proxy statement.

APPENDIX D-2

Exit Memorandum

MEMORANDUM

[DATE]

TO: Name of Departing Section 16 Reporting Person]

FROM: [Name of Section 16 Compliance Person]

RE: Continuing Reporting Obligations and Transaction Restrictions Applicable to a Departing Executive Officer or Director of the Company

With respect to your recent resignation as a[n] [executive officer/director], I am writing to remind you that any person who ceases to be an executive officer or director of the company continues to have certain obligations under the federal securities laws as follows:

Rule 10b-5 Trading Restrictions. Rule 10b-5 states that you may not buy or sell securities of the company on the basis of material non-public information obtained from the company or any party associated with the company. In addition, you may not furnish material non-public information about the company to any person who might trade on the information. We suggest that you follow these rules and the company's insider trading policy for three months from the termination of your [executive officer/director status].

Short-Swing Profit Rule Applies up to Six Months After Termination. Section 16(b) provides for the loss of profits on any sale and purchase of company common stock within a six-month period. It continues to apply to open market purchases and sales that occur within less than six months of an opposite-way, open market purchase and sale that took place while you were subject to Section 16.

For example, if you bought stock in the open market three months before you terminated your status as a Section 16 Reporting Person, any open market sales you make for three months after you have terminated your status will be reportable on a Form 4 within two business days and potentially matchable with the purchase you made while you were a Section 16 Reporting Person. Stock option exercises, however, are treated as exempt purchases and need not be reported regardless of the transactions that occurred while you were a Section 16 Reporting Person. This is equally true with respect to the delivery of previously owned shares to pay the exercise price or to pay taxes or the vesting of restricted stock. A cashless exercise in which you sell stock in the open market to pay the exercise price is reportable and matchable if you have had an open market purchase within six months while you were a Section 16 Reporting Person. With respect to any proposed transactions involving the company's common stock in the company's 401(k) plan, you should consult with me or an attorney in my office before changing your investments in the company stock fund. Any other transactions involving the 401(k) plan, need not be pre-cleared.

Form 4. You must file a Form 4 to report any open market purchases and sales in company stock after you cease to be a Section 16 Reporting Person that occurs within six months of any opposite-way, open market purchase and sale that took place while you were a Section 16 Reporting Person. Form 4 must be filed with the SEC by the second business day after the date of execution of the transaction. Please notify us so we may do the filing for you.

Form 5. You must file a Form 5 [within 45 days after the issuer's fiscal year-end] to report any pre-resignation transactions and any reportable post-resignation transactions not previously reported on Form 4. For example, a gift made while you were a Section 16 Reporting Person and not reported on a voluntary Form 4 needs to be filed on a voluntary Form 4 or mandatory Form 5. (It is the company's policy to report all gifts on a voluntary Form 4, so this should not be a problem unless we were not told of the gift.) If you have no transactions requiring a Form 5, we may ask you to so certify to the company in writing prior to the printing of the company's proxy statement to avoid being named in the company's proxy statement for failing to file a Form 5.

Exit Box. On each Form 4 or Form 5 you file after your resignation, the "exit" box in the upper left hand corner of the form should be checked.

SEC Enforcement. There may be significant civil and criminal penalties if you fail to comply with the above requirements.

Because the Section 16 reporting requirements are extremely complex, the company recommends that you consult with [Section 16 compliance person], when preparing any Form 4 or Form 5, or if you have any questions regarding the reporting requirements.

Rule 144. [Our records indicate that you do not have any restricted securities.] If you have "restricted" securities, they need to be sold under Rule 144 for at least three months after your cessation of Section 16 status, provided that you have held the restricted securities for at least one year. After three months (and the one-year holding period), you may sell the securities free of any Rule 144 restrictions.

APPENDIX D-3
Summary of Rule 144 Under the New Rules

Rule 144 is a safe harbor exemption for sales of restricted stock and control stock. Restricted stock means stock acquired from the issuer without registration of that stock. Control stock means stock held by an affiliate regardless of source, i.e., bought from the issuer or in the open market. The requirements for sale under Rule 144 are:

1. Current public information about the company must be available.
   Affiliates: Always applies
   Non-affiliates: Stock held for less than one year

2. If the stock is restricted stock, it must be held for six months before sale; unrestricted control stock does not have to be held for any period.

3. The amount to be sold during any three-month period is limited to the greater of (1) one percent of the total number of outstanding shares, or (2) the average weekly trading volume for the four calendar weeks preceding the filing of Form 144 *(applies only to affiliates).*

4. The stock must be sold in unsolicited brokers' transactions (any responsible broker will know how to do a 144 transaction) *(applies only to affiliates).*

5. Form 144 must be filed with the SEC before the sale occurs if greater than 5,000 shares or $50,000 *(applies only to affiliates).*

Notes:

Rule 144(k) permits sales of restricted stock free from the requirements of Rule 144 by non-affiliates after a one-year holding period.

If the reporting person is an affiliate, sales must be reported on SEC Form 4 no later than the second business day following the sale and are matchable against any nonexempt purchases made by the reporting person six months before or after the sale.

APPENDIX D-4
Comparison of Old Rule 144 with New Rule 144

Topic	Old Rule 144	New Rule 144
Resales of Restricted Securities by Non-affiliates Under Rule 144	–Limited resales after holding restricted securities for one year. –Unlimited resales after holding restricted securities for two years if they have not been affiliates during the prior three months. –No tolling of holding period as a result of hedging transactions.	–Unlimited resales after holding restricted securities of Exchange Act reporting companies for six months if they have not been affiliates during the prior three months, except that such resales would be subject to the current public information requirement between the end of the six-month holding period and one year after the acquisition date of the securities. –Unlimited resales after holding restricted securities of non-reporting companies for one year if they have not been affiliates during the prior three months. –Specific provision tolling the holding period when engaged in certain hedging transactions. Maximum one-year holding period.
Resales by Affiliates Under Rule 144	–Limited resales after holding restricted securities for one year. –No tolling of holding period as a result of hedging transactions.	–Limited resales after holding restricted securities of Exchange Act reporting companies for six months. –Limited resales after holding restricted securities of non-reporting companies for one year. –Specific provision tolling the holding period when engaged in certain hedging transactions. Maximum one-year holding period.
Manner of Sale Restrictions	–Apply to resale of any type of security under Rule 144.	–Would not apply to resale of debt securities by affiliates or to any resale by non-affiliates.
Form 144	–Filing threshold at 500 shares or $10,000.	–With respect to affiliates, filing threshold at 1,000 [5,000] shares or $50,000. –No Form 144 filing required for non-affiliates.

APPENDIX D-5
SEC Summary of Rule 144 from Final Release

The final conditions applicable to the resale under Rule 144 of restricted securities held by affiliates and non-affiliates of the issuer have been summarized by the SEC in Release 33-8869 as follows:

	Affiliate or Person Selling on Behalf of an Affiliate	Non-affiliate (and Has Not Been an Affiliate During the Prior Three Months)
Restricted Securities of Reporting Issuers	*During six-month holding period*—no resales under Rule 144 permitted. *After six-month holding period*—may resell in accordance with all Rule 144 requirements, including: • Current public information, • Volume limitations, • Manner of sale requirements for equity securities, and • Filing of Form 144.	*During six-month holding period*—no resales under Rule 144 permitted. *After six-month holding period but before one year*—unlimited public resales under Rule 144 except that the current public information requirement still applies. *After one-year holding period*—unlimited public resales under Rule 144; need not comply with any other Rule 144 requirements.
Restricted Securities of Non-reporting Issuers	*During one-year holding period*—no resales under Rule 144 permitted. *After one-year holding period*—may resell in accordance with all Rule 144 requirements, including: • Current public information, • Volume limitations, • Manner of sale requirements for equity securities, and • Filing of Form 144.	*During one-year holding period*—no resales under Rule 144 permitted. *After one-year holding period*—unlimited public resales under Rule 144; need not comply with any other Rule 144 requirements.

3

State Securities Law Considerations for Equity Compensation Plans

Matthew Topham

Contents

T HE TERM "BLUE SKY LAWS" refers to state statutes that prescribe the methods by which stock and other securities may be sold or offered for sale within the state. They are known as "blue sky" laws because many of the business deals that these laws were intended to address were so questionable they had no more substance to them than "air" or "blue sky."[1] As with the federal securities laws, these statutes

---

1. Paul G. Mahoney, "The Origins of the Blue Sky Laws: A Test of Competing Hypotheses," University of Virginia Law School. December 2001. See, e.g., Hall v. Geiger-Jones Co., 242 U.S. 539, 550, 37 S. Ct. 217, 220, 61 L. Ed. 480, 489 (1917) ("The name that is given to the law indicates the evil at which it is aimed; that is, to use the language of a cited case, 'speculative schemes which have no more basis than so many feet of blue sky;' or, as stated by counsel in another case, 'to stop the sale of stock in fly-by-night concerns,

generally prohibit companies and shareholders from selling (or offering to sell) stocks and securities unless the sale is registered with the state's securities commission or fits into one of the exemptions from registration provided by the state's blue sky laws. In most states, these exemptions parallel or complement many of the federal exemptions.[2] However, this chapter does not discuss exemptions from federal securities laws, which

---

visionary oil wells, distant gold mines, and other like fraudulent exploitations.'").

2. It is important to note that certain employee benefit plan securities, which are exempted from federal registration requirements by § 3(a)(2) of the Securities Act of 1933, are also preempted from state regulation (except for enforcement actions with respect to fraud), under the National Securities Markets Improvement Act of 1996, Pub. L. No. 104-290, 110 Stat. 3416 (1996). Section 3(a)(2) exempts, among other things:

> any interest or participation in a single trust fund, or in a collective trust fund maintained by a bank, or any security arising out of a contract issued by an insurance company, which interest, participation, or security is issued in connection with (A) a stock bonus, pension, or profit-sharing plan which meets the requirements for qualification under section 401 of the Internal Revenue Code of 1954, (B) an annuity plan which meets the requirements for the deduction of the employer's contributions under section 404(a)(2) of such Code, or (C) a governmental plan as defined in section 414(d) of such Code which has been established by an employer for the exclusive benefit of its employees or their beneficiaries for the purpose of distributing to such employees or their beneficiaries the corpus and income of the funds accumulated under such plan, if under such plan it is impossible, prior to the satisfaction of all liabilities with respect to such employees and their beneficiaries, for any part of the corpus or income to be used for, or diverted to, purposes other than the exclusive benefit of such employees or their beneficiaries, other than any plan described in clause (A), (B), or (C) of this paragraph (i) the contributions under which are held in a single trust fund or in a separate account maintained by an insurance company for a single employer and under which an amount in excess of the employer's contribution is allocated to the purchase of securities (other than interests or participations in the trust or separate account itself) issued by the employer or any company directly or indirectly controlling, controlled by, or under common control with the employer, (ii) which covers employees some or all of whom are employees within the meaning of section 401(c)(1) of such Code, or (iii) which is a plan funded by an annuity contract described in section 403(b) of such Code.

This chapter presumes that the securities in question do not fall within the exemption set forth in § 3(a)(2) and are not preempted from state regulation.

must also be considered before offering or selling securities (see chapter 2 for a discussion of federal securities law issues).

In many cases, in order to qualify for an exemption under state blue sky laws, the issuer must take certain steps before issuing the security. In the case of securities granted or sold pursuant to employee stock option, stock purchase, or other benefit plans, these steps may include filing the relevant plan with the state securities administrator or including specific provisions in the plan. Failure to comply with these steps could render an exemption unavailable and leave the issuer with no alternative but to register the security before it is either offered or sold. Therefore, it is critical for issuers to plan ahead and evaluate possible exemptions from registration, preferably at the time the plan is being drafted and certainly before any securities are issued. To demonstrate how this process might work, this chapter uses a fictitious company, Sample Corporation, to show how blue sky laws apply in several different states.

3.1 Identifying the Relevant Blue Sky Laws and Related Regulations

3.1.1 Determining the Relevant Jurisdiction

The first step in the process of seeking a valid exemption from registration for the grant of a stock option, the issuance of stock upon the exercise of the option, or the sale of stock pursuant to an employee stock purchase plan is identifying which blue sky laws apply. Most states require registration of securities that are offered for sale or sold in their jurisdiction. In addition, some blue sky laws treat an offer to sell as occurring in both the place from which the offer originates as well as the place where the employee receives the offer. If the issuer (the company that is issuing the securities) and employee are located in the same state, then the issuer only needs to be concerned with the blue sky laws of that one state. If, however, the issuer is located in one jurisdiction and the employee is located in another, then the issuer may be required to comply with the blue sky laws in both jurisdictions.

As a hypothetical example, take Sample Corporation, a Delaware corporation that has its headquarters in Seattle, Washington. Sample Corporation has operations in Washington, Nevada, and Texas. Sample adopted an equity incentive plan that allows for the grant of incentive stock options, nonqualified stock options, and restricted stock to employees, consultants, and directors. The plan is administered by a committee of Sample's board of directors, which includes Sample's president, who is located in Washington. After awards under the plan have been approved by the committee, Sample's president will either contact the recipient directly to make the offer or will instruct Sample's senior vice president in Nevada or senior vice president in Texas, depending upon which region the person receiving the award will be supporting, to make the offer. Sample would like to hire a software engineer who lives in Palo Alto, California, to support Sample's Nevada operations. The software engineer will telecommute from Palo Alto. After the committee approves a compensation package for the software engineer, Sample's president instructs the senior vice president in Nevada to make the offer. The senior vice president in Nevada calls the California engineer at home and offers her a job with Sample with a compensation package consisting of a salary of $15,000 per month and a stock option to purchase 100,000 shares of Sample common stock at a price of $1 per share vesting over a four-year period. The California employee accepts this offer.

Under the circumstances described in the hypothetical, which state's blue sky law will apply to the offer and issuance of the stock option? To answer this question, it is necessary to analyze where the acts essential to the offer or sale of the stock option took place. Where all acts essential to a sale or transfer of securities take place in one state only, the transaction is governed by the securities laws of that state; however, where the acts are performed in several different states, it is necessary to apply conflict of law principles to determine which state's securities law will control.[3] This analysis must be made on a case-by-case basis and will depend on the specific facts. Where there is some territorial nexus to a securities transaction, laws of two or more states may simultaneously apply without presenting a conflict of laws question.[4] Thus, issuers may be required to comply with the blue sky laws of multiple states in connection with the same transaction.

Companies should be aware that this analysis will often require the company to make a judgment call as to whether the blue sky laws of a specific state apply, particularly if there are some states that have a very limited nexus to the transaction. If after making a thorough analysis, which should include discussing the issue on an anonymous basis with the relevant state securities administrator, reasonable doubt exists as to whether a given state's blue sky laws apply, the author recommends tak-

3. 79A C.J.S. Securities Regulation § 367.
4. See *Barnebey v. E.F. Hutton & Co.*, 715 F. Supp. 1512, 1533-1536 (M.D. Fla. 1989); *Lintz v. Carey Manor Ltd.*, 613 F. Supp. 543, 550 (W.D. Va. 1985).

ing a conservative position in favor of compliance. Following is a sample analysis based on the hypothetical facts set forth above. This analysis reflects the author's views, and different practitioners may reach a different conclusion with respect to the applicability of the blue sky laws in one or more of these states.

Four states must be analyzed in connection with the transaction described in the example above: Delaware, Washington, Nevada, and California.

Delaware blue sky law provides that it is unlawful for any person to offer or sell any security in Delaware unless it is registered under the Delaware securities act, the security or transaction is exempted under Section 7309 of the Delaware securities act, or it is a federal covered security for which a notice filing has been made.[5] In the example, the only nexus between Delaware and the offer of the stock option is the fact that Sample was incorporated in Delaware and that if the stock option is exercised, the underlying stock will be issued under Delaware law. Neither Sample nor the employee is located in Delaware, and none of the communications relating to the transaction occurred or originated in Delaware. As a general rule, a transaction involving corporate stock, such as a sale, issuance, or transfer, is not governed by the securities act of the state where the corporation is organized if the transaction occurs in another state.[6] Here, the transaction occurred outside of Delaware, and the Delaware blue sky law should not apply.

Washington blue sky law provides that it is unlawful for any person to offer or sell any security in Washington unless the security is registered by coordination or qualification, the security or transaction is exempted, or the security is a federal covered security.[7] An "offer to sell" under the Washington blue sky law includes every attempt or offer to dispose of, or solicitation of an offer to buy, a security or interest in a security for value.[8] Based on the facts in the example, there is a reasonable possibility that the Securities Division of the Washington Department of Financial Institutions would take the position that an offer to sell occurred in Washington because the offer originated in Washington, although the offer was communicated to the employee by the vice president in Nevada and is

---

5. Del. Code Ann. tit. 6, § 7304.

6. See *McCullough v. Leede Oil & Gas, Inc.*, 617 F. Supp. 384, 389 (W.D. Okla. 1985).

7. Wash Rev. Code § 21.20.140.

8. Wash. Rev. Code § 21.20.005(10).

being made to an employee who will be based in California. There may be some debate as to whether the offer of the stock option in exchange for employment was "for value" for purposes of the Washington blue sky law. Although there is no Washington case law directly on point, there is authority in other jurisdictions that supports the position that when an employee bargains for compensation that includes stock or stock options, the employee has provided value for the securities.[9] Even if the stock options were not considered to have been offered for value, under Washington law, the offer of the stock option also included the

---

9. "When an individual 'commits herself to employment by a corporation in return for stock or the promise of stock,' she will be considered an investor worthy of protection under the federal securities laws. See *Yoder v. Orthomolecular Nutrition Inst., Inc.*, 751 F.2d 555, 560 (2d Cir. 1985). Where a plaintiff accepted employment with the issuer in return for an annual salary of $40,000 plus options to purchase up to 30,000 shares of the issuer's stock, the court held that plaintiff 'purchased' the options. *Yoder*, 751 F.2d at 560. Similarly, in *Rudinger v. Insurance Data Processing, Inc.*, the plaintiff bargained for and received an employment contract wherein he was to receive a certain number of stock options in addition to an annual salary of $100,000. 778 F. Supp. 1334, 1338-39 (E.D. Pa. 1991). The court declared '[a]n agreement exchanging a plaintiff's services for a defendant corporation's stock constitutes a 'sale' under the terms of the Securities Exchange Act.' Id.; see also, e.g., *Campbell v. National Media Corp.*, No. 94-4590, 1994 WL 612807 (E.D. Pa. Nov. 3, 1994) (finding that grant of options to purchase 50,000 shares in executive's employment agreement was a purchase of securities); *Collins v. Rukin*, 342 F. Supp. 1282, 1289 (D. Mass. 1972) (finding that stock options were a 'quid pro quo offered to induce plaintiff to enter into the employ of [the issuer]'). These cases indicate that where a potential employee acquires the right to options as part of his or her bargained-for compensation, courts will infer that the employees made an intentional decision to 'purchase' the options." *In re Cendant Corp. Securities Litigation*, 76 F. Supp. 2d 539, 544 (D.N.J. 1999).
   The cases cited above were decided by federal courts and considered issues based on federal securities laws. Therefore, these decisions do not create binding authority in most states. But these cases do indicate that at least some courts treat an agreement to work in exchange for securities as a purchase of such securities for value. Note, however, that under some circumstances courts have held that interests in stock-related benefit plans do not constitute a "security." See, e.g., *Childers v. Northwest Airlines, Inc.*, 688 F. Supp. 1357, 1363 (D. Minn. 1988) (holding that employees' participation in employee stock ownership plan cannot be characterized as a "purchase" of a security since participating employees did not furnish value). Therefore, the question of whether securities issued in connection with employment have been acquired for value should be considered carefully on a case-by-case basis.

offer to sell the underlying stock at $1 per share, which is probably sufficient to satisfy the requirement that the offer be for value for purposes of Washington blue sky law.[10] It should be noted that it is not certain that the Securities Division of the Washington Department of Financial Institutions would take any enforcement action under the circumstances described in the example because the transaction does not involve an offer to a Washington resident. However, because significant acts relating to the offer of the option occurred in Washington, as a precautionary measure, the author would recommend that Sample comply with Washington blue sky law.

Nevada blue sky law provides that it is unlawful for a person to offer to sell or sell any security in Nevada unless the security is registered or the security or transaction is exempt under the Nevada securities act.[11] The Nevada blue sky law uses the same definition of "offer to sell" as Washington blue sky law.[12] Based on a strict reading of the statute, it is difficult to argue that Sample's Nevada vice president did not make an offer of a security to the California employee. Sample could argue that the Nevada vice president was simply following instructions and did not have the authority to approve or make the offer, which originated in Washington. This is a reasonable argument, and given the limited nexus between Nevada and the transaction, the author believes it is unlikely that the Securities Division of the Office of the Nevada Secretary of State would take the position that Sample is required to comply with Nevada blue sky law in connection with the offer. However, Sample must accept there is a risk that the Securities Division could take that position; therefore, Sample should evaluate the requirements of Nevada blue sky law to determine how onerous compliance would be. As explained below, Nevada blue sky law has a self-executing exemption from registration, so complying with Nevada blue sky law will not impose any additional burden on Sample. In other states, compliance may not be this simple, and it will be more difficult to decide whether it is worthwhile to undertake the burdens associated with compliance where there is a very limited nexus with the state in question. This example illustrates why many issuers only allow offers of stock options or other equity incentives to be made from a single location, such as corporate headquarters. By inserting additional jurisdictions into the offer process, the issuer

---

10. Wash. Rev. Code § 21.20.005(10).

11. Nev. Rev. Stat. § 90.460.

12. Nev. Rev. Stat. § 90.280[1].

expands the list of blue sky laws that must be analyzed and creates unnecessary risk.

California blue sky law treats an offer to sell as occurring in both the location where the offer originates and the location where the offeree receives the offer.[13] The definition of an "offer to sell" under California blue sky law is similar to the definition under Washington blue sky law.[14] In addition, under California blue sky law, every sale or offer of a right to purchase another security includes an offer and sale of the other security at the time of the offer of the right to purchase such other security.[15] This means that the offer of the stock option included the offer and sale of the underlying stock. And because this offer was directed to and received by the employee in California, Sample should comply with the California blue sky law in addition to the Washington blue sky law and Nevada blue sky law with respect to the stock option grant.

3.1.2 Reviewing the Relevant Blue Sky Laws

Once the issuer has determined the relevant jurisdictions, the next step is to review the blue sky laws for those jurisdictions. The blue sky laws for a particular state are typically contained in the state's securities act (the exact title of the securities act will vary from state to state). Each state's securities act contains a section dealing with exemptions. In some states, all of the exemptions are contained in a single section, while in other states there are separate sections for exempt securities and exempt transactions. It is not sufficient to review only the exemptions listed in the state securities act. In many cases, the legislature delegates the authority to the state securities administrator[16] to create additional exemptions beyond or to further qualify those listed in the securities act. Therefore, the issuer must also review the regulations, if any, promulgated under the securities act as well as any decisions, comments, no-action letters,

---

13. Cal. Corp. Code § 25008(b) ("An offer to sell or to buy is made in this state when the offer either originates from or is directed by the offeror to this state and received at the place to which it is directed.").

14. Cal. Corp. Code § 25017(b).

15. Cal. Corp. Code § 25008(b).

16. The responsibility for administering the state securities laws varies from state to state and may rest on the department of financial institutions, a securities commission or some other department or agency. This chapter refers to the applicable agency or department generally as the "state securities administrator."

or other interpretive guidance published by the state securities administrator.

Continuing with the example of Sample Corporation, Sample should start by reviewing the Washington State Securities Act, which is contained in Title 21 of the Revised Code of Washington. However, Sample should also review Title 460 of the Washington Administrative Code, which contains rules and regulations governing the offer and sale of securities that have been adopted by the Washington Department of Financial Institutions pursuant to statutory authority. Sample should also review the Nevada Uniform Securities Act, which is contained in Chapter 90 of the Nevada Revised Statutes, and the related regulations contained in Chapter 90 of the Nevada Administrative Code. Finally, Sample should also review the California Corporate Securities Law of 1968, which is contained in Sections 25000 through 25707 of the California Corporations Code. In addition, California has blue sky regulations contained in Title 10 of the California Code of Regulations.

3.2 Identifying Applicable Exemptions

A stock option and the stock underlying the option are separate securities. Therefore, in the case of stock option plans, the issuer must have an exemption for both the grant of the stock option and the issuance of the underlying stock. In many cases, the exemption that covers the grant of a stock option will also cover the issuance of stock upon the exercise of that option. However, an issuer should not presume this will be the case and should confirm the existence of a valid exemption for both the grant of the option and the issuance of the stock upon exercise ahead of time.[17] Several states have broad exemptions either for securities or transactions relating to employee benefit plans, which are referred to in this chapter generally as "blanket exemptions." These blanket exemptions, as well as other exemptions and the requirements to qualify for those exemptions are outlined below.

3.2.1 Stock Option Grants and Sales Under Stock Purchase Plans

Exempt Securities. A number of state blue sky laws specifically exempt from registration securities issued in connection with certain employee

---

17. This issue does not arise in connection with employee stock purchase plans, because issuers typically sell shares of common stock and not derivative or convertible securities under such plans.

benefit plans, specifically including stock option plans.[18] Other blue sky laws exempt investment contracts or securities issued in connection with an employee's stock purchase, savings, pension, profit-sharing, or similar benefit plan, without specifically mentioning stock option plans.[19] The state securities administrators in many of the states with an exemption of the latter type (i.e., exemptions that do not specifically mention stock option plans), treat stock option plans as a "similar benefit plan" for purposes of the exemption. However, the issuer should confirm that this is the case with the state securities administrator before issuing stock options.[20]

Even if exemptions related to employee benefit plans apply, most attach additional requirements or conditions to that exemption. For example, some blue sky laws require that the issuer submit a plan to the state securities administrator within a set number of days before or after issuing securities under that plan or that the content of the plan include certain substantive provisions. What follows are just some of the most common requirements contained in blanket exemptions for exempt securities issued in connection with employee benefit plans.

1. *Securities must be issued in connection with a plan that meets the requirements for qualification under the Internal Revenue Code.* One common requirement contained in exemptions for securities issued in connection with benefit plans is that the applicable benefit plan must qualify under certain sections of the Internal Revenue Code. For example, Washington blue sky law provides an exemption for:

---

18. See, e.g., Ariz. Rev. Stat. § 44-1844[A][14]; Ark. Code § 23-42-503(a)(8); Cal. Corp. Code § 25102 (o); Conn. Gen. Stat. § 36b-21(a)(11); 815 Ill. Comp. Stat. 5/3 [N]; Iowa Code § 502.202 [21]; Ky. Rev. Stat. Ann. § 292.400(11); Mich. Comp. Laws (Ann) § 451.802(a)(10); N.C. Gen. Stat. § 78A-16(11); Nev. Rev. Stat. § 90.520[2](l); N.M. Stat. Ann. § 58-13B-26[K]; 70 Pa. Stat. § 1-202(g); R.I. Gen. Laws § 7-11-401(12); Utah Code Ann. § 61-1-14(1)(j).

19. See, e.g., Ala. Code § 8-6-10(10); Alaska Stat. § 45.55.900(a)(5); Colo. Rev. Stat. § 11-51-307(1)(i); Del. Code Ann. tit. 6, § 7309(a)(11); Haw. Rev. Stat. § 485-4(11) (repealed effective July 1, 2008); Ind. Code § 23-2-1-2(a)(7); Md. Code Ann., Corps. & Ass'ns § 11-601(11); Mass. Gen. Laws ch. 110A, § 402(a)(11); Miss. Code § 75-71-201(11); Mont. Code Ann. § 30-10-104(10); N.J. Stat 49:3-50(a)(11); N.Y. Gen. Bus. Law § 359-f.[2](e); Or. Rev. Stat. § 59.025(12); Va. Code Ann. § 13.1-514[A][10]; Wash. Rev. Code § 21.20.310(10).

20. Essentially every state's blanket exemption for securities issued in connection with employee benefit plans specifically lists stock purchase plans.

Any security issued in connection with an employee's stock purchase, savings, pension, profit-sharing, or similar benefit plan if: (a) The plan meets the requirements for qualification as a pension, profit sharing, or stock bonus plan under section 401 of the internal revenue code, as an incentive stock option plan under section 422 of the internal revenue code, as a nonqualified incentive stock option plan adopted with or as a supplement to an incentive stock option plan under section 422 of the internal revenue code, or as an employee stock purchase plan under section 423 of the internal revenue code; or (b) the director is notified in writing with a copy of the plan thirty days before offering the plan to employees in this state. In the event of late filing of notification the director may upon application, for good cause excuse such late filing if he or she finds it in the public interest to grant such relief.[21]

The referenced sections of the Internal Revenue Code contain requirements that must be satisfied in order for the plan to be qualified under those sections. For example, Section 422, which governs incentive stock options, includes requirements, among others, relating to exercise price, expiration, and transferability. In order for a plan to qualify under Section 422, it must include these provisions. Section 423 imposes requirements on employee stock purchase plans relating to eligibility, shareholder approval, purchase price and duration of the right to purchase. If an issuer intends to rely on an exemption such as Wash. Rev. Code Section 21.20.310(10)(a), it must satisfy the applicable requirements from the Internal Revenue Code. In the example above, Sample's equity incentive plan provides for the issuance of incentive stock options, nonqualified stock options and restricted stock grants. Although it is possible that the Washington state securities administrator might conclude that this plan would qualify as a "nonqualified incentive stock option plan adopted with or as a supplement to an incentive stock option plan under section 422 of the [I]nternal [R]evenue [C]ode" for purposes of Wash. Rev. Code Section 21.20.310(a), there is no interpretive guidance that supports this conclusion. Therefore, Sample should not rely on Wash. Rev. Code Section 21.20.310(a) and should instead submit the plan to the director of the Washington Department of Financial Institutions in accordance with Wash. Rev. Code Section 21.20.310(b) at least 30 days before offering securities under the plan to employees in Washington.[22]

---

21. Wash Rev. Code § 21.20.310(10).

22. A problem may arise if the issuer issues the securities before sending the director notice and a copy of the plan. In that situation, the issuer must ap-

2. *Securities must be issued in connection with a plan that has been submitted to the state securities law administrator.* Several jurisdictions require the issuer to submit any plan to the state securities law administrator before any securities are issued pursuant to such plan.[23] Other jurisdictions have exemptions, such as the Washington statute cited above, that require the issuer to submit the plan only if it does not qualify under certain sections of the Internal Revenue Code.[24] The state securities administrator typically has a certain number of days after receipt of the plan to disallow or deny the exemption.

3. *Securities must be issued pursuant to a plan that only applies to employees and directors.* Most exemptions for securities issued pursuant to benefit plans refer specifically to plans for employees. However, issuers frequently adopt stock option plans that provide for grants to directors and consultants as well as employees. The question is whether securities issued to directors and consultants under such plans qualify for the blanket exemption for employee benefit plans. Some state blue sky laws specifically provide that the exemption applies to directors and consultants as well as employees. In other states, the state securities administrator takes the position that the exemption only applies to consultants to the same extent Rule 701 of the Securities Act of 1933 (the "Securities Act") applies to consultants. Rule 701 is the federal law exemption covering offers and sales of securities under a written compensatory benefit plan. Rule 701 specifically allows for grants to officers, directors, consultants and advisors, but it imposes certain requirements on consultants and advisors. For example, consultants and advisors must be natural persons (i.e., individual human beings as opposed to corporations, limited liability companies, trusts, etc.) and must provide bona fide services that are not in connection with the offer or sale of securities in a capital-raising transaction and do not directly or indirectly promote or maintain a market for the issuer's securities. The issuer should research any interpretive guidance provided by the state securities administrator on whether the blanket exemption for em-

---

ply to the director, which can grant relief from the failure to meet the 30-day pre-filing requirement for good cause upon finding that it is in the public interest to grant such relief.

23. See, e.g., Del. Code Ann. tit. 6, § 7309(a)(11); Idaho Code § 30-14-202(21); Mass. Gen. Laws ch. 110A, § 402(a)(11).

24. See, e.g., Ark. Code § 23-42-503(a)(8); Ky. Rev. Stat. Ann. § 292.400(11); Md. Code Ann., Corps. & Ass'ns § 11-601(11); Wash. Rev. Code § 21.20.310(10).

ployee benefit plans applies to securities issued to consultants and directors under such plans and, if so, whether there are any restrictions with respect to such persons, such as those contained in Rule 701. If the issuer cannot find any written guidance on this issue, the issuer should contact the state securities administrator directly.

Exempt Transactions. Unlike the state blue sky laws described above that treat securities granted in connection with certain employee benefit plans as exempt *securities*, some state blue sky laws treat the issuance of securities in connection with an employee benefit plan as an exempt *transaction*.[25] Several of these blue sky laws require that in order for the transaction to be exempt, either the plan must be qualified under certain provisions of the Internal Revenue Code or the sale of securities under the plan must meet the exemption contained in Rule 701. An example of this requirement is contained in the Ohio blue sky laws, which provide the following:

> (5) The sale of any security pursuant to a pension plan, stock plan, profit-sharing plan, compensatory benefit plan or similar plan is exempt pursuant to division (V) of section 1707.03 of the Revised Code if:
>
> > (a) The security is sold pursuant to a plan qualified under sections 401 to 425 of the Internal Revenue Code of 1986;
> >
> > (b) The sale of the security is exempt from the provisions of section 5 of the Securities Act of 1933 because it meets the exemption set forth in rule 701 of the Securities Act of 1933 and any commission, discount or other remuneration paid or given for the sale of the security in this state is paid or given only to dealers or salespersons licensed by the division; or
> >
> > (c) The security is effectively registered under sections 6 to 8 of the Securities Act of 1933 and is offered and sold in compliance with the provisions of section 5 of the Securities Act of 1933.[26]

In jurisdictions such as Ohio that have a blanket exemption based on Rule 701, the issuer must comply with the requirements of Rule 701

---

25. See, e.g., Fla. Stat. § 517.061(15); Ga. Code Ann. § 10-5-9(9)(C); Haw. Rev. Stat. § 485A-202(a)(21) (effective July 1, 2008); Idaho Code § 30-14-202(21); Kan. Stat. Ann. § 17-12a202(21); La. Rev. Stat. Ann. § 51:709(9)(c); Me. Rev. Stat. Ann. tit. 32, § 16202[22]; Minn. Stat. § 80A(15) Subdivision 2(s); 26 Mo. Rev. Stat. § 409.2-202(21); Ohio Admin. Code § 1301:6-3-03(E)(5); 71 Okla. Stat. § 1-202[22]; N.D. Cent. Code § 10-04-06[11]; Tex. Rev. Civ. Stat., Art. 581-5[I](b).

26. Ohio Admin. Code § 1301:6-3-03(E)(5).

(unless the plan qualifies under an appropriate section of the Internal Revenue Code), discussed above, in order to qualify for the state blue sky law exemption.

For example, California blue sky law contains a transaction-based blanket exemption for an offer or sale of any security issued to officers, directors, general partners, trustees (where the issuer is a business trust), managers, advisors, or consultants of the issuer pursuant to an option plan or agreement where the security at the time of issuance is exempt from registration under the Securities Act pursuant to Rule 701, provided that the terms of the option plan or agreement comply with Sections 260.140.41, 260.140.45, and 260.140.46 of Title 10 of the California Code of Regulations and the issuer files a notice of transaction with the state securities administrator and pays a filing fee no later than 30 days after the initial issuance of any security under that plan.[27] Section 260.140.41 requires the plan to contain specific provisions, such as restrictions on the maximum exercise period. Sections 260.140.45 and 260.140.46 contain requirements relating to the maximum number of securities issuable under a plan and the delivery of financial statements to security holders, respectively, but neither of these sections applies to a plan or agreement that complies with all conditions of Rule 701. This California exemption highlights the importance of planning ahead to make sure that the necessary provisions are included in the option plan or agreement. A company such as Sample, which is based in Washington but may periodically grant options to employees in California, should consider adding a separate section to its option plan that contains the language required by Sections 260.140.41, 260.140.45, and 260.140.46 and applies only to options granted to California employees, officers, directors, advisors, or consultants. Alternatively, Sample could leave these provisions out of the plan and handle grants to California employees, officers, directors, advisors, and consultants through separate agreements that contain the required language.

Limited Offering Exemptions. In the event the issuer does not qualify for a blanket exemption of the type described above, another alternative is to issue the stock options under a private offering exemption. Because these exemptions typically limit the number of purchasers to somewhere between five and thirty-five persons, they are not a practical alternative for an issuer seeking an exemption for the issuance of stock options to

---

27. Cal. Corp. Code § 25102(o).

a large number of employees. However, these exemptions are useful in situations where the issuer only plans to issue options to a few key executives or wants to grant options without a written plan or agreement that qualifies for the blanket exemption. These exemptions may require providing advance notice to the state securities administrator and generally have specific restrictions that may include limitations on the number of offerees, the number of purchasers, the aggregate value of securities sold, the number of shareholders after the offering, and written material that must be provided to offerees. Therefore, as is the case with the blanket exemptions, it is imperative that the issuer research the exemption before the offering.

One limited offering exemption that is important to mention in this context is Rule 506 of Regulation D, which was adopted pursuant to the Securities Act. Although Rule 506 is a federal law exemption, it is relevant in the context of a chapter on state blue sky laws because, pursuant to the National Securities Markets Improvement Act of 1996, offers and sales under Rule 506 are exempt from state blue sky laws with the exception of notice requirements in certain jurisdictions. Some of the advantages of Rule 506 over state law limited offering exemptions are (1) Rule 506 does not limit the dollar amount of securities that can be offered; (2) if the offering is only made to "accredited investors" as defined in Rule 501 of Regulation D, then the issuer is not required to provide the participants with any specific disclosure materials; and (3) the number of purchasers is limited to 35, but accredited investors do not count against this number (i.e., there can be an unlimited number of accredited investors). The definition of "accredited investor" includes, among others, (1) any corporation, partnership or limited liability company not formed for the specific purpose of acquiring the securities offered, with total assets in excess of $5,000,000; (2) any director, executive officer, or general partner of the issuer of the securities being offered or sold, or any director, executive officer, or general partner of a general partner of that issuer; (3) any natural person whose individual net worth, or joint net worth with that person's spouse, at the time of his purchase exceeds $1,000,000; and (4) any natural person who had an individual income in excess of $200,000 in each of the two most recent years or joint income with that person's spouse in excess of $300,000 in each of those years and has a reasonable expectation of reaching the same income level in the current year.[28]

---

28. On August 3, 2007, the Securities and Exchange Commission issued proposed revisions to Regulation D and requests for comment, including comments on the definition of "accredited investor." Before relying on Regulation D,

Including nonaccredited investors in a Rule 506 offering destroys much of the benefit the rule provides because issuers must provide nonaccredited investors who participate in a Rule 506 offering with extensive disclosure. In some cases, this disclosure is comparable to what would be required in a registration statement. Rule 506 offerings are frequently used for sales to institutional investors or high net worth individuals. However, because the definition of accredited investor includes executive officers and directors, Rule 506 can be an effective tool for issuing stock options or selling stock to officers and directors before a benefit plan has been established or outside of a plan that does not have enough shares available. Note that it is impermissible to elect a person to be an officer or director solely for the purpose of making that person an accredited investor.

3.2.2   Issuance of Stock Upon Exercise of Options

As discussed above, the stock issued upon exercise of a stock option is a security distinct from the option itself and must either be registered or exempt from registration. In general, if a stock option was granted pursuant to a valid exemption, then there will be a valid exemption for the issuance of stock upon the exercise of that stock option. This chapter presumes that, as is typically the case, employee stock purchase plans only involve the sale of common stock and do not involve the sale of any derivative or convertible security that can subsequently be exercised for or converted into common stock. Accordingly, this section does not address employee stock purchase plans.

Blanket Exemptions. Although some of the blanket exemptions referenced above specifically cover the issuance of stock upon the exercise of stock options that were granted pursuant to the exemption,[29] most of the blanket exemptions refer broadly to any securities issued in connection with particular types of benefit plans. The question is whether this language is broad enough to cover stock issued upon the exercise of a stock option that was granted pursuant to an employee benefit plan. In order to answer this question in a particular jurisdiction, the issuer should review any regulations or interpretive guidance created by the applicable state securities administrator. If these sources do not provide

---

issuers should review any final revisions to Regulation D to ensure the issuer is in compliance.

29. See La. Rev. Stat. Ann. § 51:709(9)(d).

an answer, the issuer should contact the state securities administrator directly and confirm that the exemption covers both the grant of the stock option and the issuance of stock upon the exercise of the option. In all likelihood the state securities administrator will confirm such is the case, but it is best to clarify this in advance.

For example, as discussed above, Wash. Rev. Code Section 21.20.310(10) exempts "[a]ny security issued in connection with an employee's stock purchase, savings, pension, profit-sharing, or similar benefit plan." The Washington state securities administrator has issued interpretive guidance clarifying that this language covers both the stock option and the stock issued upon exercise of the option. Therefore, the issuance of stock upon the exercise of Sample's stock options granted pursuant to the plan should be exempt pursuant to Wash. Rev. Code Section 21.20.310(10).

Section 90.520[2](l) of the Nevada Revised Statutes provides an exemption for "A security issued in connection with an employees' stock purchase, savings, option, profit-sharing, pension or similar employees' benefit plan." The Securities Division of the Nevada Secretary of State has not issued written guidance clarifying whether this exemption covers the issuance of the underlying stock. However, even if this section does not cover the issuance of the underlying stock, Section 90.530[14] of the Nevada Revised Statutes provides an exemption for a transaction pursuant to an offer to sell to existing security holders of the issuer, which should cover the issuance of stock upon the exercise of a stock option.

California's blue sky law treats the grant of a stock option as a sale of the underlying stock at the time the option is granted.[30] Therefore, assuming the grant of the options was exempt pursuant to Cal. Corp. Code Section 25102(o), Sample does not need to find a separate exemption for the issuance of the stock upon exercise because the issuance of that stock does not constitute an offer or sale for purposes of California blue sky law.

---

30. See Cal. Corp. Code § 25017(e). "Every sale or offer of a warrant or right to purchase or subscribe to another security of the same or another issuer, as well as every sale or offer of a security which gives the holder a present or future right or privilege to convert the security into another security of the same or another issuer, includes an offer and sale of the other security only at the time of the offer or sale of the warrant or right or convertible security; but neither the exercise of the right to purchase or subscribe or to convert nor the issuance of securities thereto is an offer or sale."

Exemption for Transactions Pursuant to an Offer to Existing Security Holders. In the event that a blanket exemption is not available to cover the issuance of stock upon the exercise of a stock option, the issuer should research whether the applicable blue sky laws provide an exemption for transactions with existing security holders, such as the Nevada statute referenced above. This is a common exemption that is generally appropriate for the issuance of a security upon the exercise or conversion of an already outstanding security, such as a warrant or a convertible security (for example, preferred stock). In most states, this exemption requires that either no commission or other remuneration is paid or given directly or indirectly for soliciting any security holder in the state or the issuer first files a notice specifying the terms of the offer and the state securities administrator does not disallow the exemption within a set number of days, which ranges from thirty days to five business days, depending on the jurisdiction.[31]

Limited Offering Exemption. If a blanket exemption or an exemption for transactions with existing security holders is not available, the issuer should research whether a limited offering exemption is available. As discussed above, limited offering exemptions are subject to a variety of qualifications, which the issuer must carefully research before relying upon the exemption. If the issuer is unable to find a valid exemption, then the issuer must consider registration, which is discussed below.

Additional Exemptions Available for Public Companies. In addition to the exemptions above, which are available for both public and private companies, the blue sky laws of most states contain an exemption that may cover the issuance of stock of public companies upon the exercise of stock options. This exemption is for securities that are listed, or authorized for listing, on the New York Stock Exchange, the American Stock Exchange, the national market system of the NASDAQ stock market, or any successor to such entities. This exemption does not apply to the grant of the stock options themselves because the stock options are not listed on any

---

31. See, e.g., Alaska Stat. § 45.55.900(b)(7); Col. Rev. Stat. § 11-51-308(1)(l); Conn. Gen. Stat. § 36b-21(b)(12); Del. Code Ann. tit. 6 § 7309(b)(11); Fla Stat. § 517.061(6); Haw. Rev. Stat. § 485-6(11) (repealed effective July 1, 2008, and replaced by Haw. Rev. Stat. § 485A-202(a)(14)); Idaho Code § 30-14-202(15); 815 Ill. Comp. Stat., 5/4[B]; Ind. Code § 23-2-1-2(b)(11); La. Rev. Stat. Ann. § 51:709(8); Mass. Gen. Laws, ch. 110A, § 402(b)(11); N.M. Stat. § 58-13B-27[N]; 70 Pa. Stat. § 1-203(n); Tex. Rev. Civ. Stat., Art. 581-5[E]; Utah Code Ann. § 61-1-14(2)(j); Va. Code Ann. § 13.1-514[B][8]; Wash. Rev. Code § 21.20.320(11).

exchange or the national market system. However, this exemption would apply to listed stock issued upon the exercise of stock options.

3.3 Registration

If an issuer is unable to find an applicable exemption for granting stock options, issuing stock upon the exercise of stock options, or selling stock pursuant to an employee stock purchase plan, then the issuer must register the securities that the issuer intends to offer (i.e., stock options or stock). Registration is typically done through coordination or qualification and involves the filing of a registration statement with the state securities administrator. The registration statement generally includes information about the issuer, its subsidiaries, officers and directors, capitalization, kind and amount of securities to be offered, anticipated proceeds from the offering and use of the proceeds, a copy of any prospectus or offering circular to be used in connection with the offering, an opinion of counsel as to the legality of the security being registered, and financial statements meeting specified requirements. In many states, registration by coordination is available only if the issuer has already filed a registration statement with respect to such securities under the Securities Act. Registration by coordination generally requires filing with the state securities administrator a copy of the documents filed pursuant to the Securities Act and an abbreviated registration statement as compared to what is required for registration by qualification.

3.4 Conclusion

While blue sky laws vary from state to state and can cause confusion about whether or not an issuer needs to register securities, in most cases companies can qualify for an exemption when it comes to the offering and sale of stock options or stock under employee benefit plans. Working with an experienced attorney who thoroughly understands and can carefully review blue sky laws in the state in which the issuer is based (as well as in those states in which the issuer's employees participating in the plan might reside), companies should be able to avoid the time and expense of registration.

4

Preparing for an Initial Public Offering

Mark A. Borges

Contents

OR MANY COMPANIES, an initial public offering (IPO) of securities is a significant measure of the success of the enterprise. There are several reasons for conducting an IPO. The most frequently cited motive is to raise additional capital for the business. Other reasons include enhancing the image of the company, spreading the risk of future development activities, and providing an avenue to liquidity for the company's founders and other shareholders.

The IPO process can be quite complex and involves the combined efforts of many parties: the company's management; the underwriters for the transaction; and the company's attorneys, accountants, and other professional advisors. If the company maintains an employee stock option plan, several issues related to the IPO must be addressed. Identifying and preparing for these issues will greatly ease the transition from a closely held business to a public reporting company.

In addition, administering the employee stock option plan in an environment where there is a public market for the company's securities is significantly more complex than when the company was closely held. Exercises of outstanding stock options are much more common and more complex. Officers and directors are subject to a multitude of restrictions on their ability to trade in the company's securities, which affect their participation in the stock option plan. Regulatory compliance increases, particularly as it relates to the public disclosure of plan activity. It becomes imperative to have a stock plan administrator to manage these increased responsibilities.

This chapter summarizes some of the key issues involving a company's stock option plan both before and immediately after an IPO. While it is intended to provide a checklist of matters that the company should consider in connection with its IPO, it is not exhaustive. Because the requirements for conducting an IPO are revised from time to time and the regulatory considerations affecting stock option plans are constantly changing, a company should consult its professional advisors to ensure the appropriate application of the rules discussed here to its particular situation.

4.1   Overview of the IPO Process

While a comprehensive discussion of the IPO process is beyond the scope of this chapter, it is helpful for the stock plan administrator to have a basic understanding of the regulatory framework in which the offering takes place.

An IPO represents a company's first sale of securities to the general public. Typically, the company engages one or more investment banks to "underwrite" the offering; that is, to act as intermediaries for the distribution of the securities to public investors.

Any offering of securities is subject to compliance with the Securities Act of 1933 (the "Securities Act"), the basic purpose of which is to ensure that complete and accurate information about the securities being offered to the public and the company offering them is available. To meet this objective, the Securities Act requires that the offering either be registered with the Securities and Exchange Commission (SEC) or satisfy the conditions of an appropriate exemption from the registration requirement. Because an IPO is aimed at reaching a broad audience of prospective investors, it is almost always conducted as a registered transaction with the SEC.

One common misconception regarding an IPO is that it registers all of the company's securities. In fact, registration under the Securities Act covers only the specific securities actually being offered (typically, common stock) and only for the specific purposes of the offering described in the registration statement. While the securities sold in the IPO are previously authorized but unissued shares of the common stock of the company, frequently the founders and other shareholders of the company also sell some of their shares in the offering.

In addition to complying with the Securities Act, the company must satisfy the securities laws in each state in which the shares of stock will be offered. For most IPOs, this means compliance with the securities laws of virtually all 50 states. Fortunately, most states have exemptions that can be used to avoid the registration process in those states. Most state securities laws provide exemptions for securities that are listed or approved for listing on a national securities exchange or quoted for trading through a national securities association. Other states exempt sales of securities to registered broker-dealers or financial institutions.

The securities offered in the IPO also must be designated for trading on a stock market—either an "exchange" market such as the New York Stock Exchange (NYSE), or the "over-the-counter" (OTC) market. Unless and until a company can meet the stringent listing requirements of an exchange, its securities will be traded on the OTC market. The National Association of Securities Dealers, Inc. (NASD), the self-regulatory organization that oversees the OTC market, maintains an electronic automated quotations system to facilitate the trading of many OTC stocks (the NASDAQ). Listing on the NYSE or the NASDAQ requires, among other things, agreement by the company to observe the market's corporate governance requirements, which reflect minimum standards for conducting its internal corporate affairs.

4.2 Planning Considerations Before an IPO

A number of matters involving the company's employee stock option plan will require the attention of the company's management before an IPO.

4.2.1 Amending the Stock Option Plan

While a stock option plan will, in most material respects, operate similarly whether a company's securities are closely held or publicly traded, there will be some features of the plan that company management should consider modifying before the company's IPO. Some of these changes may require shareholder approval, either for regulatory purposes or as required by the plan itself. Preplanning is desirable because it is generally easier to obtain shareholder approval while the company's securities are still closely held. Typical amendments to consider include the following:

Increase Plan Share Reserve. Company management should review the plan share reserve to ensure that there is a sufficient number of shares available to cover projected future stock option grants for a predetermined period of time (generally, at least one to two years).

Revise Plan Eligibility Criteria. The stock plan administrator should review the plan eligibility provision to determine whether the plan permits grants to the appropriate categories of individuals. For example, if the company has not provided for grants to non-employee consultants and advisors in the past, it may be desirable to expand the category of eligible participants to include such individuals. Conversely, if the company has granted stock options to consultants and advisors in the past but now plans a shift in philosophy as a public reporting company, the plan can be amended to restrict future grants to such individuals. Finally, the company should determine how the participation of the company's board of directors, including non-employee directors, will be handled after the IPO, either under the general stock option plan or through a separate directors' stock option plan.

Individual Grant Limitations. Section 162(m) of the Internal Revenue Code (the "Code") limits the ability of public reporting companies to deduct from their corporate income taxes compensation expense in excess of $1 million paid to certain executive officers. An exception to this deduction limit is available for "performance-based" compensation. In order for stock options granted to these executive officers to qualify for this exception, among other things, the stock option plan must contain a maximum per-employee share limitation. (The plan also must be approved by the company's shareholders.)

This per-employee share limitation will be deemed to have been satisfied if the stock option plan states the maximum number of shares of stock for which stock options may be granted during a specified period to any employee. Accordingly, company management, in consultation with the company's professional advisors, should select an appropriate limitation that will act as the maximum number of shares subject to a stock option that can be granted under the plan during a specified period to any employee.

Eliminate Contractual Restrictions. The stock option plans of most closely held companies impose certain contractual restrictions on the ability of an optionee to sell or otherwise transfer his or her option shares following the exercise of a stock option. Typically, these restrictions take the form of a right of first refusal (on third-party transactions), a vested share repurchase option, or a similar arrangement. To the extent that such provisions do not automatically terminate upon the IPO, they should be deleted from the plan.

Revise Exercise Payment Methods. In anticipation of the establishment of a public market for the company's securities, company management should consider expanding the range of permissible payment methods under the stock option plan. To the extent that the stock option plan does not expressly permit broker-assisted same-day exercise and sale transactions, such a provision should be added to the stock option plan.

As permitted under Regulation T, a securities brokerage firm may advance funds to an optionee to cover the exercise price and any associated withholding taxes as if the firm had the certificate for the shares of stock underlying the stock option in its possession, provided the optionee has delivered to the firm an executed notice of exercise and a copy of irrevocable instructions from the optionee directing the company to deliver the option shares to the firm. The instructions must designate the account into which the option shares are to be deposited (either a margin account or a cash account). Where the option shares are to be immediately sold by the securities brokerage firm, a cash account will be designated from which the sale proceeds would fund the exercise.

While it is not required, the company may find that it is more expedient to amend its stock option plan to permit this type of exercise. This will provide the company with more flexibility in structuring its same-day exercise and sale arrangements with one or more securities brokerage firms. The company will also want to consider any applicable tax, securities law, and accounting issues that may be associated with amending the stock option plan to add this provision. Under Section 13(k) of the Securities Exchange Act of 1934 (the "Exchange Act"), reporting companies are prohibited from making personal loans, or facilitating the extension of credit, to their directors and executive officers. Presently, it is unclear whether stock option exercises by a director or executive officer using a broker-assisted same-day exercise and sale program constitute prohibited loans under this statute. Consequently, a company should consult its professional legal advisors when amending a plan to establish a broker-assisted same-day exercise and sale program to determine whether the program may be extended to its directors and executive officers.

Because of the prohibition on personal loans mandated by Section 13(k) of the Exchange Act, the company should consider modifying any provision in its stock option plan that permits the use of a promissory note to pay the exercise price of an option to either eliminate the provision or to restrict this payment method to optionees who are neither directors nor executive officers.

Finally, company management should consider whether it is appropriate to amend outstanding stock options to add a brokers' same-day exercise and sale provision for those options. Once again, applicable legal and accounting implications should first be considered before taking such action.

Composition of Plan Administration Committee. Typically, a stock option plan will identify the body authorized to administer the plan and will also set forth certain guidelines for the committee's composition and operation. Most stock option plans provide that the company's board of directors or a committee of the board, such as the compensation committee, is responsible for administering the plan. While it may not require a formal plan amendment, company management should seek to coordinate the composition of the plan administration committee to comply with the conditions of the Exchange Act Rule 16b-3 exemption, the "performance-based" compensation exception to Section 162(m) of the Code, and, if the company is to be listed on the NYSE or NASDAQ, the applicable corporate governance listing standard.

For purposes of Rule 16b-3, stock option grants may be approved by a committee of two or more "non-employee" directors. For purposes of the "performance-based" compensation exception of Section 162(m), the compensation committee must be composed solely of two or more "outside" directors. For purposes of the NYSE and NASDAQ corporate governance listing standards, the compensation committee of the board of directors must be comprised solely of "independent" directors. The definition of a "non-employee" director differs in several respects from the definition of an "outside" director. The definition of a "non-employee" director tends to be less restrictive than the definition of an "outside director" because it focuses only on a director's current, rather than past, status. Both of these definitions vary, in several ways, from the "independence" definitions contained in the NYSE and NASDAQ corporate governance listing standards.

Under Rule 16b-3, a "non-employee director" is an individual who is not currently an officer or otherwise employed by the company or a parent or subsidiary corporation; does not receive compensation, directly or indirectly, from the company or its parent or subsidiary corporations for services rendered as a consultant or in any capacity other than as a director (except for an amount for which disclosure would not be required under the "related-person transaction" rules of SEC Regulation S-K); does not possess an interest in any other transaction for which disclosure would be required under the "related-person transaction" rules of Regulation S-K; and is not engaged in a business relationship with the company for which disclosure would be required under the "related-person transaction" rules of Regulation S-K.

For purposes of the "performance-based" compensation exception of Section 162(m), a director is considered to be an "outside" director if the director (1) is not a current employee of the publicly held corporation, (2) is not a former employee of the publicly held corporation who is receiving compensation for prior services (other than benefits under a tax-qualified retirement plan) during the taxable year, (3) has not been an officer of the publicly held corporation either currently or at any time in the past, or (4) does not currently receive remuneration, either directly or indirectly, in any capacity other than as a director (including any payment in exchange for goods or services).

"Current remuneration" includes remuneration paid by the company, directly or indirectly, to the director personally; remuneration paid by the company to an entity in which the director has a beneficial ownership interest of more than 50%; remuneration paid by the corporation in its preceding taxable year to an entity for which the director is employed or self-employed other than as a director (unless it is a de minimis amount that is less than the lesser of $60,000 or 5% of the entity's gross revenue for the entity's taxable year ending within the publicly held corporation's taxable year); or remuneration paid by the corporation in its preceding taxable year to an entity in which the director beneficially owns a 5% to 50% interest (unless it is a de minimis amount that is less than the lesser of $60,000 or 5% of the entity's gross revenue for the entity's preceding taxable year ending within the publicly held corporation's taxable year).

For purposes of Section 162(m), whether a director is a current employee or a former officer is determined on the basis of the facts at the time that the individual serves as a director on the compensation committee. For purposes of these rules, an officer is an administrative executive who is or was in regular and continued service. The determination of whether an individual is or was an officer is based on all of the facts and circumstances in the particular case, including, without limitation, the source of the individual's authority, the term for which the individual is elected or appointed, and the nature and extent of the individual's duties.

For purposes of the NYSE corporate governance listing standards, a director is "independent" if the board of directors affirmatively determines that the director has no "material relationship" with the listed company (either directly or indirectly), and, within the past three years, the director has not:

- been an employee, or had an immediate family member who was an executive officer, of the company;
- received, or had an immediate family member who received, more than $100,000 per year in direct compensation from the listed company (other than director and committee fees, and pension or other deferred compensation for prior service);
- been affiliated with or employed by, or had an immediate family member who was affiliated with or employed in a professional capacity by, a present or former internal or external auditor of the listed company;

- been employed, or had an immediate family member who was employed, as an executive officer of another company where any of the listed company's present executives served on that company's compensation committee; or

- been an executive officer or an employee, or had an immediate family member who was an executive officer, of a company that made payments to, or received payments from, the listed company for property or services in an amount which, in any single fiscal year, exceeded the greater of $1 million or 2% of such other company's consolidated gross revenues.

For these purposes, a "material relationship" includes commercial, industrial, banking, consulting, legal, accounting, charitable, or familial relationships.

The NASDAQ corporate governance listing standards provide a similar, although not identical, definition of "independence." A company that will be listed on NASDAQ should consult the specific "independence" definition in the NASDAQ rules in conjunction with structuring its plan administration committee.

Once the company has determined its strategy for complying with Rule 16b-3, Section 162(m), and the corporate governance listing standards, if applicable, it should identify the appropriate directors to comprise the compensation committee of the board of directors. It may be necessary to add individuals to the board of directors to ensure that one or both of the exemptions will be available for future transactions and periods and that the applicable listing requirements are satisfied. Company management should review the stock option plan to determine if any coordinating amendments need to be made to the stock option plan.

Other Amendments. Because of limitations on the ability of the company's officers and directors to obtain liquidity for their option shares due to federal and state insider trading restrictions, company management may want to consider amending the stock option plan to permit optionees subject to Section 16 of the Exchange Act to tender shares of stock to satisfy any income tax withholding obligations that arise in connection with the exercise of their stock options.

Company management should also review the "change of control" provisions in the stock option plan and outstanding stock option agreements and employment agreements, if any, for consistency and to ensure that future stock option grants will contain the desired features and for the impact, if any, of Sections 280G and 4999 of the Code (the "golden parachute" provisions). In addition, the company's accountants should be consulted to consider the effect that the change of control provisions and any contemplated changes may have on the accounting treatment of a future acquisition of the company.

Finally, the company may want to consider changing the standard form of employee stock option grant from an incentive stock option to a nonstatutory (nonqualified) stock option. Generally, this change does not require a formal amendment to the stock option plan; instead, it requires a change to the company's philosophy for stock options. If the company anticipates that most employees will use a broker-assisted same-day exercise and sale procedure to exercise their stock options, it may find that, for practical purposes, nonstatutory stock options are preferable because they are simpler to administer and ensure that the company will receive a corporate income tax deduction upon exercise of the options.

4.2.2 Adoption of Employee Stock Purchase Plan

Concurrent with an IPO, some companies implement a broad-based employee stock purchase plan. Often, this plan will supplement the company's stock option plan. Occasionally, the plan will substitute for a stock option plan where the company believes that it may no longer be possible to grant meaningful stock options to all employees.

Generally, an employee stock purchase plan provides eligible employees with the opportunity to purchase shares of the company's stock at certain predetermined intervals (generally once or twice each year). Shares are usually purchased at a discount from the fair market value of the company's stock. Before the adoption of Statement of Financial Accounting Standards No. 123 (revised 2004) ("FAS 123(R)"), it was customary for the purchase price to be based on a formula providing that shares may be purchased at 85% of the lesser of the fair market value of the company's stock at the beginning or end of a specified period of time. Today, many plans provide that the discount will be 5% (or sometimes 10%) of the fair market value of the company's stock on the purchase date. Typically, the purchase price for the shares is paid in the form of payroll deductions authorized by the employee. Unless an employee withdraws from the plan before the date of purchase, shares are automatically purchased on that date by dividing the applicable purchase price into the accumulated payroll deductions for the employee.

If the company is to be listed on the NYSE or NASDAQ, the plan will need to be submitted to the company's shareholders for their approval.

In addition to the economic benefits provided by these plans, a company can, by satisfying the conditions of Section 423 of the Code, ensure that employees participating in the plan receive preferential tax treatment for federal income tax purposes in connection with their acquisition and disposition of shares.

By satisfying several statutorily enumerated requirements, a Section 423 employee stock purchase plan can offer several distinct tax advantages to participants. First, a Section 423 plan offers employees the opportunity for tax deferral. Participants in a Section 423 plan are not required to recognize income in connection with the purchase of shares of stock under the plan until the shares are sold. In addition, a Section 423 plan offers the opportunity for the recharacterization of most of the income ultimately recognized upon a disposition of the shares into capital gain. Specifically, if certain holding period requirements are met, a portion of the discount from current fair market value that results on the purchase of the shares will be subject to tax as capital gain income rather than as compensation income taxable at ordinary income rates.

To qualify for preferential tax treatment under Section 423, an employee stock purchase plan must meet the following requirements:

- Participation in the plan must be limited to employees.
- The plan must be approved by shareholders of the company within 12 months before or after its adoption by the board of directors.
- The purchase price for the shares of stock may not be less than 85% of the lesser of the fair market value of the company's stock at the time an employee enrolls in the plan or the fair market value of the company's stock on the date of purchase.
- The term of an option granted pursuant to the plan may not exceed 27 months (or five years if the purchase price is determined only on the date of purchase).
- All employees must be allowed to participate in the plan (with certain exclusions).
- All participants in the plan must have the same rights and privileges.
- Employees owning stock possessing 5% or more of the total combined voting power or value of all classes of the stock of the company

or its parent or subsidiary corporations may not participate in the plan.

- An employee may not purchase more than $25,000 worth of stock on a cumulative basis (based on the fair market value of the company's stock at the time of enrollment) for each calendar year in which an option is outstanding at any time.

By offering shares of stock at a discount from fair market value, an employee stock purchase plan provides employees with an opportunity to obtain a favorable return on their investment. An employee stock purchase plan enables employees to acquire an equity interest in their company, an objective beneficial to the company because it provides both incentive and motivation for employees to work harder in the common interest, thereby aligning the interests of the employees with those of its shareholders. From the company's perspective, an employee stock purchase plan can be a convenient means by which the company can raise capital on a continuing basis. It also can be used to promote widespread stock ownership among employees and to recruit and retain talented employees. For a company that may be unable or unwilling to grant stock options to all employees, an employee stock purchase plan allows the company to offer a company-wide equity participation program while limiting stock option grants. In recognition of the tendency of employees participating in an employee stock purchase plan to regularly liquidate their stock holdings, some companies will offer stock options as an investment program and an employee stock purchase plan as a liquidity mechanism.

To an employee, an employee stock purchase plan provides an easy way to purchase company stock at a discount. And, if the plan is qualified under Section 423, the employee incurs no federal income tax liability at the time of purchase. The plan may provide a strong motivational tool for an employee, since the employee recognizes that his or her individual performance can directly affect the company's prospects and, therefore, the value of the company's stock.

In considering whether to implement an employee stock purchase plan and the appropriate design of such a plan, the company's accountants should be consulted to evaluate the accounting consequences of the plan. Under FAS 123(R), a company must calculate and recognize a compensation expense for its employee stock purchase plan over each purchase period unless the plan qualifies for a limited exception available for "non-compensatory" plans.

4.2.3 Adoption of Directors' Stock Option Plan

The company also may want to consider adopting a separate stock option plan for the members of its board of directors. While it is quite common to grant stock options to non-employee directors out of the company's primary stock option plan while the company is closely held, separate arrangements are often implemented after an IPO.

Historically, such plans were "formula" plans under which eligibility was limited to non-employee directors; the plan, by its terms, specified the amount, price, and timing of option grants; and the company's ability to amend these plan provisions more than once every six months was limited. These "formula" plans played an important role in ensuring that a company could provide stock options to its non-employee directors without jeopardizing their "disinterested" status for purposes of administering the company's discretionary employee stock plans. Under current SEC rules, "disinterested" status is no longer needed to ensure that grants or awards to officers and employee-directors under a company's discretionary stock plans are exempt from the "short-swing profits" recovery provisions of Section 16(b) of the Exchange Act. Still, many companies continue to use "formula" plans as a way of minimizing conflict-of-interest issues that might arise where non-employee directors are both administrators and beneficiaries of the companies' stock option program.

Exchange Act Rule 16b-3 does not prohibit non-employee directors (or the full board, for that matter) from awarding themselves grants of the company's securities or stock options on those securities. Nor does it automatically subject these transactions to shareholder scrutiny. Instead, such transactions will be subject to state laws governing corporate self-dealing. As a result, companies must decide whether to use a separate "formula" plan or to simply include them as participants in their general employee stock option plan. For shareholder relations purposes, as well as to maintain the impartiality of the directors, a company may find that it is still prudent to implement a non-employee director "formula" plan.

If the company is to be listed on the NYSE or NASDAQ, the plan will need to be submitted to the company's shareholders for their approval.

4.2.4 Assisting Employees in the Disposition of Their Stock Options

Tax Considerations. Once the company's employees are informed of the impending IPO, most individuals will have questions concerning the impact of the transaction on their stock options. Some employees will seek counseling concerning their stock options and may look to the stock plan administrator to advise them on how to proceed. While the stock plan administrator should avoid giving individual tax and financial advice, it may be prudent to schedule one or more informational meetings for employees to provide them with basic information about their stock options and outline the key planning considerations they should address with financial advisors.

Securities Law Restrictions. In addition, it will be helpful to educate the employees on the resale limitations imposed contractually and under the federal securities laws that will affect their ability to sell their option shares following the IPO.

Generally, an employee who has acquired shares of stock under the company's stock option plan will hold "restricted securities." For purposes of the federal securities laws, "restricted securities" are securities acquired from a company in a transaction or series of transactions that has not been registered under the Securities Act. Under the Securities Act, any proposed sale of the option shares must either be registered or exempt from registration.

Rule 144 under the Securities Act provides an exemption from the registration requirement of the Securities Act for a person seeking to resell "restricted securities." To sell "restricted securities" in reliance on Rule 144, several conditions must be satisfied. First, the company must be subject to the reporting requirements of the Exchange Act and must be current in meeting its reporting obligations. Next, the securities to be sold must have been fully paid for and held for a specified minimum period (recently, this period was reduced from one year to six months). Third, the amount of securities that can be resold during any three-month period must not exceed the greater of (1) 1% of the outstanding stock of the company or (2) the average weekly trading volume of the company's stock during the four calendar weeks preceding the date of the proposed sale. Fourth, all sales must be made in unsolicited brokers' transactions or directly to market makers. Finally, a notice of the proposed sale, on Form 144, must be filed with the SEC (and any national securities exchange on which the securities are admitted for trading) before or concurrently with the sale if the proposed sale involves more than 5,000 shares or has an aggregate sale price over $50,000.

For purposes of Rule 144, the specified holding period is measured from the date that the securities are paid for in full. Payment with a promissory note that is essentially financed by the company does not constitute full payment unless the note is a full-recourse obligation and is collateralized by property other than the shares of stock being purchased, which property has a fair market value at least equal to the total purchase price of the shares. In addition, the promissory note must be repaid in full before the sale of the restricted securities.

In addition to transactions in "restricted securities," Rule 144 is the primary exemption from the registration requirements of the Securities Act for resales of securities by "affiliates" of the company. For purposes of the federal securities laws, an "affiliate" includes any person directly controlling or controlled by the company or any person under direct or indirect common control with the company. While the determination of "affiliate" status ultimately depends on the facts and circumstances of each individual case, the officers, directors, and principal shareholders of a company generally are considered "affiliates" of the company.

Rule 144 applies to any sale of securities by an affiliate (whether of registered securities or "restricted securities"). The conditions of the rule to be satisfied in the case of an affiliate transaction depend on the nature of the securities to be resold. If the securities are "restricted securities," all of the conditions of Rule 144 described above must be met. If the securities have previously been registered, then all of the conditions of Rule 144, other than the holding period condition, must be met.

Typically, a company will place a restrictive legend on the certificate for shares of stock that are either "restricted securities" or held by an affiliate. This legend is intended to alert the company's transfer agent and/or a stock brokerage firm assisting with the proposed sale to the fact that the shares are subject to the conditions of Rule 144. In addition, the company may issue "stop transfer" instructions to its transfer agent as a precaution against inadvertent sales that do not comply with Rule 144. Rule 144 is applicable to resales of "restricted securities" and securities held by affiliates, however, whether or not a legend appears on the certificate or stop transfer instructions have been issued.

Following the IPO, unless an employee's option shares acquired before the offering are first registered with the SEC, such shares only may be sold in reliance on Rule 144. One significant exception to this requirement exists. If the stock option was granted under the exemption provided by Securities Act Rule 701 for employee benefit plans, a special resale provision in the rule will be triggered following the IPO. While option shares acquired pursuant to Rule 701 are deemed to be "restricted securities" for resale purposes, 90 days after the company becomes subject to the reporting requirements of the Exchange Act, non-affiliates may sell their Rule 701 option shares without regard to Rule 144 (other than the manner-of-sale condition) and affiliates may sell their Rule 701 option shares pursuant to Rule 144 (but without regard to the holding period condition).

Contractual Restrictions. Notwithstanding compliance with applicable securities laws, employees may still be restricted contractually from selling their option shares immediately following an IPO. Frequently, the underwriter for the offering will require the officers, directors, and principal shareholders of the company to agree not to sell any shares of stock in the public market for a period of up to 180 days following the IPO. This is done primarily to ensure stabilization of the market price for the company's stock during the post-IPO period. This restriction is often called the "underwriters' lockup" or "market standoff" requirement.

Where there are a large number of stock options outstanding at the time of the IPO, it is not uncommon for the underwriters to request that each optionee agree to be bound by the lockup provision. This may require the stock plan administrator to obtain written agreements from each optionee, agreeing to the applicable restrictions. Consequently, many companies include a contractual lockup provision in their standard stock option agreements to avoid having to obtain lockup agreements individually in connection with the offering. An explanation of these provisions and their applicability should be included in the information provided to the employees about the IPO.

4.3   Regulatory Considerations Before an IPO

4.3.1   Section 16

The officers, directors, and principal shareholders of any company that has a class of equity securities registered under Section 12 of the Exchange Act are subject to the provisions of Section 16 of the Exchange Act. Generally, registration of a class of securities is required under Section 12(b) of the Exchange Act where a company elects to have equity securities listed for trading on a national securities exchange or under Section 12(g) of the Exchange Act where the company has more than 500 shareholders of record and total assets exceeding $10 million as of the end of the company's fiscal year. In addition, a company may voluntarily register a class of its equity securities under Section 12(g).

Where a company intends to have its securities listed for trading on a national securities exchange in connection with its IPO, compliance with Section 16 is required. While such a situation arises from time to time, it is far more common today for a company to seek to have its securities listed on the NASDAQ NMS or the OTC Bulletin Board. Under NASDAQ rules, a company must comply with the NASDAQ corporate governance requirements, which among other things require registration under Section 12 of the Exchange Act on a voluntary basis. Consequently, today many companies file under Section 12 concurrently with their IPOs, thereby subjecting their officers, directors, and principal shareholders to compliance with Section 16 at the effective date of the IPO.

Under Section 16, officers and directors and beneficial owners of more than 10% of the class of equity securities registered under the Exchange Act must disclose their holdings of, and transactions involving, the equity securities of their company and further must return to the company any profits that they realize in the event of any "short-swing" trading in such securities.

Determination of Corporate Insiders. Initially, the stock plan administrator must assist in the determination of who will be subject to Section 16 as a result of the Section 12 registration. Section 16 applies to any officer or director of a Section 12 company, as well as any beneficial owner of more than 10% of the company's registered equity securities. The determination of directors subject to Section 16 is generally straightforward: it includes each member of the company's board of directors. The determination of officer status for purposes of Section 16 can be more challenging.

The rules under Section 16 contain a specific definition of who is to be considered an "officer" for purposes of Section 16. A Section 16 "officer" includes a company's (1) president; (2) principal financial officer; (3) principal accounting officer (or, if there is none, the controller); (4) any vice president in charge of a principal business unit, division, or function (such as sales, administration, or finance); (5) any other officer performing a significant policy-making function; (6) any other person performing a significant policy-making function; and (7) officers of parent or subsidiary companies who are performing policy-making functions for the company.

The rules under Section 16 make it clear that function, rather than title, will be determinative of "officer" status. In establishing whether an individual is to be treated as a Section 16 officer, the policy-making responsibilities of the individual will be a key factor. The rules further provide that if a company identifies an individual as an "executive officer" (in its proxy statement or annual report on Form 10-K), a presumption will arise that the board of directors made this judgment and that the individual is a Section 16 officer. Consequently, once the initial group of Section 16 officers has been identified, the company's board of directors should formally confirm this status. Thereafter, the board of directors should consider taking action annually to review and confirm the identities and titles of its officers subject to Section 16.

Section 16 Reporting. A corporate insider must prepare and file an initial report concerning the insider's holdings of equity securities of the Section 12 company on Form 3, the initial statement of beneficial ownership of securities. Generally, a Form 3 must be filed with the SEC within 10 days after the corporate insider first becomes subject to Section 16, listing the insider's holdings of equity securities as of that date. In the case of a company registering a class of equity securities under Section 12 of the Exchange Act for the first time, however, a Form 3 must be filed with the SEC for each corporate insider by the effective date of the Section 12 registration. Where Section 12 registration is being made concurrent with the IPO, such filings must take place by the effective date of the IPO. The Form 3 must list and describe all of the equity securities of the company beneficially owned by the corporate insider before the effective date of the Section 12 registration. A Form 3 must be filed whether or not the corporate insider owns any equity securities of the company. The Form 3 must be filed electronically with the SEC on its Electronic Data Gathering and Retrieval (EDGAR) system.

A corporate insider must prepare and file subsequent reports concerning changes to the insider's holdings of equity securities on either Form 4 or Form 5 within the prescribed deadlines set forth in the applicable Exchange Act rules as discussed below. These forms must be filed electronically with the SEC on its EDGAR system.

4.3.2 "Cheap" Stock

Before an IPO, company management should closely monitor the prices at which the company grants stock options to its employees. The SEC will scrutinize the methodology used to set the exercise price for these stock option grants to ensure that the company has not issued "cheap" stock, that is, stock issued at prices below the stock's true market value. The SEC often presumes that stock options granted during the period immediately before an IPO involve "cheap" stock unless the options were granted at the offering price, and will require the company to record a compensation expense for these stock options to the extent that the exercise price is less than the offering price. Disputes are common in which a company and the SEC will disagree about whether the stock options were properly valued and accounted for in the company's financial statements.

Where the SEC presumes that the stock options were not priced at fair market value at the time of grant, it will require the company to record a compensation expense for the "discount" reflected in the stock options. Such a result can both delay the offering (as the parties wrangle over the proper valuation for the stock options) and change the financial statements, altering investors' views of the company and the proposed offering.

To minimize potential problems, the company should begin documenting the methodology employed to price its stock option grants during the 12- to 18-month period before the IPO. Important factors in responding to an SEC inquiry include the number of months between the stock option grant and the IPO, the difference between the exercise price and the offering price, and whether significant changes in the company's business prospects have taken place since the grant date. The most persuasive factor is whether the company used the services of an independent professional appraiser in setting the stock option exercise price. Many companies retain an independent appraiser to assist in the stock option valuation process during the months before the offering.

The possibility that stock options were not priced at fair market value at the time of grant may also raise issues under Section 409A of the Code. Section 409A governs the federal income tax treatment of non-qualified deferred compensation (NQDC). A discount stock option, i.e., an option with an exercise price that is less than the fair market value of the granting company's stock on the date of grant, is considered to involve a deferral of compensation and is subject to Section 409A. (Where an option is determined to involve a deferral of compensation, Section 409A requires that the optionee make an advance election as to when to exercise the option.) A stock option that has an exercise price that is never less than the fair market value of the granting company's stock on the date of grant is not subject to Section 409A.

Thus, stock valuation will be important for purposes of determining whether outstanding stock options must comply with the restrictions governing NQDC under Section 409A. For the stock of a closely held business, fair market value may be determined using any reasonable valuation method that takes into account a number of specified factors (such as the value of the company's assets or the present value of its cash flows) and is consistently applied. Under regulations adopted by the Internal Revenue Service (IRS), the following valuation methods will be presumed to be "reasonable":

- appraisals that satisfy the Internal Revenue Code's requirements for the valuation of ESOP stock (which will be presumed to be reasonable for a one-year period after the appraisal unless new information becomes available);

- formula valuations based on non-lapse restrictions as defined in Section 83 of the Code (for example, a permanent requirement that an optionee sell the option shares back to the company at a formula price), but only if the valuation method is used consistently for both compensatory and noncompensatory purposes; and

- for illiquid stock of a "start-up corporation," special valuations that meet the following requirements: the company is in its first 10 years of active trade or business, has no readily traded securities, does not anticipate a change in control or initial public offering within a specified period after the valuation, and applies the valuation to stock that is not subject to a put or call or repurchase obligation.

Thus, the potential application of Section 409A is another reason why a company will want to closely monitor the prices at which it grants stock options to its employees and the valuation methodologies used for this purpose. A valuation method is considered to be consistently used if it is used for all equity awards and for all terms of the award.

4.3.3 Preparing the Registration Statement

The purpose of a formal registration statement is to ensure that complete and accurate information is available about the company and the securities to be offered. The registration statement contains certain detailed information as required by the Securities Act and the SEC rules and forms.

Generally, a registration statement contains two parts: (1) the "prospectus," which must be furnished to each prospective and ultimate purchaser of the securities, and (2) "Part 2," which is filed with the SEC and is available to the public. The basic registration form is Form S-1, which must be used in any offering of securities for which no other form is authorized or prescribed.

Under the SEC's "integrated disclosure system," the basic disclosure requirements for all of the Securities Act and Exchange Act documents are set forth in a series of SEC regulations. The required disclosures with respect to the company's financial statements are set forth in Regulation S-X. The textual disclosures for the registration statement itself are contained in Regulation S-K (or, in the case of certain small entities, Regulation S-B). The requirements under the SEC's Electronic Data Gathering and Retrieval (EDGAR) system, which prescribes electronic filing of all required disclosure documents, are set forth in Regulation S-T.

Compliance with these requirements results in a disclosure document that is both comprehensive and complex. While most of the registration statement will be prepared by the company's corporate securities attorneys, there are certain portions of the document that require detailed disclosure of the company's equity compensation plans and arrangements and other related information.

4.3.3.1 *Executive Compensation Disclosure*

Under Item 402 of Regulation S-K as revised by the SEC in July 2006, the company must disclose information concerning the various forms of compensation paid to senior executives and directors and explain its compensation philosophy and decisions involving senior executive compensation. These disclosure requirements consist of approximately 10 items, which are sometimes grouped into "soft" and "hard" disclosures. The "soft" (subjective) disclosures include the Compensation Discussion and Analysis, the Compensation Committee Report, the Compensation Committee Interlocks and Insider Participation Report, and the narrative disclosure to accompany the required tabular disclosure. In addition to this subjective disclosure, extensive tabular disclosure is required covering the actual compensation packages of a company's senior executive officers. The compensation of each of these executives is highlighted in up to eight separate tables or charts. The stock plan administrator will frequently be called upon to assist with the preparation of the specific tabular disclosure.

The executives subject to this heightened disclosure include (1) all individuals who have served as the chief executive officer of the company (or acted in a similar capacity) during the last completed fiscal year (regardless of the level of compensation paid to the individual during that year), (2) all individuals who have served as the chief financial officer of the company (or acted in a similar capacity) during the last completed fiscal year (regardless of the level of compensation paid to the individual during that year), (3) each of the company's three most highly compensated executive officers (other than the CEO and CFO) who were serving as executive officers at the end of the last completed fiscal year whose total compensation exceed $100,000 for the fiscal year, and (4) up to two additional individuals who would have been among the three most highly compensated executive officers but for the fact that the individual was not serving as an executive officer of the company at the end of the last completed fiscal year. These individuals are referred to as the "named executive officers." For purposes of determining a company's most highly compensated executive officers, "total compensation" includes all amounts that are included in the Summary Compensation table (as described below) except for the amounts required to be disclosed in the "Change in pension value and nonqualified deferred compensation earnings" column of that table.

Compensation Discussion and Analysis. The Compensation Discussion and Analysis (CD&A) replaces the previous board compensation committee report and performance graph. A company disclosure, rather than a compensation committee disclosure, the CD&A is supposed to set the context for the other required executive compensation disclosures. The CD&A is to address the objectives and policies of a company's executive compensation program as well as how that program is implemented. The CD&A is to be a "principles-based" discussion; that is, the company must tailor the disclosure to its own individual situation. To assist in this process, the disclosure requirements provide that the following broad topics be addressed in the CD&A:

- the objectives of the company's compensation programs;
- what each program is designed to reward;
- the different elements of compensation offered by the company;
- why the company chooses to pay each element;
- how the company determines the amount (and where applicable, the formula) for each element; and

- how each element and the company's decisions regarding that element fit into the company's overall compensation objectives and affect decisions regarding other elements.

While the company must provide detailed information about the measures and targets that it uses in its performance-based compensation arrangements, it is not required to disclose these performance metrics to the extent that they involve confidential information the disclosure of which would cause competitive harm to the company. In response to concerns about stock option backdating and the timing of option grants around the disclosure of material information, the company is also required to address its executive grant practices. This disclosure needs to describe why the company selects particular dates for granting options and how it sets an option's terms and conditions, including the option exercise price.

Summary Compensation Table. The centerpiece of the tabular disclosure requirements, the Summary Compensation table is designed to provide a comprehensive overview of a company's executive pay practices in a single location within the registration statement. This information is intended to enable prospective investors to understand clearly the compensation paid for the prior fiscal year, to evaluate the company's pay policies in light of its overall performance, and to compare trends in compensation practices between companies.

The Summary Compensation table covers the compensation paid to each of the named executive officers during the last three completed fiscal years. If the company has not been a reporting company under the Exchange Act for the prior three years (as will typically be the case in an IPO), the table need only cover the shorter period that the company has been a reporting company, but it must cover at least the last completed fiscal year.

The Summary Compensation table divides the compensation of the named executive officers into several categories, each of which is then reported in a separate column of the table. The amounts to be disclosed for each named executive officer include:

- his or her base salary earned for the covered fiscal year;
- his or her bonus earned for the covered fiscal year;
- the value of stock awards granted for the covered fiscal year;

- the value of stock options granted for the covered fiscal year;

- the value of non-equity incentive plan compensation earned for the covered fiscal year;

- the aggregate change in the actuarial present value of his or her accumulated benefit under all defined benefit and actuarial pension plans (including supplemental plans) during the covered fiscal year, and any above-market or preferential earnings on nonqualified deferred compensation;

- all other compensation for the covered fiscal year that could not be properly reported in any other column of the table (which elements are to be aggregated and reported as a single amount); and

- the total compensation for the covered fiscal year (the sum of all of the columns in the table).

Restricted stock awards, stock options, or other long-term incentive compensation that is received in lieu of salary or bonus should be reported in the appropriate column for that award type and must be included in determining whether a person is a named executive officer.

The dollar amount reported for stock and option awards is to be based on the amount of compensation expense recognized for financial reporting purposes in accordance with FAS 123(R) during the covered fiscal year. Consequently, this amount will include both stock and option awards granted during the last completed fiscal year, as well as stock and option awards granted in prior years for which compensation expense is still being recognized.

Non-equity incentive plan compensation generally involves performance-based awards that are payable in cash. These awards can be either annual or long-term incentive awards. Thus, most annual incentive awards that were previously reported as bonuses will be reported in this category where they are subject to the achievement of objective performance criteria that were established at the beginning of the year, were substantially uncertain when established, and were communicated to the named executive officers at that time.

The items to be included in the "all other compensation" category include (1) perquisites and other personal benefits; (2) tax "gross-ups" or other reimbursements; (3) preferential discounted stock purchases; (4) amounts paid or accrued in connection with a termination of employment or a change in control of the company; (5) company contributions to defined contribution plans; (6) the dollar value of any insurance premiums paid for life insurance for the benefit of a named executive officer; and (7) the dollar value of any dividends or other earnings paid on stock or option awards (where those amounts were not factored into the award's grant date fair value). Perquisites and other personal benefits are reportable where the aggregate amount is $10,000 or more. Each perquisite must be separately identified, and where an individual perquisite exceeds the greater of $25,000 or 10% of the total amount of perquisites reported for a named executive officer, that perquisite must be quantified and the valuation methodology described.

Grants of Plan-Based Awards Table. The Grants of Plan-Based Awards table requires disclosure of supplemental information about the incentive and equity awards granted during the last fiscal year to each of the named executive officers. Unlike the Summary Compensation table, this disclosure covers only the last completed fiscal year. Each award must be identified and discussed separately in one of four broad categories: (1) non-equity incentive plan awards; (2) equity incentive plan awards; (3) service-based stock awards; and (4) service-based stock option awards.

Among other things, this table must include the grant date for each equity award, as well as its full grant date fair value. If the award's grant date differs from the date on which the board or compensation committee took action to grant such awards, a separate, adjoining column must be added to the table showing such date. In addition, in the case of stock options, the per-share exercise price of the option must be disclosed. If the exercise price is less than the closing market price of the option stock on the grant date, a separate, adjoining column must be added showing the closing market price on the grant date. Whenever the reported exercise price reported is not the closing market price, the company must describe the methodology for determining its exercise price.

The company must supplement the Summary Compensation table and the Grants of Plan-Based Awards table with a narrative description of any material factors necessary to an understanding of the information disclosed in the tables. Such information may include (1) the material terms of each named executive officer's employment agreement (if any); (2) the details of any stock option repricing or the material modification of an option or other equity awards during the last fiscal year; (3) the material terms of any award reported in the Grant of Plan-Based Awards table; and (4) an explanation of the amount of salary and bonus in proportion to total compensation.

Outstanding Equity Awards at Fiscal Year-End Table. The Outstanding Equity Awards at Fiscal Year-End table requires disclosure of each stock option and other equity award outstanding at the end of the last fiscal year held by each named executive officer.

Among other things, this table must include in the case of stock options (which must be disclosed on a grant-by-grant basis) the number of securities underlying unexercised service-based options that are currently exercisable, the number of securities underlying unexercised service-based options that are currently unexercisable, the total number of shares underlying unexercised performance-based options that have not been earned, the option exercise price, and the option expiration date. In the case of other stock awards (which may be disclosed on an aggregated basis), this table must include the total number of unvested shares of stock subject to service-based awards; the aggregate market value of these unvested share of stock; the total number of unvested shares of stock, units, or other rights subject to performance-based awards; and the aggregate market or payout value of these unvested shares of stock.

Option Exercises and Stock Vested Table. The Option Exercises and Stock Vested table requires disclosure of stock option exercises (as well as exercises of free-standing SARs) and the vesting of outstanding stock awards that occurred during the last fiscal year for each of the named executive officers. While this disclosure covers only the last completed fiscal year, unlike the Outstanding Equity Awards at Last Fiscal Year-End table, these transactions may be aggregated and reported as a single amount in each general category.

Among other things, this table must include the number of shares received upon exercise (or, if no shares were received, the number of securities with respect to which the option and/or SAR was exercised) and the aggregate dollar value realized upon exercise. In the case of other stock awards, this table must include the number of shares of stock that have vested and the aggregate dollar value realized upon the vesting of these shares of stock.

Pension Benefits Table. The Pension Benefits table requires disclosure of the potential payments and benefits payable to the named executive officers under the company's defined benefit pension plans (both tax-qualified and nonqualified plans).

Among other things, this table must include the name of each plan in which a named executive officer participates, the number of years of service credited to the named executive officer under the plan, the actuarial present value of the named executive officer's accumulated benefit under the plan, and the dollar amount of any payments and benefits paid to the named executive officer during the last completed fiscal year

For purposes of computing the present value of the current accrued benefit to be reported in the table, the company must use the same assumptions used by the company for financial reporting purposes, except that retirement age is to be assumed to be the normal retirement age as defined in the plan (or if not defined, the earliest time at which a participant may retire under the plan without any benefit reduction due to age). The company must disclose the valuation method and all material assumptions used in quantifying the present value of the current accrued benefit. If a named executive officer's years of credited service with respect to any plan differ from his or her actual years of service with the company, the disclosure must quantify the difference and any resulting benefit augmentation.

The company must supplement the Pension Benefits table with a narrative description of any material factors necessary to an understanding of the information disclosed in the table. Such information may include (1) the material terms and conditions of payments and benefits available under the plan; (2) where a named executive officer is currently eligible for early retirement under a plan, the plan's early retirement payment and benefit formula and eligibility standards; (3) the specific elements of compensation (for example, salary and bonus) included in applying the payment and benefit formula; (4) with respect to named executive officer's participation in multiple plans, the reasons for each plan; and (5) company policies with regard to such matters as granting extra years of credited service.

Nonqualified Deferred Compensation Table. The Nonqualified Deferred Compensation table requires disclosure of information about each nonqualified defined contribution plan or other nonqualified deferred compensation plan or arrangement.

Among other things, this table must include the dollar amount of aggregate named executive officer contributions during the last fiscal year, the dollar amount of aggregate company contributions during the last fiscal year, the dollar amount of aggregate interest or other earnings accrued during the last fiscal year (all earnings, not just above-market or preferential amounts), the aggregate dollar amount of all withdrawals by and distributions to the named executive officer during the last fiscal year, and the dollar amount of total balance of the named executive officer's account as of the end of the last fiscal year.

To avoid possible double-counting of this information with amounts that have been previously disclosed, the company must quantify the extent to which amounts reported in the contributions and earnings columns are reported as compensation in the last completed fiscal year in the company's Summary Compensation table and amounts reported in the aggregate balance at the last fiscal year end previously were reported as compensation to the named executive officer in the company's Summary Compensation table for previous years.

The company must supplement the Nonqualified Deferred Compensation table with a narrative description of any material factors necessary to an understanding of the information in the table. Such information may include (1) the type(s) of compensation permitted to be deferred, and any limitations (by percentage of compensation or otherwise) on the extent to which deferral is permitted; (2) the measures for calculating interest or other plan earnings (including whether such measure(s) are selected by the named executive officer or the company and the frequency and manner in which selections may be changed), quantifying interest rates and other earnings measures applicable during the company's last fiscal year; and (3) the material terms applicable to payouts, withdrawals, and other distributions.

Potential Payments Upon Termination or Change in Control. The company must disclose information about each contract, agreement, plan, or arrangement that provides for payment(s) to a named executive officer at, following, or in connection with any termination of employment, including resignation, severance, retirement, or a constructive termination of employment, or a change in control of the company or a change in the named executive officer's responsibilities. While this information need not be provided in tabular form, as a practical matter the company will probably use one or more tables to disclose the required information.

Among other things, the disclosure must describe the specific circumstances that would trigger payment(s) or the provision of other benefits (including perquisites and health care benefits); quantify the estimated annual payments and benefits that would be provided in each covered circumstance (including whether they would or could be lump-sum or annual, disclosing the duration, and by whom they would be provided); explain how the appropriate payment and benefit levels are determined under the various circumstances that trigger payments or provision of benefits; explain any material conditions or obligations that apply to the receipt of payments or benefits (including non-compete, non-solicitation, non-disparagement, or confidentiality agreements); and describe any other material factors regarding each contract, agreement, plan, or arrangement.

In calculating the potential payments and benefits that may be received by a named executive officer, the company is to assume that the triggering event took place on the last business day of the last completed fiscal year, and the price per share of the company's securities is the closing market price as of that date. If uncertainties exist as to the provision of payments and benefits or the amounts involved, the company must make a reasonable estimate (or provide a reasonable estimated range of amounts) of the payment or benefit and disclose the material assumptions used to make such estimates or estimated ranges in its disclosure. Perquisites may be excluded only if their aggregate amount will be less than $10,000. A company need not provide information about contracts, agreements, plans, or arrangements that do not discriminate in favor of the company's executive officers and that are available generally to all salaried employees.

4.3.3.2 *Director Compensation*

Under the disclosure rules, the company must provide a Director Compensation table that covers the compensation paid to each member of the company's board of directors during the last completed fiscal year. This table divides the compensation of the directors into several categories, each of which is then reported in a separate column of the table. The amounts to be disclosed for each director include

- the aggregate dollar amount of all fees earned or paid in cash for services as a director, (including annual retainer fees, committee, and/or chairmanship fees, and meeting fees);
- the amount recognized as compensation expense for stock awards during the covered fiscal year in accordance with FAS 123(R);
- the amount recognized as compensation expense for stock options during the covered fiscal year in accordance with FAS 123(R);
- the value of non-equity incentive plan compensation earned for the covered fiscal year;

- the aggregate change in the actuarial present value of his or her accumulated benefit under all defined benefit and actuarial pension plans (including supplemental plans) during the covered fiscal year, and any above-market or preferential earnings on nonqualified deferred compensation; and

- all other compensation for the covered fiscal year that could not be properly reported in any other column of the table (which elements are to be aggregated and reported as a single amount); and

- the total compensation for the covered fiscal year (the sum of all of the columns in the table).

Non-equity incentive plan compensation generally involves performance-based awards that are payable in cash. These awards can be either annual or long-term incentive awards.

The items to be included in the all other compensation category include (1) perquisites and other personal benefits; (2) tax "gross-ups" or other reimbursements; (3) preferential discounted stock purchases; (4) amounts paid or accrued in connection with a termination of employment or a change in control of the company; (5) company contributions to defined contribution plans; (6) consulting fees earned from, paid, or payable by the company and/or its subsidiaries; (7) the annual costs of payments and promises of payments pursuant to director legacy programs and similar charitable award programs; (8) the dollar value of any insurance premiums paid for life insurance for the benefit of a director; and (9) the dollar value of any dividends or other earnings paid on stock or option awards (where those amounts were not factored into the award's grant date fair value). Perquisites and other personal benefits are reportable where the aggregate amount is $10,000 or more. Each perquisite must be separately identified, and where an individual perquisite exceeds the greater of $25,000 or 10% of the total amount of perquisites reported for a director, that perquisite must be quantified and the valuation methodology described.

4.3.3.3 *Securities Ownership*

The registration statement must disclose the identities and certain related information concerning beneficial ownership of the company's securities, including stock options, by certain principal shareholders (primarily 5%-or-more shareholders), members of management and the board of directors, and any selling shareholders.

4.3.3.4 *Shares Eligible for Future Sale*

The registration statement must disclose, with specificity, the number of shares of stock of the company that are eligible for future sale following the IPO. This discussion typically sets forth the source of these shares of stock, the basis for such future sales, and any contractual or securities law restrictions on such sales. To the extent that the company intends to register its stock option plan and other employee stock plans following the IPO, disclosure of these plans is required. This information provides prospective investors with a complete description of the potential dilutive effect that sales of these shares of stock could have once any restrictions on resale have lapsed.

4.3.4 **Establishing a Same-Day Exercise and Sale Program**

As noted above, the company will probably elect to establish a broker-assisted same-day exercise and sale program to provide optionees with an efficient means to finance the exercise of their stock options. A broker-assisted same-day exercise and sale is a means by which an employee can finance the exercise of a stock option by immediately selling through a securities brokerage firm that number of option shares from the stock option being exercised necessary to satisfy the payment of the total required option price for the option shares being purchased plus any withholding taxes due to the company.

The company may elect to make formal arrangements with one or more securities brokerage firms to facilitate these transactions. Not only do such arrangements, sometimes referred to as "captive broker" programs, simplify the administration of these programs, they also enable the transactions to be completed more expeditiously. The company will keep the securities brokerage firm or firms updated on outstanding stock options and vested shares, thereby enabling optionees to contact the brokerage firm directly when they want to exercise their stock options. To further simplify the administration of these transactions, some companies will establish an "omnibus" account with one or more securities brokerage firms and transfer a block of shares to the account for the purpose of ensuring that sufficient shares are available to deliver upon the settlement of the sale.

Under Section 13(k) of the Exchange Act, reporting companies are prohibited from making personal loans, or facilitating the extension of credit, to their directors and executive officers. Presently, it is unclear whether stock option exercises by a director or executive officer using a broker-assisted same-day exercise and sale program constitute prohibited loans under this statute. Consequently, a company should consult its professional legal advisors when establishing a broker-assisted same-day exercise and sale program to determine whether the program may be extended to its directors and executive officers.

4.3.5 Financial Statement Disclosures

Stock Option Valuation. All companies, including closely held companies, must estimate and recognize a compensation expense for their employee stock options using the "fair value" method of accounting under FAS 123(R). An option's "fair value" is to be determined using an option-pricing model, such as the Black-Scholes or a binomial model, that takes into account, as of the grant date, the option price and the expected life of the option, the current price of the underlying shares of stock and its expected volatility, expected dividends on the stock, and the risk-free interest rate for the expected option term.

While under FAS 123(R)'s predecessors, a closely held company could calculate the "minimum value" rather then the "fair value" for its employee stock option grants, under FAS 123(R) both closely held and public reporting companies are generally subject to the same rules for valuing stock options and other stock-based awards that are classified as equity instruments. The most challenging aspect of valuation for closely held (or, as they are designated under FAS 123(R), "nonpublic" companies) is estimating stock price volatility—a required assumption in option-pricing models. Public reporting companies typically estimate volatility using their historical volatility or, if available, the implied volatility of their stock derived from publicly traded options or other derivative securities. These sources are generally unavailable to nonpublic companies.

Some nonpublic companies may be able to estimate volatility based on the internal market for their shares, private sale transactions, or issues of new equity securities. If volatility cannot be estimated using this type of information, however, FAS 123(R) prescribes the use of a "calculated value" method. (Under this methodology, a company substitutes the historical volatility of an appropriate industry sector index for its own stock price volatility in the option-pricing model.) In the rare circumstance in which a closely held company cannot estimate either fair value or calculated value, because of the complexity of an award's terms, the award's intrinsic value must be used and be remeasured at each reporting date.

4.4　Regulatory Considerations After an IPO

After an IPO, the company's compliance obligations will increase substantially, primarily as a result of the application of the Exchange Act to the company. The Exchange Act regulates the trading of securities following their initial issuance by a company. Among other things, the Exchange Act imposes certain disclosure and reporting requirements on public reporting companies, prohibits the use of fraudulent and deceptive or manipulative practices in connection with trading in securities, restricts the trading activities of certain corporate insiders, and regulates the use of credit in connection with the purchase of securities. These compliance obligations have been significantly enhanced as a result of the enactment of the Sarbanes-Oxley Act of 2002.

Section 12 of the Exchange Act requires companies to register a class of equity securities with the SEC if the class is listed for trading on a national securities exchange or if the company has more than 500 shareholders of record and total assets exceeding $10 million as of the end of the company's fiscal year. In addition, a company may voluntarily register a class of its equity securities under Section 12.

Under Section 13(a) of the Exchange Act, any company that has registered a class of equity securities under Section 12 must file periodic reports with the SEC. These reports include the quarterly report on Form 10-Q, the annual report on Form 10-K, and the current report on Form 8-K, which is used to disclose certain significant nonrecurring events (such as entry into, or the material modification of, a material definitive agreement, or the appointment or departure of a new principal officer or director).

In addition, the company is subject to the proxy rules of Section 14 of the Exchange Act, and the officers, directors, and principal shareholders of the company must file reports and conduct their trading activities in conformity with the requirements of Section 16 of the Exchange Act.

Even where a company has not registered a class of equity securities under Section 12 of the Exchange Act, Section 15(d) of the Exchange Act requires companies with an effective registration statement under the Securities Act that are not otherwise subject to the registration requirements of Section 12 of the Exchange Act to comply with the reporting requirement of Section 13(a) of the Exchange Act until such time as they have less than 300 shareholders of record at the beginning of any subsequent fiscal year.

Some of the primary compliance requirements that affect administration of the company's stock option plan include the following:

4.4.1 Form 8-K

In 2004, as part of its initiative to implement "real time" disclosure of important corporate information, the SEC adopted new rules expanding the number of events that must be reported on a current report on Form 8-K and shortening the deadline for filing the report. The new disclosure items covered a range of significant corporate events, such as the departure of a director or principal officer and an amendment to the company's articles of incorporation or bylaws. It also included some events that are potentially applicable to the administration of a company's stock option plan, such as the entry into a definitive material agreement involving a compensatory purpose.

Because the initial rule changes led to a flood of filings about compensatory transactions, many of which were not significant, in July 2006 the SEC revised the Form 8-K disclosure requirements for compensation-related transactions and events to reduce the number of required filings. The changes consolidate the reporting of compensation-related transactions with the reporting of appointments and departures of directors and principal officers

Effective November 2006, a publicly traded company must file a Form 8-K for only the following compensation-related transactions and events:

- where a director resigns or refuses to stand for reelection to the board of directors because of a disagreement with the company that is known to at least one of the company's executive officers on any matter involving the company's operations, policies, or practices, or if a director is removed for cause;

- where the company's principal executive officer, president, principal financial officer, principal accounting officer, or principal operating officer (a "principal officer"), or any named executive officer, retires, resigns, or has his or her employment terminated, or if a director retires, resigns, is removed, or refuses to stand for re-election (except because of a disagreement, as noted above);

- where the company appoints a new principal officer (in this case, the required disclosure must describe any material plan, contract, or arrangement to which the officer is a party or in which he or she participates as a result of the appointment and any grant or award made to the officer under the plan, contract, or arrangement);

- where the company elects a new director at a time other than in connection with an annual or special meeting of shareholders (in this case, the required disclosure must briefly describe any material plan, contract, or arrangement to which the director is a party or in which he or she participates as a result of the election and any grant or award made to the director under the plan, contract, or arrangement); and

- where the company adopts or starts a material compensatory plan, contract, or arrangement in which the company's principal executive officer, principal financial officer, or a named executive officer participates or is a party, or a material grant or award is made to any such person under the plan, contract, or arrangement (in this case, the required disclosure must briefly describe the terms and conditions of the plan, contract, or arrangement and the amounts payable to the officer thereunder).

In the case of this last disclosure trigger, a Form 8-K need not be filed in the case of grants or awards (whether involving cash or equity) that are materially consistent with the previously disclosed terms of such plan, contract, or arrangement, provided the company has previously disclosed such terms and the grant or award is subsequently included in the company's proxy disclosure about executive compensation. In addition, a company does not need to file a Form 8-K about a plan, contract, or arrangement that does not discriminate in scope, terms, or operation in favor of executive officers or directors and that is available generally to all salaried employees.

It is important to note that this Form 8-K filing requirement is in addition to an individual executive's obligation to file a Section 16(a) insider report within two business days of the receipt of an equity grant or award from the executives company (as discussed below).

A Form 8-K must be filed with the SEC within four business days of a triggering event. Because companies will sometimes need to file a Form 8-K (to meet the four-day filing deadline) when all of the details about the disclosure may be unclear, the rules contain a limited "safe harbor" from liability under the federal anti-fraud rules solely for situations where the company adopts a new material compensation plan or makes a material grant or award under such a plan or arrangement. For example, if a company does not make a required Form 8-K filing for the grant of an equity award (because it originally thought the award was not material), it will not be subject to possible anti-fraud liability as long as the award is disclosed in its next required quarterly or annual report.

4.4.2 Section 16

Assuming the company has registered a class of its equity securities with the SEC under Section 12 of the Exchange Act in connection with its IPO, the officers and directors of the company will be subject to Section 16 following the offering. Section 16 governs the reporting obligations and regulates the trading activities of the directors, officers, and principal shareholders of public reporting companies in the equity securities of their own companies. Specifically, directors and officers of a company that has a class of equity securities registered under the Exchange Act and beneficial owners of more than 10% of the class of equity securities so registered (often called "corporate insiders") must disclose their holdings of, and transactions involving, the equity securities of their company, and further must return to the company any profits that they realize in the event of any "short-swing" trading in such securities.

Section 16 Reporting. Under Section 16(a), a corporate insider must file reports with the SEC (which reports are available to the public) disclosing their holdings of, and transactions involving, the equity securities of the insider's company. This reporting is required for any equity securities that the corporate insider beneficially owns. Typically, the stock plan administrator, or other designated individual, will be responsible for assisting the company's officers and directors in complying with their filing obligations. Since the summer of 2003, all Section 16(a) reports must be filed electronically with the SEC.

The filing of Form 3 in connection with an IPO is discussed above. Following a company's registration of a class of equity securities under Section 12 of the Exchange Act, each time an individual joins the company as an officer or director, or is promoted to officer or director status, a Form 3 must be filed with the SEC by the new corporate insider.

With limited exceptions, a Form 4, the current statement of changes in beneficial ownership, must be filed with the SEC within two business days after the date of execution of a transaction that results in a change in the corporate insider's beneficial ownership of the company's equity securities that is not otherwise eligible for deferred reporting under a specific SEC rule. In other words, a Form 4 must be filed within two business days whenever there is an acquisition or disposition of equity securities by a corporate insider (such as an open-market purchase or sale), including any exercise or conversion of a derivative security, such as an employee stock option. Under the Section 16 rules, any transaction that may be reported on a deferred basis on Form 5 may be reported on an earlier filed Form 4.

Generally, a Form 5, the annual statement of changes in beneficial ownership, must be filed with the SEC within 45 days after the end of the company's fiscal year to report any change in the corporate insider's beneficial ownership of the company's equity securities that is otherwise eligible for deferred reporting. In other words, a Form 5 must be filed whenever there is an acquisition or disposition of equity securities by a corporate insider (such as a bona fide gift) that is eligible for deferred reporting and that has not been previously reported on Form 4.

Special "Look-Back" Rule. Before an IPO, a closely held company may grant stock options and otherwise issue shares of stock to its officers and directors. In addition, such individuals may have other transactions involving the company's equity securities during the pre-IPO period.

To discourage officers and directors of pre-public reporting companies from using their knowledge of the impending offering for their own economic advantage, Exchange Act Rule 16a-2 provides that purchase and sales of the company's equity securities during the six-month period preceding the IPO are subject to Section 16 if carried out by officers or directors who become subject to Section 16 solely as a result of the IPO.

This means that any pre-IPO purchase or sale must be disclosed if it occurs within six months of any Form 4 reportable transaction taking place after the IPO. Likewise, such pre-IPO transactions can be matched for purposes of the Section 16(b) "short-swing profits" recovery provision with any IPO sale of securities or any post-IPO transaction that takes place within a six-month period. Consequently, it is important for the stock plan administrator to ensure that any pre-IPO stock option grants or other awards of stock under an employee stock plan comply with the applicable conditions of the Exchange Act Rule 16b-3 exemption (as discussed below).

Section 16 "Short-Swing Profits" Liability. Under Section 16(b), a company that has registered a class of equity securities under Section 12 of the Exchange Act may recover from a corporate insider any profits that are realized as a result of the purchase and sale, or sale and purchase, of the company's equity securities within a period of less than six months. Section 16(b) imposes strict liability on a corporate insider who meets the required elements of the provision. In other words, disgorgement of any profits realized from the "short-swing" transactions is required whether or not the corporate insider actually used material, nonpublic information to conduct the trades. Moreover, Section 16(b) may operate to require that the corporate insider forfeit "short-swing profits" to the company even where the insider has, in fact, realized no economic gain from the transactions.

For purposes of Section 16(b), the terms "purchase" and "sale" are interpreted broadly and may include acquisitions and dispositions involving derivative securities as well as acquisitions and dispositions arising in connection with a merger or other corporate transaction. Certain types of transactions, however, such as a bona fide gift, are exempt from "purchase" or "sale" status by virtue of a specific SEC rule and thus are outside the scope of Section 16(b). In addition, under the broad definition of "beneficial ownership," transactions by other persons can be attributed to a corporate insider for purposes of Section 16(b). For example, in certain situations, the equity securities of a Section 12 company held by relatives of a corporate insider will be deemed to be beneficially owned by the insider. Thus, a purchase or sale of the securities by a member of an insider's immediate family may be matched with a sale or purchase by the insider that occurs within the same six-month period to trigger "short-swing profits" recovery.

Where "short-swing" trading has occurred, the amount of "profits" recoverable by the Section 12 company is to be determined by pairing the corporate insider's transactions within the six-month period so as to match the transaction with the highest sale price and the transaction with the lowest purchase price. It does not matter whether the purchase or the sale occurred first, and it is not necessary for the same securities to have been involved in each of the matched transactions. The sum of the "profits" from these matched purchases and sales is the amount that the corporate insider must turn over to the company. As previously noted, because gains are not offset by losses, it is possible for a corporate insider to realize "profits" for purposes of Section 16(b) even though the insider actually lost money from the trading activities.

Typically, the stock plan administrator will assist the company's officers and directors in avoiding the operation of Section 16(b) when planning and executing their transactions involving the company's equity securities. In addition, the stock plan administrator should ensure that transactions involving the company's employee stock plans satisfy an appropriate exemption of Exchange Act Rule 16b-3 so as to ensure that such transactions are not considered to involve either a "purchase" or a "sale" for purposes of Section 16(b). Under Rule 16b-3, a transaction between a company (including an employee benefit plan sponsored by the company) and its officers and directors is exempt from the "short-swing profits" recovery provisions of Section 16(b) if it satisfies the applicable conditions of the exemption.

Typically, routine, non-volitional transactions pursuant to a "tax-conditioned plan" (which generally encompasses most Section 401(k) plans, tax-qualified profit-sharing plans, and Section 423 employee stock purchase plans) are exempt from the operation of Section 16(b) without having to satisfy any specific conditions. Fund-switching transactions or volitional cash withdrawals from an employer securities fund in an employee benefit plan will be exempt if the election to engage in the transaction is at least six months after the last election to engage in an "opposite way" (purchase vs. sale) transaction under any company plan.

Other acquisitions of a company's equity securities by an officer or director from his or her company, including grants of stock options, are exempt from the operation of Section 16(b) if the transaction is approved by the company's board of directors, approved by a committee of two or more non-employee directors, approved or ratified by the company's shareholders, or a six-month holding period requirement is satisfied. While these conditions make it much easier to qualify the grant or award of a company's equity securities, including the stock option grant, for exemptive treatment, the stock plan administrator must make sure that the required approval has been obtained for each grant or award to a corporate insider.

Proxy Statement Disclosure. A public reporting company is required to disclose in its annual proxy statement and annual report on Form 10-K under the caption "Section 16(a) Beneficial Ownership Reporting Compliance" a list of any corporate insiders who have been delinquent in filing or failed to file the required Section 16(a) reports with the SEC during the last completed fiscal year. This disclosure is to include (1) the name of the corporate insider who failed to file reports on a timely basis during the fiscal year, (2) the number of late reports by the insider, (3) the number of transactions not reported on a timely basis, and (4) any known failures to file a required report.

This disclosure is based solely on the information contained in the reports furnished to the company during the fiscal year and any written representations delivered to the company by corporate insiders stating that no Form 5 was required. The company may rely on a written representation from a corporate insider that no Form 5 was required if the company maintains a file of such representations for two years and makes copies available to the SEC upon request.

4.4.3 Equity Compensation Disclosure

A company is required to disclose in tabular form each year in its annual report on Form 10-K, and in its proxy statement in years in which the company is submitting a compensation plan for shareholder approval, certain information about the number of securities to be issued upon the exercise of outstanding stock options, the weighted-average exercise price of outstanding stock options, and the number of securities remaining available for future issuance under all of the company's equity compensation plans. This disclosure is to be made on an aggregated basis in two categories: plans that have been approved by shareholders, and plans that have not been approved by shareholders. Individual equity compensation arrangements, such as individual stock options that have been granted outside a formal plan, and equity compensation plans that have been assumed in a merger, consolidation, or other acquisition transaction may be aggregated in the appropriate category with the company's plan disclosure.

In addition, where a company has one or more equity compensation plans that have not been approved by shareholders, the company must disclose the material features of each non-shareholder-approved plan and attach a copy of the plan as an exhibit to the Form 10-K, unless the plan is immaterial in amount or significance.

4.4.4 Shareholder Approval of Equity Plans

Companies that are listed on the NYSE or NASDAQ must obtain shareholder approval of their equity compensation plans, including stock option plans, and material revisions or amendments to such plans, subject to the limited exemptions discussed below.

Under the NYSE standard, an "equity compensation plan" is a plan or other arrangement that provides for the delivery of shares (either newly issued or treasury shares) of a listed company to any employee, director, or service provider as compensation for services, including a compensatory grant of options or other equity securities that is not made under a formal plan. Certain plans are not considered "equity compensation plans" for purposes of the standard, including:

- Plans that provide for the payment of cash based on the value of shares, rather than for the delivery of actual shares;

- Plans that are made available to shareholders generally (such as a typical dividend reinvestment plan); and

- Plans that merely allow employees, directors, or service providers to elect to buy shares on the open market or from the listed company for their current fair market value, regardless of whether the shares are delivered immediately or on a deferred basis, or the payments for the shares are made directly or by giving up compensation that is otherwise due (for example, through payroll deductions).

The NASDAQ standard does not define the types of plans that must be approved by shareholders. Instead, the standard provides that it covers stock option and purchase plans and other equity compensation arrangements pursuant to which options or stock may be acquired by officers, directors, employees, or consultants, except for warrants or rights issued generally to all shareholders, stock purchase plans available on equal terms to all shareholders (such as a typical dividend reinvestment plan), and plans that merely provide a convenient way to purchase shares on the open market or from the company at fair market value.

Both standards require shareholder approval of any material revision or amendment of an equity compensation plan, such as a stock option plan. Generally, a "material revision" or "material amendment" is a modification that expands, rather than curtails, the scope of the plan.

The NYSE and NASDAQ standards do not require shareholder approval for the adoption or amendment of certain specified types of plans and arrangements. These plans and arrangements are exempt, however, only if approved by the listed or quoted company's independent compensation committee or a majority of the company's independent directors. In addition, in the case of a listed company, the NYSE must be notified in writing when one of these exemptions is relied upon.

Generally, the exemptions under the standards include:

- "inducement" awards to individuals being hired by the company or being rehired following a *bona fide* period of interruption of employment;

- the conversion, replacement, or adjustment of outstanding options or other equity compensation awards to reflect the terms of a merger or other acquisition transaction;

- post-transaction grants of options and other equity awards of shares under certain pre-existing plans acquired in a corporate merger or acquisition;

- grants and awards pursuant to tax-qualified, non-discriminatory employee benefit plans (such as Section 401(a) plans and Section 423 plans); and

- grants and awards pursuant to pension plans designed to work in parallel with tax-qualified employee benefit plans that meet certain conditions.

Finally, special rules apply to so-called "formula" and "discretionary" plans as defined in the relevant standard.

4.4.5 Form S-8 Registration

Following the IPO, the company will need to ensure that the securities issued to employees under the company's employee stock option plans satisfy the requirements of federal and state securities laws. Generally, securities cannot be issued under an employee stock option plan unless a registration statement is in effect or an exemption from registration is available.

Form S-8 is a simplified registration statement that may be used by a company that is subject to the reporting requirements of the Exchange Act to register the securities to be offered and sold pursuant to the company's employee stock option plan. The registration statement reflects an abbreviated disclosure format and incorporates by reference information contained in the company's other publicly available documents.

Unlike other registration statements, the preparation and distribution of a formal prospectus is not required. Instead, the company need only deliver to employees certain required information about the employee stock option plan and a statement of the documents that are available upon request to participants. This information can be provided separately or integrated into the company's customary employee communications. The information must be identified as comprising part of the Form S-8 "prospectus," which is accomplished by including a specific legend at the beginning of each document that contains the required plan information.

A company may use a registration statement on Form S-8 at any time after becoming subject to the reporting requirements of the Exchange Act. In addition, Form S-8 becomes effective immediately upon filing with the SEC.

Form S-8 covers offers and sales of securities under an employee stock option plan to consultants and advisors, as well as to employees, officers, and directors. Transactions by former employees are also covered in certain instances. Form S-8 applies to transactions pursuant to individual written compensatory contracts, as well as actual employee stock plans.

Option shares acquired under a Form S-8 registration statement may be resold by non-affiliates without restriction. Affiliates may sell their Form S-8-registered option shares pursuant to Rule 144 (but without regard to the holding period condition).

4.4.6 Section 162(m)

Under Code Section 162, a company is entitled to deduct from gross income all ordinary and necessary expenses paid or incurred during a taxable year in connection with carrying on a trade or business. The expenses contemplated by this provision include a reasonable allowance for salaries or other compensation for personal services actually rendered. Thus, amounts expended by a company to compensate its employees, including equity compensation, are deductible as long as the amounts are "reasonable."

Code Section 162(m) contains a limitation on the deductibility of certain executive compensation. Section 162(m) limits the ability of publicly held corporations to deduct from their corporate income taxes compensation in excess of $1 million paid to certain executive officers. While the limit is clearly aimed at limiting the deductibility of cash compensation, such as salary and bonus, it is also potentially applicable to compensation income realized in connection with the receipt of stock under an employee stock plan. For example, the limit would apply in the case of compensation income realized upon the exercise of a nonqualified stock option and upon the vesting of restricted stock.

The deduction limit of Section 162(m) applies only to "publicly held corporations." For these purposes, a corporation is considered to be "publicly held" if a class of its common equity securities is required to be registered under Section 12 of the Exchange Act as of the last day of the company's taxable year. Thus, companies that voluntarily register under Section 12 are not subject to Section 162(m).

The deduction limit of Section 162(m) applies only to the compensation paid to specific "covered employees." These are (1) the chief executive officer of the company (or the individual acting in that capacity) on the last day of the taxable year, and (2) the three most highly compensated officers of the company (other than the chief executive officer) whose compensation is required to be reported to shareholders under the executive compensation disclosure rules of the Exchange Act. Note that the current "covered employee" definition is not congruent with the named executive officer group as determined under SEC rules. It does not incorporate either the 1993 or the 2006 amendments to the executive compensation disclosure rules. As a result, it does not cover either a company's chief financial officer or certain former executive officers. Thus, the deduction limit does not apply to a CEO who leaves the company before the end of the taxable year, to an officer who would be among the most highly compensated officers for the year but for the fact that he or she was not with the company at year-end, or to the company's CFO.

For purposes of the deduction limit, "applicable employee remuneration" with respect to any covered employee includes all otherwise deductible remuneration for services performed by the employee (whether or not such services were performed during the taxable year). Thus, covered compensation can include the compensation income recognized upon the exercise of a nonqualified stock option, the disqualifying disposition of an incentive stock option, or the vesting of restricted stock, even if the option or restricted stock was granted in a prior year.

Certain types of compensation are expressly excluded from the deduction limit of Section 162(m) and thus need not be taken into account in determining whether an employee's total compensation for the year exceeds the $1 million threshold. These include (1) compensation payable solely on a commission basis; (2) certain "fringe" benefits that are not included in the employee's gross income; (3) payments made to or from certain tax-qualified retirement plans; (4) compensation payable under any written binding contract that was in effect on February 17, 1993 (and which has not been subsequently modified in any material respect); and (5) "performance-based" compensation.

Performance-Based Compensation. Certain performance-based compensation is excluded from the deduction limit of Section 162(m) if several conditions are satisfied. To be considered "performance-based," (1) the compensation must be payable solely upon the attainment of one or more performance goals that are determined by a compensation committee of the board of directors comprised solely of two or more "outside" directors; (2) the material terms of the plan or arrangement under which the compensation is to be paid, including the performance goals, must be disclosed to shareholders and approved by a majority of the vote in a separate shareholder vote before the payment of the compensation; and (3) before the payment of the compensation, the compensation committee must certify that the performance goals and any other material terms of the arrangement were in fact satisfied.

Transition for Closely Held Companies. Unless a company has been publicly held for the entire taxable year, the deduction limit of Section 162(m) does not apply to any compensation plan or agreement that was in effect while the company was closely held, as long as the plans and agreements are adequately disclosed at the time of the company's IPO and are not thereafter materially modified. In other words, the deduction limit would not apply to stock options granted under stock option plans that are in existence when a company becomes publicly held, provided that such plans are disclosed as part of the prospectus accompanying the company's IPO.

This exception may be relied upon until the earliest to occur of (1) the expiration or material modification of the plan or agreement, (2) the issuance of all the securities or other compensation that has been allocated under the plan, or (3) the first meeting of shareholders at which the directors are to be elected that occurs after the close of the third calendar year following the calendar year in which the IPO took place. Thus, corporations can rely on the exemption for any compensation received as the result of the exercise of a stock option or the vesting (or receipt) of restricted stock if the grant or award (rather than the exercise or vesting) occurs before the end of the reliance period.

4.4.7 Section 409A

Section 409A of the Code, added by the American Jobs Creation Act of 2004, governs the design and operation of plans and arrangements that provide for the deferral of compensation. While the definition of a "deferral of compensation" for purposes of Section 409A is broad enough to encompass employee stock options and other types of equity awards, IRS regulations provide the following guidance:

- Incentive stock options (ISOs) and options granted under employee stock purchase plans that comply with Section 423 of the Code are not subject to Section 409A.

- Nonstatutory stock options are not subject to Section 409A if they can never have an exercise price less than the fair market value of the underlying stock on the grant date and do not contain any deferral feature other than the right to exercise the option.

- Stock appreciation rights (SARs), whether settled in stock or cash, are not subject to Section 409A as long as (1) the amount payable upon exercise of the SAR does not exceed the difference between the fair market value of the underlying stock on the grant date and the exercise date, (2) the exercise price of the SAR can never be less than the fair market value of the underlying stock on the grant date, and (3) the SAR does not include any deferral feature other than the right to exercise the SAR in the future.

Any stock option or SAR that does not qualify for the exemptive treatment described above is considered to involve a deferral of compensation and must comply with the requirements of Section 409A—which involve the timing of deferral elections and permissible distribution events—to avoid early inclusion of the award's appreciated value in employees' income, plus a 20% penalty and interest.

To be exempt from Section 409A, a stock option or SAR may only be exercisable for so-called "service recipient stock." The definition of a "service recipient" is defined broadly and includes an employer company; a 50% subsidiary; and, given a legitimate business reason (for example, in some joint ventures), a 20% subsidiary. The IRS regulations also indicate that "service recipient stock" may include American Depository Receipts (ADRs) and "units" in mutual insurance companies. However, "service recipient stock" is limited to *common stock*. For public companies, the common stock must be readily tradable on an established securities market; for private companies, common stock must be the class of common stock having the greatest aggregate value of all the classes of common stock outstanding.

Because stock options and SARs with an exercise price that is less than the fair market value of the underlying stock on the grant date (discounted options and SARs) are subject to Section 409A, valuation of a company's stock in connection with an option or SAR grant will be a critical aspect of compliance with Section 409A. For stock that is readily tradable on an established securities market (including over-the-counter markets and many foreign markets), the IRS regulations provide that fair market value may be determined using the stock's trading price (using a method that is determined on a reasonable basis using actual market transactions and that is consistently applied).

For the stock of a closely held company, fair market value may be determined using any reasonable valuation method that takes into account a number of specified factors and is applied consistently. The IRS regulations include some valuation methods that will be presumed to be reasonable:

- appraisals that satisfy the Internal Revenue Code's requirements for valuation of ESOP stock;

- formula valuations based on non-lapse restrictions as defined in Section 83 of the Code, but only if the valuation method is used consistently for both compensatory and noncompensatory purposes; and

- for illiquid stock of a "start-up corporation," special valuations that meet the following requirements: the company is in its first 10 years of active trade or business, has no readily traded securities, does not anticipate a change in control or initial public offering within a specified period after the valuation, and applies the valuation to stock that is not subject to a put or call or repurchase obligation.

Because the exemption for stock options and SARs is limited to awards that were not granted at a discount *and* do not contain any additional deferral feature, amending an option or SAR may convert an otherwise-exempt award into a discount option or an SAR subject to Section 409A. Under the IRS regulations, certain changes to an option or SAR will cause the award to be treated either as a new award on the amendment date (which is then retested for Section 409A compliance) or as an award with an additional deferral feature that is considered to have been subject to Section 409A from the original grant date. This issue exists not only for nonstatutory stock options but also for ISOs and Section 423 ESPP options. Any change in the terms of an award that provide the employee a direct or indirect reduction in the award's exercise price, an additional deferral feature, or an extension or renewal of the award is potentially subject to this principle.

4.4.8 Insider Trading

Under the federal securities laws, any person, including a corporate insider, possessing "material" nonpublic information about a company must refrain from engaging in transactions in the company's securities until adequate public disclosure of this information has been made. The penalties for trading in securities while in the possession of material nonpublic information are severe and include injunctive actions or actions for civil penalties that may be brought by the SEC, actions for monetary damages that may be brought by private parties, and criminal penalties. The federal securities laws also prohibit persons, including corporate insiders, from "tipping" third parties, either by disclosing confidential information to such persons or by making trading recommendations based on such information.

Of the various antifraud provisions found in the federal securities laws, Section 10(b) of the Exchange Act has enjoyed the broadest application. Generally, Section 10(b) makes it unlawful for any person, directly or indirectly, to use or employ, in connection with the purchase or sale of a security (whether or not registered on an exchange), "any manipulative or deceptive device or contrivance" which contravenes such rules and regulations as the SEC may adopt.

Pursuant to this authority, the SEC has adopted Exchange Act Rule 10b-5, which states that it is unlawful for any person, directly or indirectly, to employ any "device, scheme or artifice to defraud," to make any untrue statement of a material fact, to omit to state a material fact necessary to make statements not misleading, or to engage in any "act, practice or course of business which operates" as a fraud or deceit upon any person.

One of the primary uses of Exchange Act Rule 10b-5 over the years has been to prohibit trading in securities by persons having knowledge of material, undisclosed information, thereby promoting full and fair disclosure of material information to all investors. This prohibition on "insider trading" is applied broadly by the courts and covers not only directors, officers, and principal shareholders of the company, but essentially anyone who comes into possession of confidential information and has a duty to disclose (or to abstain from trading), including an insider's spouse and immediate family members. The prohibition covers trading in the equity, debt, and derivative securities of the company.

"Material" Information. While there is no specific definition of what constitutes material information for purposes of the insider trading prohibitions, at least two standards are commonly applied to determine the "materiality" of specific information. First, if the information would be expected to significantly affect the market price of the company's stock, then it is probably material. Alternatively, if the information would influence or affect the investment decisions of a reasonable investor, then, once again, it is probably material. Typical examples of "material" information might include a company's quarterly and annual financial results (or components thereof); major proposed or pending transactions; changes in a company's capital structure; research and development projects or plans; pricing, sales, or market plans or projections; management or other key personnel changes; and litigation developments.

Nonpublic Information. Generally, information is considered to be "nonpublic" until it has been disseminated throughout the securities markets. As construed by the courts, this means that the information must have first been distributed through the media of widest circulation. Typically, this is accomplished by disclosure of the information in one or more of the company's periodic reports or filings under the federal securities laws or through the issuance of a press release.

The prohibitions against insider trading not only restrict a person from making use of the confidential information but also prohibit "tipping," or passing the information on to another person who then trades on the basis of the information (where the person could have reasonably foreseen that the recipient would make use of the information).

Trading Policies. Because of the difficulties associated with determining the materiality of undisclosed information, many companies maintain internal trading policies to prevent inadvertent violations of the insider trading prohibitions. A typical trading policy will restrict transactions in the company's stock to certain designated periods following the release of quarterly financial information about the company. These trading periods are commonly referred to as "window periods." In addition, the company may designate an employee, usually a member of management, to act as a compliance officer. In this capacity, the compliance officer must clear in advance any trade in the company's stock by an employee subject to the policy.

At a minimum, corporate trading policies will be applied to its directors, officers, and other corporate insiders. Some companies extend the policy to several additional levels of employees, while others apply the policy to all employees. Even where a company limits its trading policy to corporate insiders, most companies take steps to ensure that, at a minimum, all employees are aware of their obligations under the federal securities laws.

Exchange Act Rule 10b5-1. Under Exchange Act Rule 10b5-1, for purposes of Section 10(b) of the Exchange Act, an individual will be considered to have traded "on the basis of" material non-public information if he or she was aware of the information at the time he or she made the subject purchase or sale of securities. The rule goes on, however, to provide an affirmative defense to this "awareness" standard for determining insider trading liability. If an individual has (1) entered into a binding contract, provided instructions to another person, or adopted a written trading plan before becoming aware of the material, nonpublic information, (2) the binding contract, instructions, or written plan expressly provides (by amount of formula) the amount, price, and date of the transaction, and (3) demonstrated the transaction in question was pursuant to the binding contract, instructions, or written plan, then the binding contract, instructions, or written plan will act as an affirmative defense to a claim of insider trading.

Because a written program for trading securities may cover any securities owned by an individual, many officers and directors of public reporting companies have taken to adopting written trading plans as a means for implementing liquidity strategies for their employee stock options. Unlike a trading "window" instituted to ensure compliance with Exchange Act Rule 10b-5, a trading plan does not permit any discretion on the part of the individual adopting the plan. It does, however, permit trading at any time, as long as the criteria for trading were established at a previous time when the individual was not aware of any material, nonpublic information about the company. If a trading plan involves the disposition of "restricted securities" for purposes of Rule 144, the parties must ensure compliance with the resale conditions of that rule.

Insider Trading Prohibition During Pension Fund Blackout Periods. Section 306(a) of the Sarbanes-Oxley Act of 2002 prohibits the directors and executive officers of public reporting companies from, directly or indirectly, purchasing, selling, or otherwise acquiring or transferring any equity security of the company during a pension plan blackout period that prevents plan participants or beneficiaries from engaging in equity security transactions, if the equity security was acquired in connection with the director or executive officer's service or employment as a director or executive officer. In addition, the company must provide timely notice to its directors and executive officers, as well as to the SEC, of an impending blackout period.

The SEC has adopted Regulation BTR, which contains rules that clarify the application of this insider trading prohibition, including rules that define when an equity security is acquired "in connection with" service of employment as a director or executive officer. Generally, these rules provide that equity securities, including stock options, acquired under an equity compensation plan maintained by the company are to be considered acquired in connection with service or employment. Accordingly, companies will need to assist their directors and executive officers in identifying the equity securities that are subject to the trading prohibition and in monitoring any pension plan blackout periods to avoid violations of the prohibition.

Where a director or executive officer engages in a prohibited transaction, he or she is subject to possible enforcement action by the SEC. In addition, the company may recover from the director or executive officer any profits that are realized as a result of the purchase, sale, acquisition or transfer that occurred during the blackout period. Similar to Section 16(b) of the Exchange Act, Section 306(a) of the Sarbanes-Oxley Act imposes strict liability on a director or executive officer who violates the trading prohibition. In other words, disgorgement of any profits realized from the prohibited transaction is required whether or not the director or executive officer intended to trade in violation of the statutory provision.

Other Insider Trading Restrictions. Over the past 20 years, the existing body of insider trading law has been supplemented by a number of statutory provisions. The adoption of these provisions has been frequently cited as a significant influence in the development of insider trading policies and other internal controls by many publicly held companies. In the mid-1980s, the Insider Trading Sanctions Act of 1984 was enacted by Congress. Among other things, the Act authorized the SEC to seek civil penalties of up to three times the profit gained or the loss avoided where a person purchased or sold securities while in possession of material nonpublic information.

In 1988, Congress enacted the Insider Trading and Securities Fraud Enforcement Act, which added Section 21A to the Exchange Act. Among other things, Section 21A authorizes the SEC to seek civil penalties against employers and other controlling persons who "knew or recklessly disregarded" the fact that a controlled person was likely to engage in insider trading and failed to take appropriate steps to prevent such act before it occurred. While the Exchange Act does not define what constitutes appropriate steps, most companies have concluded it is necessary to communicate regularly with all employees, especially those most likely to have access to confidential information, about their responsibilities under the federal securities laws and to establish some control over trading by directors and officers.

Section 21A retained the civil remedy established by the Insider Trading Sanctions Act against primary traders. In addition, it authorizes the imposition of a penalty against controlling persons of the greater of $1 million or three times the profit gained or loss avoided as a result of the controlled person's violation.

In 1990, the Securities Enforcement Remedies and Penny Stock Reform Act was enacted. The Act substantially increased the enforcement powers of the SEC for violations of the federal securities laws. Among the remedies available under the Act, the SEC has the authority to issue both permanent and temporary cease-and-desist orders to enforce the various federal securities laws, the power to seek in federal district court monetary penalties ranging from $5,000 to $500,000 for securities law violations, and the ability to seek to have individuals who have violated specific provisions of the federal securities laws barred from serving as a director or officer of a public reporting company.

4.4.9 Financial Statement Information

Stock Option Valuation. The company will need to use the "fair value" method of accounting in order to comply with FAS 123(R). While previously the "fair value" method was used primarily to meet a company's disclosure obligations under FAS 123, commencing with its first fiscal year beginning after December 31, 2005, the company will need to comply with FAS 123(R) for purposes of calculating the expense associated with its stock option programs even if the IPO has not yet occurred.

"Fair value" is to be determined using an option-pricing model, such as the Black-Scholes or a binomial model, that takes into account, as of the grant date, the option price and the expected life of the option, the current price of the underlying shares of stock and its expected volatility, expected dividends on the stock, and the risk-free interest rate for the expected option term. The determination of the required assumptions for input into the option-pricing model will be more challenging for the initial years following adoption of the accounting standard. This will be the case for the expected option life and stock price volatility assumptions.

One potential problem in formulating the expected option life assumption can arise if there are differences in the terms and conditions of the stock options being valued and the stock options that will form the basis of the historical information to be analyzed to determine the assumption. Where the terms and conditions of the stock options being valued differ from those of the historical option grants (for example, different vesting schedules), the stock plan administrator will need to decide to what degree the historical data is relevant to determining the expected life of the stock options being valued. This issue may be of particular significance if the company has revised or updated the terms and conditions of its stock option plan in connection with the IPO.

In addition, the IPO will likely result in a large number of stock option exercises related to the offering. These transactions should be given less weight in the evaluation of the company's historical data for purposes of establishing the expected option life assumption because the economic conditions that influenced the exercise decisions are not likely to be duplicated in the near future.

With respect to the stock price volatility assumption, because the company will not have a trading history that is commensurate with the expected life of the stock options being valued, it will need to consider the historical volatility of similar companies following a comparable period in their lives. Consequently, the stock plan administrator will need to assist in selecting the group of companies to be compiled for this purpose. Alternatively, FAS 123(R) prescribes the use of a "calculated value" method. In the rare circumstance in which a publicly traded company cannot estimate either fair value or calculated value because of the complexity of an award's terms, the award's intrinsic value must be used and be re-measured at each reporting date.

Earnings per Share. Under current generally accepted accounting principles, an earnings-per-share computation must be presented by publicly held corporations. This information is used by investors to assess the profitability and the performance of the company from period to period and to compare the company to other businesses. Simply put, the earnings-per-share (EPS) computation involves spreading the company's earnings for the period being reported over the number of common equity securities outstanding during such period. For purposes of this computation, the company's shares of stock are weighted for the actual time that such shares were outstanding during the period.

The current requirements for calculating earnings per share are set forth in FAS No. 128. The standard requires the presentation of both "basic" and "diluted" earnings per share. The basic earnings-per-share computation does not take into consideration the effects of dilution. It is calculated by dividing the total income available to common shareholders for the reporting period by the weighted average number of shares of common stock actually outstanding during that period, without factoring in any potentially issuable securities that could have a dilutive effect on the company's outstanding shares of stock, such as employee stock options. Shares of stock issued during the period and shares reacquired during the period are weighted for the portion of the period that they were outstanding.

The diluted earnings-per-share computation reflects the potential dilutive effect of outstanding stock options and other common stock equivalents by treating them as if they were exercised or converted into common stock that then shared in the total income of the company available to shareholders. The calculation of diluted earnings per share is similar to the calculation of basic earnings per share except that the denominator is increased to include the number of additional shares of common stock that would have been outstanding if the dilutive potential common shares had been issued. In addition, the calculation does not take into consideration the exercise or conversion of any securities that would have an antidilutive effect on earnings per share (that is, the exercise or conversion would result in an increase to earnings per share because the acquisition of the shares of stock would result in the payment to the company of more than the current value of the shares). Generally, the dilutive effect of options and warrants is to be reflected in the calculation through the application of the so-called "treasury stock" accounting method. Under this method, (1) the exercise of options and warrants is to be assumed at the beginning of the reporting period (unless actually exercised at a later time during the period) and shares of common stock are assumed to be issued, (2) the proceeds from the assumed exercise are further assumed to be used to repurchase outstanding shares of common stock at the average fair market value of the company's stock for the reporting period, and (3) the incremental shares of common stock (the difference between the number of shares assumed to be exercised and the number of shares assumed to be repurchased) are included in the denominator of the diluted earnings-per-share calculation.

Disgorgement of Bonuses and Profits upon Financial Restatement. Under Section 304 of the Sarbanes-Oxley Act of 2002, if a public reporting company is required to restate its financial statements because of the material noncompliance of the company, due to misconduct, with any financial reporting requirements, the company's chief executive officer and chief financial officer are required to return to the company any bonus or other equity or incentive based compensation, including stock options, received from the company during the one-year period preceding following the issuance of the original financial statements (that are now being restated) and any profits realized from any sale of the company's securities during the same one-year period.

4.5   Conclusion

While the reasons for an IPO can be compelling, most companies underestimate the amount of work involved in getting ready to "go public." A fundamental understanding of the process and adequate advance preparation are essential to a successful offering. Because the company's stock option plan may be the primary source of equity for the company's employees before and after the IPO, it is important to understand both the impact the plan will have on the offering and the impact the offering will have on the plan. In addition, administering the stock option plan following an IPO can be very complex and challenging. The stock plan administrator must have a thorough familiarity with the applicable legal and other requirements to ensure a smooth transition from a closely held to a public reporting company.

5

Handling Death Under a Stock Option Plan

Donna Yip and Mark Poerio

Contents

WHILE HANDLING DEATH UNDER a stock option plan depends largely on the situation, there are various issues that consistently present themselves at both the corporate and individual level. These issues include, but are not limited to, probate administration, tax consequences, and securities laws. This chapter provides general guidance on these specific issues.

5.1   Probate Administration

A traditional view of probate administration focuses on the management, organization and disposition of the decedent's estate—i.e., the role of the estate administrator. However, in evaluating probate administration in conjunction with stock options, it is clear that the role of the corporate-level stock plan administrator is essential to this discussion.

5.1.1 From the Estate Administrator's Perspective

At the estate administration level, there is flexibility, however limited, in determining who will handle the issues arising from the decedent's estate. Generally, the decedent has stipulated in the will who the estate representative (the "Representative") should be. Upon death, a court confirms or newly appoints a Representative to handle the administration of the decedent's estate.

The Representative is charged with a number of responsibilities concerning the decedent's estate. These responsibilities include, but are not limited to (1) organizing and filing the relevant paperwork surrounding the decedent's estate; (2) inventorying and managing the assets of the decedent's estate; (3) taking possession of all of the decedent's property that is subject to probate; (4) filing an inventory and appraisal of the estate's assets; (5) paying (and filing where necessary for) the debts, taxes, and liabilities of the estate; and (6) distributing the remaining assets to the persons entitled to receive them.

Focal to this discussion is the Representative's responsibility to inventory and manage the assets of the decedent's estate. Generally, where the decedent "owns" stock options, the value of these options must be included in the decedent's gross estate,[1] which creates additional responsibilities for the Representative. Depending on the type of option or equity award held by the decedent and whether such options are transferable to the estate, the Representative may need to determine whether he or she has the authority under the will or state law to exercise stock options, hold stock, sell stock, or transfer the option or stock. The tax consequences of these various forms of disposition are discussed below. Other issues may arise, such as whether the Representative has sufficient funds to exercise any options and whether the Representative has the authority to borrow or pledge stock.[2]

5.1.2 From a Stock Plan Administrator's Perspective

At the corporate level, there is no court-appointed representative to handle the issues surrounding stock options at death. Additionally, where the court appoints the Representative to handle the estate issues after death, companies must handle corresponding and different issues for the periods before and after the death of the optionee.

---

1. Rev. Rul. 53-196.

2. When borrowing funds to exercise options, an institutional fiduciary may be restricted by Regulation U of the Federal Reserve System Board of Governors.

A prudent stock plan administrator knows that handling death in a stock option plan requires planning before the death of any employee. The best time to accommodate for the various issues that arise in administering a stock option plan (such as a retirement or change in control) is in the plan design phase. The stock plan administrator and legal counsel should carefully review the terms of all stock option plans as well as each form of grant agreement for provisions relating to the death of an optionee.

Many issues must be considered regarding the impact of death on outstanding options. For example, is the option extinguished or is it transferable pursuant to the optionee's will or the laws of descent and distribution? Does vesting accelerate on the optionholder's death? How long is the option exercisable after death—three months, six months, one year, or more? Does the individual award agreement modify or expand upon relevant plan provisions?

If a plan or the individual award agreement provides for the designation of death beneficiaries, those records should be examined upon notice of the death of the optionee. Unlike tax-qualified or ERISA retirement plans, there is no legal requirement that the optionee's spouse be named as the beneficiary. If the option survives the death of the optionee and a beneficiary designation was not executed, then the optionee's estate would become the beneficiary, subject to any specific bequest in the optionee's will. In some states, beneficiary designations for stock options may not be valid, and a dispute could arise as to the rightful beneficiary.

In the event of the death of an optionee, the stock plan administrator should obtain a copy of the death certificate and the court order appointing the Representative. Note that the probate process generally requires that following the optionee's death, the stock plan administrator must correspond and interact with the Representative, not the surviving spouse or children. (In many cases, however, the surviving spouse will be appointed as the Representative.) The Representative should request a copy of the notice of exercise form and prospectus, a summary of the optionee's grants and exercises, and related plan materials.

For additional concerns posed at the stock plan administrator level, please refer to the discussion of tax and securities issues below.

5.2 Tax Consequences

Upon satisfactory resolution of stock plan and estate administration issues, the Representative, the beneficiaries of the estate, and the former employer must consider the tax consequences associated with the various transactions subsequent to the employee's death. These tax consequences vary depending on the underlying equity and for purposes of this discussion are mainly distinctions between (1) incentive stock options (ISOs) and (2) nonqualified stock options (NSOs).

5.2.1 Incentive Stock Options

An ISO is a form of equity that receives tax-favored treatment by satisfying certain statutory requirements, including employment and holding requirements enumerated in the Internal Revenue Code (the "Code"). Section 422 of the Code requires that an optionee be an employee of the company granting the option (or an employee of its parent or a subsidiary) at all times during the period beginning on the date of grant through the day three months before exercise. This three-month period is waived in the event an optionholder's death causes employment to terminate (although most plans or award agreements limit the post-death exercise period). The Code also requires that stock purchased through exercise of an ISO be held for two years from the date of grant of an ISO and one year from the date of exercise. If these requirements are met, the employee will not be taxed until the sale of the shares and will be entitled to long-term capital gains tax treatment on the difference between the sales price and the exercise price. Additionally, the employer will not be entitled to any compensation deduction.[3]

Exercisability and Transferability in the Event of Death. While Section 422 lays out various exercisability and transferability rules, the transfer of an ISO to a beneficiary or estate is not treated as a modification of the option (although an extension of an exercise period to accommodate an estate or beneficiary will be treated as a modification and will disqualify the ISO), and the transfer of stock to a beneficiary or an estate is not deemed to be a "disqualifying disposition."[4] As noted above, the regular ISO requirement that the option be exercised within three months of the optionee's leaving the company does not apply if an employee dies while in service or up to three months later. However, if the optionee dies more than three months after terminating employment, and thereafter the option is exercised by the estate then the option cannot be treated as an ISO.[5]

---

3.   Code §§ 421(a) and 422(a).

4.   Code § 424(c)(1)(A); Treas. Reg. § 1.421-2(b)(2); Code § 421(c)(1); Treas. Reg. § 1.421-2(c)(1); Treas. Reg. § 1.421-2(d).

5.   Id.

If an optionee exercised an ISO before death, the stock acquired by the ISO exercise may be sold by the estate without satisfying the one- and two-year holding periods generally required for long-term capital gains tax treatment on the post-option grant appreciation.[6] In such a situation, the estate would receive a step-up in basis in the stock equal to its fair market value determined at the date of death of the optionee.[7]

If the optionee has unexercised ISOs at the time of death, the estate receives a step-up in basis in the option itself. When the option is exercised by the estate, the estate will have a basis in the underlying shares equal to the sum of the exercise price and the fair value of the option at the optionee's death.[8] Note that in this case, the holding period of the option does not "tack" (i.e., add to) with holding period of the resulting stock for capital gains purposes. Thus, if the ISO is exercised by the estate, the underlying shares must be held for more than a year to obtain long-term capital gains treatment on the post-grant appreciation.

The Representative should review the ISO award agreements and consult a tax adviser before determining the tax liability relating to the ISO award because there may be further issues to consider. One such example is that certain award agreements provide accelerated vesting of all unvested ISOs at the optionee's death. The amount that is accelerated may be greater than the Section 422 $100,000 annual limit, a disqualifying disposition which will cause the estate to incur additional federal tax liability and, depending on the applicable state laws, independent state tax liability and timing of tax payments.

Disqualifying Disposition: Income Tax and AMT. Generally, if an employee fails to meet the employment or holding period requirements, the employee will have a so-called "disqualifying disposition."[9] If the price of the stock has gone up since the exercise, the employee will have ordinary income in the year of disposition equal to the amount by which the fair market value of the stock received (determined as of the time of exercise) exceeds the exercise price. The balance of the gain (e.g., the amount by which the sale price exceeds what the fair market value was at the date of exercise) would be capital gains. If the price of the stock has gone down since exercise (e.g., the exercise price was $10 per share,

---

6. Code § 421(c)(1); Treas. Reg. § 1.421-2(d).
7. Code § 1014(a).
8. Treas. Reg. § 1.421-2(c)(4)(i); Code § 421(c)(3).
9. Code § 422.

the fair market value at exercise was $15, and now the market price at which the employee sells is $13), the employee will have ordinary income in the year of disposition equal to the amount by which the sales price exceeds the exercise price.[10] In the case of a disqualifying disposition, the employer would receive a tax deduction equal to the amount that the employee must include in ordinary income as long as the employer reports the income on Form W-2. No withholding is required for federal income tax (FIT) or FICA purposes.[11]

The exercise of an ISO also has consequences for the alternative minimum tax (AMT) that must be addressed. AMT is a tax determined under a separate tax system originally designed to require the wealthy to pay their fair share of taxes. The calculations can be quite complex. The calculations start with adjusted gross income minus itemized deductions. That figure is increased by the amount of certain deductions (e.g., state and local property and income taxes), certain items of income (e.g., ISO spread at exercise), and certain items of tax preference to obtain alternative minimum taxable income (AMTI). Next, AMTI is reduced by the applicable AMT exemption amount ($33,750 for single filers and $45,000 for married joint filers as of this writing, but subject to phasing out) to obtain the AMT base. To obtain the amount of AMT owed, apply the 26% AMT rate to up to $175,000 of the AMT base, and apply the 28% AMT rate for amounts above.[12] The taxpayer pays the larger of AMT or "regular tax" liability. Often, the exercise of an ISO will cause the employee to pay AMT because the spread increases the AMT base but not the regular income tax base. In many cases, all or a part of extra taxes owed for the year of exercise of an ISO can be recovered through a tax credit in later tax years when the taxpayer's "regular tax" liability exceeds the AMT liability (but only to the extent of excess). Usually, the bulk of the tax credit cannot be recovered until the sale of the ISO stock. No AMT is owed if the stock is sold in the year of exercise.

The exercise of an ISO by an estate raises complicated AMT issues, specifically where an estate exercises an ISO, an estate sells a share acquired through an ISO, or where bequests by will are concerned. Where

---

10. Code §§ 421(b) and 422(c)(2).

11. Section 251 of the American Jobs Creation Act of 2004 provides that companies do not have to withhold taxes for disqualifying dispositions of shares acquired through ISOs and Section 423 ESPPs.

12. The AMT information included in this discussion relates to tax information for 2007 or based on information available at the time this chapter was revised.

an estate exercises an ISO, there is a positive AMT adjustment equal to the difference between the fair market value of the stock acquired at the date of exercise over the estate's basis in the stock. The basis of the shares for this purpose is the sum of the exercise price plus the date of death value of the option.[13] Thus, if the company's stock has appreciated, the estate may owe AMT tax. Where an estate sells the shares in the same year of exercise, the estate could reverse the AMT adjustment.[14] Under certain circumstances (the discussion of which is beyond the scope of this chapter), the AMT may in effect be passed on to beneficiaries through distributions in the same tax year of the estate as the year of exercise.[15] If neither tax event occurs, the estate could be stuck with the AMT liability. Lastly, if the ISO is specifically bequeathed in a will to a beneficiary, then the beneficiary will receive the same regular tax basis as the estate. The beneficiary will also be forced to address the AMT consequences of the ISO upon exercise.

Additional Employer Considerations. Generally, in employee transactions under a stock option plan, the employer's concerns revolve around withholding and reporting requirements. When administering a stock option plan in a death scenario, the employer would not have any withholding obligations upon the exercise of an ISO or the sale of the underlying stock by the Representative or beneficiary, but the employer must report certain information regarding any ISO exercise to the Representative or beneficiary in January of the following year.[16] Although a stock option plan administrator is generally not involved with the estate tax aspects of an option, it is worth mentioning here that for reporting requirements for estate tax purposes, ISOs are generally given a value equal to the option spread (if any) at date of death.[17]

5.2.2 Nonqualified Stock Options

NSOs are options other than statutory stock options. No employment or holding requirements apply as a matter of law at the time of an NSO grant. Upon the exercise of an NSO, the optionee realizes ordinary in-

---

13. Rev. Rul. 78-182, 1978-1 C.B. 265.
14. Code § 56(b)(3).
15. Code §§ 661-663.
16. Code § 6039(a).
17. Rev. Rul. 53-196, 1953-2 C.B. 178.

come equal to the spread between the fair market value of the stock at the date of exercise and the exercise price.[18] Any gain over the optionee's adjusted basis upon disposition (i.e., the price paid plus the amount included in income) is treated as capital gain. The capital gain is given favorable tax treatment as long-term capital gains if the shares are held for more than a year.[19] The employer is entitled to receive a deduction upon exercise equal to the amount that the employee includes in income, but only if the employer reports such amount to the Internal Revenue Service (IRS) on Form W-2.[20] The spread at exercise is treated as wages for purposes of FIT and FICA withholding, and FUTA.[21]

Unlike ISOs, NSOs exercised after the death of the optionee constitute an item of "income in respect of the decedent" (i.e., an amount that is not includable on the employee/decedent's final tax return as earned compensation but that retains its character as a gross income item in the hands of the recipient).[22] The estate will not be entitled to a step-up in basis on the value of the option.[23] Consequently, the estate or beneficiary must recognize ordinary income equal to the difference between the fair market value of the option on the date of exercise and the exercise price of the option. The long-term capital gain holding period begins upon the exercise of the option.

If the NSO is specifically bequeathed to a beneficiary, the beneficiary obtains the same tax basis as the estate, i.e. there is no step-up in basis. Similarly, the beneficiary would have ordinary income upon exercise of the NSO.[24] Note that if the NSO is immediately exercisable, the transfer precludes those options from being included in the decedent's estate and subjects the beneficiary to gift tax liability.[25]

Additional Employer Considerations. The employer is entitled to a tax deduction equal to the spread upon exercise. In the case of an NSO exercise following the optionee's death, the employer is not required to

---

18. Treas. Reg. § 1.83-7(a).

19. Code § 1222(3).

20. Code § 83(h); Treas. Reg. § 1.83-6.

21. Rev. Rul. 78-185, 1978-1 C.B. 304.

22. Code § 691(a); Treas. Reg. 1.691(a)-1; Treas. Reg. 1.83-1(d).

23. Code § 1014(c).

24. Code § 691(a); Treas. Reg. 1.83-1(d).

25. PLR 9350016. Note that this concept is also subject to Code Sections 2701 and 2703.

withhold for FIT.[26] The employer will be required to withhold for FICA purposes if the exercise of the option occurs in the same calendar year as the optionee's death. If the option exercise occurs thereafter, the income is not considered to be FICA or FUTA wages.[27] In addition to these withholding requirements, the employer is required to report income realized by the estate or beneficiary attributable to the exercise of the NSOs on Form 1099-MISC and any FICA wages attributable to the exercise of the options during the year of death on the optionee's final Form W-2.

Generally, NSOs are valued for estate tax purposes by reference to the option spread (if any) at the optionee's date of death. However, for vested non-statutory stock options of publicly traded companies, the IRS has issued safe-harbor guidance that uses a Black-Scholes valuation model with an additional variable involving the underlying stock's expected dividend yield.[28]

5.3 Securities Law Considerations

5.3.1 Registration

The Securities Act of 1933 (the "1933 Act") requires all "offers" or "sales" of "securities" to be registered by filing a registration statement with the Securities and Exchange Commission (SEC) unless an exemption is available. Generally, the grant of an option is exempt from registration because there usually is no sale and the underlying securities are not considered offered until the options are exercisable. However, a stock option plan must be registered at exercise unless an exemption applies. Options granted with respect to public companies that are exercised by Representatives and beneficiaries are covered by an S-8 registration statement.[29] To register a stock option plan on Form S-8, the employer must also deliver a description of the plan and its tax consequences (known as a "prospectus") to the eligible employees, together with a copy of the

---

26. Rev. Rul. 86-109, 1986-2 C.B. 196; PLR 8113058 (December 31, 1980); PLR 9738009 (June 17, 1997).

27. Id.

28. Rev. Proc. 98-34, 1998-1 C.B. 983. Note that this valuation technique is for transfer tax purposes only.

29. General Instruction A1 to Form S-8. Public companies subject to the reporting requirements of the Securities Exchange Act of 1934 (the "1934 Act") usually register a stock option plan for purposes of the 1933 Act on Form S-8.

company's latest annual report to stockholders.[30] If an employer is aware of outstanding unexercised options held by an estate or beneficiary, then the employer should deliver a copy of the prospectus and latest company annual report to the Representative or beneficiary.

5.3.2 Reporting

The transfer of an option or the resulting shares held by an executive to the executive's estate or beneficiary is not reportable per se. Generally, Section 16(a) of the 1934 Act requires "insiders" (generally, officers, directors, and persons who beneficially own more than 10% of any class of securities) to report various securities transactions. The exercise of a stock option and the sale of the underlying stock by the executive's estate would not be reportable under Section 16 unless the estate is a 10% owner or the Representative is an insider and such transactions occurred more than 12 months after the executive's death.[31] Additionally, an insider who acquires additional shares as a beneficiary of another person's estate must report the acquisition on Form 5 or a voluntary Form 4. Option grants are to be reported on Form 4 by the end of the second business day following the day of grant. Option exercises and resales must be reported on Form 4 by the end of the second business day following the day on which the option is exercised. Form 5 is used to annually report certain other changes in beneficial ownership within 45 days of the end of the company's fiscal year.

---

30. The employer must advise the plan participants that certain shareholder information is available upon request. The information provided must be periodically updated. The shares acquired under a plan registered on Form S-8 may be resold without registration or delivery of a prospectus, except that officers, directors, and 10% owners are subject to certain conditions. These "affiliates" may sell securities only in compliance with the applicable limitations of Rule 144 or under another exemption from registration. (Private companies usually rely on Rule 701 for an exemption from the registration requirements for the offer and sale of shares under a stock option plan. Unless a company goes public, securities issued under Rule 701 may be resold only pursuant to registration or an exemption.) If option grants are limited to a small group of executives, an employer may elect to rely on the private placement exemption of Section 4(2) of the 1933 Act for a registration exemption.

31. Rule 16a-2(d).

5.3.3 Short-Swing Profit Recovery

Any profits resulting from the purchase and sale (or sale and purchase) of stock of a company registered under the 1934 Act within a period of less than six months by any insider may be recovered by an action brought by the company, or on behalf of the company by another stockholder, against the insider under Section 16(b) of the 1934 Act. This disgorgement provision is intended to discourage the unfair use of inside information. Rule 16b-3 provides an exemption for certain transactions between officers or directors and the company. Option grants and exercises of options are exempt from the matching of purchases and sales if the grants are authorized by the company's board of directors or by a committee composed of two or more non-employee directors.[32] Sales of stock acquired by exercises of options can be matched with other purchases.

An executive or director ceases to be an insider upon death. Thus, the transfer of an option or the resulting shares held by an executive to an insider's estate or beneficiary is not subject to short-swing profit recovery. The exercise of a stock option and the sale of the underlying stock by the insider's estate would not be subject to Section 16(b) if it occurs during the first 12 months after the insider's death. Thereafter, such sales would be subject to Section 16 only if the estate is a 10% owner or the Representative is an insider.[33]

If an heir is already an insider, the acquisition of shares as a beneficiary is not deemed to be a purchase for purposes of Section 16(b) of the 1934 Act.[34] If a beneficiary is an insider or receives sufficient stock to become an insider following the executive's death, then the individual would be required to comply with Section 16 following the transfer.

5.4 Section 409A Considerations

Section 409A of the Internal Revenue Code was enacted under Section 885 of the American Jobs Creation Act of 2004 (the "Act") and imposes various rules, several of which include exemptions in the event of death under a stock option plan.[35] Section 409A does not cover ISOs, qualified

---

32. Rule 16b-3(d)(1).

33. Rule 16a-2(d); See also SEC No-Action Letter, American Soc. of Corp. Secretaries (Dec. 11, 1996).

34. Rule 16b-5.

35. Note that Section 409A effectively applies to those deferred compensation arrangements that are not vested as of December 31, 2004.

employee stock purchase plans (ESPPs), or restricted stock awards, but it does cover certain stock appreciation rights (SARs).[36] The Act specifically excludes death benefit plans, which are not discussed in this chapter. Three key rules discussed below involve the moment of taxation, distribution rules, and subsequent election rules.

One rule affected by the issue of death under the Act is the moment of taxation for discounted stock options, i.e. options granted with an exercise price less than the fair market value on the day of grant. Discounted stock options qualify as deferred compensation under Section 409A and are subject to tax at vesting (rather than at exercise), unless an exemption applies. One viable exemption is the exercisability of the option upon death.

Another rule affected by the issue of death under the Act is the distribution rules. Generally, the Section 409A rules stipulate that the form of payment of properly deferred compensation must be specified either in the stock option plan or by the participant at the time of his or her Section 83(b) election. However, this rule is overridden in certain events, including death.

Finally, the Section 409A rules stipulate that there are specific limitations to delaying the payment of compensation properly deferred, including the disallowance of an additional deferral period. However, the exception to this rule is in the case of a participant's death; in that case, an additional period of at least five years from the date end of the original deferral period may be tacked on.

---

36. Notice 2005-2.

6

Evergreen Provisions for Stock Plans

Thomas LaWer

Contents

S TOCK OPTION AND EMPLOYEE STOCK PURCHASE PLANS (throughout this chapter, these will be referred to as "stock plans" or "plans") typically reserve a fixed number of shares for issuance under the plan. To add more shares to a plan, the company's board of directors must amend the plan, and in many cases, the company's shareholders must approve the amendment. If a publicly traded company's stock option or employee stock purchase plan runs out of shares, there is often significant time, expense, and uncertainty involved in receiving shareholder approval of share increases.

To avoid the issues involved with frequent shareholder approval of share increases, a company can incorporate an automatic replenishment feature (commonly referred to as an "evergreen" provision) into its stock plans. An evergreen provision automatically increases the number of shares reserved under the company's stock plans at regular intervals.

The evergreen provision can eliminate the expense and difficulty of seeking frequent shareholder approval of a plan share increase. In addition, a company may plan its stock awards for several years with greater certainty because it has a reliable supply of reserved shares. Finally, the evergreen provision detaches equity compensation strategies from the vagaries of the company's stock price. Publicly traded companies may have a more difficult time obtaining shareholder approval for share reserve increases when the stock has performed poorly. Because employers often need to motivate people more in a downturn, this can be the worst time for a company to curtail its stock award grants.

This chapter discusses the issues involved with designing and implementing an evergreen provision.

6.1 Evergreen Design

The simplest evergreen provision annually increases the number of shares reserved under the stock plan by a percentage of the outstanding shares of the company on the date of increase. (See example 1 below.) This evergreen provision allows the stock plan to continue to grow as the company's outstanding capital stock increases. Unfortunately, this design does not meet the requirements of the tax laws for incentive stock options (ISOs) and tax-qualified employee stock purchase plans (ESPPs). (Thus, such a provision cannot be used for plans granting ISOs or in an ESPP.) However, a "percentage of the outstanding" evergreen provision does work for non-employee director plans and for stock plans that grant nonqualified stock options rather than ISOs.

> *Example 1.* The maximum number of shares reserved for issuance under the Plan is 1,000,000 shares, plus an annual increase to be added on each anniversary date of the adoption of the Plan equal to four percent (4%) of the outstanding Common Stock on such date.

To qualify for preferential tax treatment, ISOs and ESPPs must comply respectively with the requirements of Sections 422(b) and 423(b) of the Internal Revenue Code of 1986, as amended (the "Code"). One of the conditions for preferential tax treatment is that the option must be granted under a plan specifying "the aggregate number of shares which may be issued."[1] The maximum aggregate number of shares that may be issued

---

1. Section 422(b)(1) of the Code, Treasury Regulation ("Treas. Reg.") §§ 1.422-2(b)(3) and 1.423-2(c)(3).

under a plan must be determinable at the *time the plan is adopted.* That is, on the date the board of directors adopts the plan, the total number of shares that can possibly be granted under the plan must be calculable. The use of a "percentage of the outstanding" as in example 1 does not meet this requirement.[2] For companies that wish to grant ISOs or have an ESPP, this requirement limits the flexibility of the evergreen provision. The evergreen provision must provide for periodic increases of a fixed number of shares (see Example 2 below).

> *Example 2.* The maximum number of shares reserved for issuance under the Plan is 1,000,000 shares, plus an annual increase to be added on each anniversary date of the adoption of the Plan equal to 400,000 shares.

However, many companies would prefer to add an amount determined as a percentage of the outstanding shares on a specified date each year, such as each anniversary date of the plan adoption. As discussed above, such a provision, by itself, violates the requirement of the ISO and ESPP rules for a determinable number of shares. One possible way to remedy this problem is to draft a tiered evergreen provision that provides that the number of shares to be added each year is equal to the *lesser* of (1) a fixed number of shares or (2) a percentage of the outstanding shares on each anniversary of the plan adoption.[3] (See example 3 below.) In drafting this provision, it is important to select as the fixed number of shares an amount that is significantly greater than the anticipated percentage of the outstanding shares. Otherwise, if there is rapid growth in the number of shares of the company outstanding, the provision can quickly be constrained by the fixed limit. In the example, the tiered evergreen provision satisfies the maximum-determinable-number-of-shares condition because the maximum number of shares reserved under the plan is equal to the initial reservation of 1,000,000 shares plus 1,000,000 (the fixed number to be added each year) multiplied by the term of the plan.

> *Example 3.* The maximum aggregate number of shares reserved for issuance under the Plan is 1,000,000 shares, plus an annual increase to be added on each anniversary date of the adoption of the Plan equal to the lesser of (1) 1,000,000 shares, and (2) four percent (4%) of the outstanding shares on such date.

---

2. Treas. Reg. § 1.422-2(b)(3)(ii).
3. See PLR 9531031, which specifically approves this design structure for an automatic replenishment feature.

A company may retain even greater control over the number of shares being added to the plan by adding to the formula a third variable, the ability of a company's board of directors to provide for a lesser amount each year, to the tiered evergreen provision described above. (See example 4 below.) If either the fixed number of shares or the number of shares equal to a percentage of the outstanding shares provides more generous benefits than is required or appropriate, this refinement lets the board of directors limit the number of shares that would otherwise be added to the plan.

> *Example 4.* The maximum aggregate number of shares reserved for issuance under the Plan is 1,000,000 shares, plus an annual increase to be added on each anniversary date of the adoption of the Plan equal to the least of (1) 800,000 Shares, (2) four percent (4%) of the outstanding shares on such date, and (3) an amount determined by the Board.

Another variation is to reload the option grants made in the prior year (a "top-up" evergreen provision). The number of shares to be added to the plan is still determinable: it is the number of shares reserved under the plan, multiplied by the number of years in the plan term. In example 5 below, the evergreen provision will add the number of shares granted in options in the prior year up to the maximum number of shares reserved under the plan of 400,000. If the plan in example 5 had a five-year term, then the maximum number of shares issuable under the plan would be 2,000,000. There are many variations possible for the top-up provision. However, in all these variations, the basic concept of the top-up is the same.

> *Example 5.* The maximum aggregate number of shares that may be optioned and sold under the Plan is 400,000 shares, plus an annual increase to be added on each anniversary date of adoption of the Plan equal to the lesser of (1) the number of shares of common stock subject to options granted in the immediately preceding year and (2) an amount determined by the Board.

A final variation used in omnibus equity compensation plans (i.e., plans that permit the grant of incentive stock options, nonqualified stock options, restricted stock, stock appreciation rights, phantom stock, and other equity awards) is to combine the use of a fixed share reserve for the grant of incentive stock options with the evergreen provision described in example 1. The ISO regulations finalized in 2004 permit this approach.[4]

---

4.   Treas. Reg. § 1.422-2(b)(3)(i) and Treasury Decision 9144, Aug. 2, 2004, p. 4.

This allows a company to get the full benefit of an uncapped evergreen provision for all award types except incentive stock options. Example 6 below provides that 4% of the outstanding shares as of the anniversary of the adoption of the plan will be added to the reserve each year, provided that the maximum number of shares that may be granted as incentive stock options is limited to 2,000,000.

> *Example 6.* The maximum number of shares reserved for issuance under the Plan is 1,000,000 shares, plus an annual increase to be added on each anniversary date of the adoption of the Plan equal to the lesser of (1) four percent (4%) of the outstanding Common Stock on such date and (2) an amount determined by the Board. Notwithstanding the foregoing, the aggregate maximum number of shares that may be issued as Incentive Stock Options shall be 2,000,000 shares.

6.2 Shareholder Approval Considerations

Shareholder approval is required in most circumstances to add an evergreen provision to a stock plan. The shareholder requirements vary based on the type of plan and the specific situation of the company.

6.2.1 Tax Law Requirements

For a stock plan that issues ISOs or for a tax-qualified employee stock purchase plan, shareholder approval is required to add an evergreen provision. The shareholder approval requirement for an evergreen provision is the same as is required for any increase in the shares reserved under a stock plan.

Section 162(m) of the Code, the $1 million compensation deduction limitation rule, generally does not require shareholder approval specifically for the addition of shares to a plan and thus does not directly affect an evergreen provision. However, Section 162(m) does require that if a stock plan is approved while a company is "private" (i.e., the company does not have to register any class of common equity securities under Section 12 of the Securities and Exchange Act of 1934, as amended[5]), shareholder approval will be required to the extent the company wishes to exempt options and performance-based stock awards from the Section 162(m) deduction limitations after the company is "public."[6] With

---

5. Treas. Reg. § 1.162-27(c)(1)(i).
6. Treas. Reg. § 1.162-27(f).

a company that has become "public," the maximum time period before Section 162(m) applies, and shareholder approval is thus necessary for Section 162(m) compliance, is the period up to the shareholder meeting in which members of the company's board of directors are elected that occurs in the fourth calendar year following the calendar year in which the initial public offering (IPO) occurs.[7] Until this time, the provisions of Section 162(m) are not applicable (assuming the material terms of the plan were described in the IPO prospectus for companies that become public in connection with an IPO).[8] Shareholder approval for purposes of Section 162(m) may be required before the annual meeting in the fourth calendar year upon the occurrence of any of the following events: (1) the expiration of the plan, (2) the material modification of the plan within the meaning of Section 162(m), or (3) the issuance of all stock that has been allocated under the plan.[9]

This means that a company that adopts an evergreen provision immediately before its IPO and has enough shares at the end of the Section 162(m) exemption period will still have to submit its plan for shareholder approval if it wants future option grants and performance-based awards to be exempt from the Section 162(m) compensation deduction limitations. Therefore, implementing an evergreen provision while a company is private delays seeking approval from the company's public shareholders for several years, but it does not entirely avoid the need for such approval.

6.2.2 Stock Exchange Requirements

For both NASDAQ-listed companies that do not meet one of NASDAQ's exceptions to shareholder approval[10] and New York Stock Exchange (NYSE)-listed companies that do not meet one of the NYSE's exceptions,[11] shareholder approval will be required to add an evergreen provision to a stock plan, whether or not the stock plan will issue ISOs. In addition,

---

7. Treas. Reg. § 1.162-27(f)(2)(iv).

8. Treas. Reg. § 1.162-27(f)(1).

9. Treas. Reg. § 1.162-27(f)(2).

10. Rule 4350(i)(1)(A) of *the NASD Manual for The NASDAQ Stock Market*. Rule 4350(i)(1)(A) provides an exemption from shareholder approval for the compensatory grant of stock in very limited circumstances.

11. Rule 312.03(a) of the *NYSE Listed Company Manual*. Rule 312.03(a) provides an exemption from shareholder approval for the compensatory grant of stock in very limited circumstances.

both NASDAQ and the NYSE limit the term of a shareholder-approved plan that has an evergreen provision to 10 years. If a plan with an evergreen provision has a term longer than 10 years, then NASDAQ will require shareholder approval of the plan every 10 years, and the NYSE will require shareholder approval for each increase in the share reserves from the evergreen provision. Stock plans approved by the shareholders before a company goes public and is listed on the NYSE or NASDAQ generally will be considered to have met the NYSE's and NASDAQ's listing requirements for shareholder approval.

6.2.3 Securities Law Requirements

Generally, the securities laws do not require shareholder approval of stock plans for any reason. However, companies granting stock awards in California that are not exempt from California's securities laws[12] will need to obtain shareholder approval of an evergreen provision to the same extent shareholder approval would be required for any increase in the shares reserved under a plan.[13] However, it is unusual for a private company to adopt an evergreen provision, because the shareholders of a private company are usually very involved with the management of the company and generally prefer to keep a tight control over the dilution of their positions. The only exception to this practice is when a private company is on the eve of having an initial public offering. At this time, private company shareholders generally have been willing to approve stock plans containing an evergreen provision for use after the company's IPO.

6.2.4 Shareholder Reaction

At this time, institutional investors rarely vote in favor of evergreen provisions. Institutional investors want to retain control of any increases in the shares reserved under the stock plans and thereby limit the dilution of their ownership. Before the end of the technology bubble in 2000, there were examples of institutional investors approving evergreen provisions that caused limited dilution. However, in the current busi-

---

12. Companies that are listed for trading on the NYSE, the NASDAQ National Market, and certain other U.S. stock exchanges are exempt from registration under California's securities laws. California Corporations Code § 25100(o) and California Code of Regulations §§ 260.004 and 260.101.2.

13. California Code of Regulations §§ 260.140.41 and 260.140.42.

ness environment, it is extremely unlikely that an institutional investor will vote in favor of an evergreen provision. Historically, there appears to be less resistance from institutional investors for approving evergreen provisions in (1) employee stock purchase plans, which by their broad-based, nondiscretionary nature appear to require less shareholder oversight, and (2) not surprisingly, for companies whose stock price has performed well.

One of the ways RiskMetrics Group's ISS Governance Services (ISS) (formerly Institutional Shareholder Services), an important proxy adviser to institutional investors, judges stock plans is based on the shareholder value transfer (the estimate of the cost of the shareholder's equity transferred to stock award recipients).[14] For purposes of these calculations, the maximum number of shares that would be available under the evergreen provision is used without taking into account the timing of the share increases. For example, if the proposal for the evergreen provision is to add 100,000 shares per year for 10 years, ISS would consider the proposal to be a request for an additional 1,000,000 shares. By increasing the number of shares reserved under a plan based on the maximum potential increase, an evergreen provision significantly increases the cost of the stock plan under this ISS calculation. Therefore, by increasing the potential dilution from the stock awards, an evergreen provision will usually make a stock plan too "expensive" to the shareholders, in ISS's opinion. This would result in ISS recommending that shareholders vote against a stock plan with an evergreen provision.

In the past, to make an evergreen provision more palatable to institutional investors, a company would limit the evergreen provision to a specified period of years. For example, the evergreen may last for three or four years, after which it expires and the company must go back to the shareholders for any further increase in the shares reserved under the plan (see example 8 below). This tactic somewhat undercuts the purpose of the evergreen by limiting the number of shares that can be added to the plan.

> *Example 8.* The maximum aggregate number of shares that may be optioned and sold under the Plan is 1,000,000 shares, plus an annual increase to be added on each anniversary date of the adoption of the Plan for the next three years beginning in the year 2006 equal to the lesser of (1) 800,000 Shares, (2) four percent (4%) of the outstanding shares on such date, or (3) a lesser amount determined by the Board.

---

14. ISS Proxy Voting Manual, Chapter 10.

In the current business environment, it is rare for public companies to propose any type of evergreen provision because their chances of approval are slim. Currently, the most common time for a company to add an evergreen provision to its stock plans is while the company is still private but on the eve of an initial public offering. At this time, private company shareholders are usually willing to approve the evergreen provision, and institutional investors have not objected to the potential dilution caused by a stock plan in the initial public offering context. This is likely because the decision on whether to purchase stock in an IPO is determined by the persons at the institutional investors who are concerned whether the company's stock price will appreciate and not by the persons responsible for determining how to vote on proxies of companies in which the institutions have already invested.

6.2.5 Voting Issues

For public companies, the NYSE and NASDAQ broker voting rules limit when a broker may vote for a stock plan proposal. Under the 2003 revision of these rules, shares held in street name (i.e., shares owned by a client of the broker but registered under the broker's name to facilitate trading) may not be voted by the broker on stock plan proposals without instructions from the beneficial holders. Where a retail investor throws away his or her proxy, his or her shares cannot be voted on stock plan proposals. In the past, when brokers were able to vote these shares, the likelihood of approval of stock plan proposals was greater, since the brokers generally voted in favor of company proposals. These broker voting rules increase the power of the institutional investors because, unlike individual investors, institutional investors almost always vote. As discussed above, since institutional investors generally do not favor evergreen provisions, these voting rules make it even more difficult for a public company to obtain shareholder approval of an evergreen provision.

6.3   Federal Securities Law Issues

Each year, when the evergreen provision replenishes the stock plan, the S-8 registration statement under which the stock plan shares are registered must be amended to register the increase. This is an important administrative matter that needs to be completed in a timely fashion after the increase to ensure that shares issued under the stock plan are registered and tradable.

6.4   Stock Splits, Dividends, and Tracking Stock

The stock option or employee stock purchase plan should contain a provision to adjust the shares reserved under the plan, including the evergreen provision, for any stock split or stock dividend, or for the creation of different classes of stock or tracking stock. With such a provision incorporated into the plan at the time the evergreen provision is adopted, the evergreen provision can automatically be adjusted for the split, dividend, or change in class of shares without any concern about obtaining shareholder approval.

6.5   Conclusion

An evergreen provision can be a useful tool for a company. It reduces the administrative expense involved with adding shares to a stock plan and provides a company with a reliable supply of reserved shares for stock awards. Since 2000, however, unfavorable shareholder reaction to an evergreen provision has generally prevented the adoption of an evergreen provision by most publicly traded companies, except for companies that adopt an evergreen provision in connection with an initial public offering.

Underwater Stock Options and Repricing Strategy

Daniel N. Janich

Contents

ALTHOUGH STOCK OPTIONS have been a part of the compensation package of members of the highest reaches of management for quite some time, particularly in public companies, it has been the cash-starved Internet startups and emerging high-tech companies that have led the way in making broad-based stock options popular among rank-and-file employees in more recent years. As a result of the popularity of these broad-based plans, stock options have assumed a major role as incentive-based compensation available to employees and independent contractors.[1] In fact, the reality today is that many such workers consider compensatory stock options to be an essential part of their total compensation package. Until recently, favorable accounting treatment made stock options particularly attractive to use as a compensatory device because the compensation cost was allowed to be largely unrecognized on the issuing company's financial statements.[2]

When the U.S. economy declined after bursting of the tech bubble in the late 1990s, many companies that had issued stock options found their grants "underwater," that is, with an exercise price above the current fair market value of the underlying shares, thereby stripping the option of its purpose as an incentive or its value as compensation. During those dark days, few companies were undertaking any meaningful hiring, and even fewer workers felt the time was right to leave their current employment. However, in more recent years, as the economy has improved and the job market along with it, these same companies have faced increasing pressure to develop an effective strategy to revive their option programs before losing valuable talent to a competitor.

This chapter is an update to an essay originally published in 2001 and titled "Underwater Stock Options and Repricing Strategy: Is Your Company Drowning in Confusion?" that discussed stock option repricing and its alternatives. Since its publication, the Financial Accounting Standard Board (FASB) issued Statement of Financial Accounting Standards No. 123 (revised 2004) ("FAS 123(R)"), which repealed the "intrinsic value"

---

1. The requirements of Code Section 422(b) restrict incentive stock options to employees. Therefore, non-employee service providers, such as independent contractors, are eligible to receive only nonqualified stock options, and employees are eligible to receive both incentive stock options and nonqualified stock options.

2. Before 2005, many companies accounted for their stock options using APB Opinion No. 25 ("APB 25"), under which compensation cost was measured using the "intrinsic value" method of accounting. This method allowed companies to avoid recognition of their compensation cost as an expense. Under Statement of Financial Accounting Standards No. 123 (revised 2004), APB 25 has been repealed and replaced with a mandate that all equity awards granted to employees be accounted for by using a "fair value" method of accounting. This fair value is measured at grant for stock-settled awards and at subsequent exercise or settlement for cash-settled awards.

method of accounting for equity compensation and replaced it with a mandated "fair value" method for all equity awards granted to employees. Congress was no less busy comprehensively revising the deferred compensation rules under Section 409A of the Internal Revenue Code (the "Code"), which was enacted in 2004 as part of the American Jobs Creation Act.[3] Both of these recent developments and, in particular, the changed accounting rules, prompt us to take a fresh look at repricing and its alternatives. Is repricing still subject to adverse accounting treatment that renders its use inadvisable? Are there alternatives to repricing that are remain viable today? What additional concerns arise under the new accounting rules and Section 409A compliance requirements that companies must now consider when developing an effective strategy to address the underwater stock option problem? These and other questions are addressed below.

7.1 Repricing

7.1.1 What Is Stock Option Repricing?

Stock option repricing generally refers to a company's decision to effectively lower the exercise price of its outstanding options whose underlying shares have declined in value. In addition to amending the existing options to lower the exercise price, a repricing is also accomplished by cancelling the existing option and granting the optionee one or more new options at a lowered exercise price.

Until recently, unfavorable accounting treatment resulted if the cancellation and new grant of options occurred within six months of each other.[4] This six-month look-back/look-forward period was far-reaching in scope, covering any action that either had the effect of lowering the exercise price on the underwater option, such as payment of a cash bonus to the optionee upon exercise of the option or a below-market interest loan to facilitate option exercise, or had the effect of cancelling the option, such as modifying the option to reduce the exercise period, restart or extend the vesting period, increase the exercise price, or reduce the number of shares of the award, or otherwise reach any other agreement

---

3. The American Jobs Creation Act of 2004 was enacted into law on October 22, 2004. See Public Law No. 108-357, 118 Stat. 1418.

4. See FASB Interpretation No. 44, "Accounting for Certain Transactions Involving Stock Compensation" ("FIN 44"), which FASB adopted on March 31, 2000.

with the optionee that would reduce the likelihood that the option would be exercised.[5] With the adoption of FAS 123(R), the six-month look-back/ look-forward period is no longer of concern for repricing purposes, as discussed below.

7.1.2 Accounting Treatment

Until December 1998, companies desiring to do so simply repriced their underwater stock options by offering their employees the opportunity to exchange their old, unexercised options for entirely new ones granted at a lower exercise price in order to permit optionees to "profit" by any subsequent increase in share value.[6] A straight repricing conducted in this manner would not entail any adverse accounting treatment. Interpretation No. 44, *Accounting for Certain Transactions Involving Stock Compensation* ("FIN 44"), which was adopted by FASB on March 31, 2000, and applied retroactively to December 15, 1998, changed all of that by requiring the exercise price to be treated as "variable" for the life of the option, resulting in "variable accounting treatment" for the remaining life of the repriced option.[7] When the exercise price is subject to variable accounting treatment, the difference between the revised (lower) exercise price and the value of the underlying stock when the repriced option is exercised (or forfeited or expires unexercised) must be recognized as a compensation expense for financial reporting purposes. Since the value of the underlying stock when the repriced option would be exercised would be unknown at the time of repricing, this approach made the amount of expense to be recognized difficult to predict. To make matters worse, under variable accounting, as the company's stock price increased, a periodic charge to earnings was required to be reported.[8] Needless to say, the accounting treatment for repricing of options under FIN 44 discouraged companies from using repricing to address their underwater stock option problems, and caused them to seek out alternatives with relatively less onerous consequences.

With FASB's adoption of FAS 123(R), the accounting conundrum raised by variable accounting treatment for repriced options may no

---

5. FIN 44.

6. Id.

7. Id.

8. Id. Variable accounting occurs when the exercise price at grant is not certain. The grant must be expensed against the company's earnings in each quarter, based on the spread between the exercise and market price of the stock.

longer be of as much importance as it had been previously.[9] Companies are no longer subject to variable accounting treatment when they reprice their options and, therefore, no longer need to wait six months and a day to replace cancelled options in order to avoid unfavorable accounting treatment.[10] Rather than impose variable accounting treatment, FAS 123(R) applies the "fair value" method of accounting to repricing and treats a cancellation of an award accompanied by the concurrent grant of a replacement award (or other valuable consideration) as a modification.[11] For purposes of measuring the recognized expense, FAS 123(R) compares the fair value of an award immediately before and immediately after a modification, as of the modification date.[12] If the fair value of the replacement award is higher, the company must recognize as an expense the incremental value of the modified award over the remaining service period.[13] However, that expense will be fixed at the time of repricing. As a result, option repricing has become easier.

---

9. FAS 123(R) applies only to stock-based awards to employees and to non-employee directors. The revised standard does not apply to stock-based compensation issued to non-employees, such as independent contractors or other non-employee service providers. Share-based payment transactions with non-employees continue to be accounted for under FAS 123. FASB intends to consider these accounting standards for non-employees at a later date.

10. The six-month look-back/look-forward strategy was not without risks. The company was not allowed to compensate the optionee for any appreciation in the stock price during the six-month period, and option holders who terminated their employment with the company before the six-month waiting period before receiving reissued options were not eligible to receive the new grant.

11. FAS 123(R).

12. Under FAS 123(R), "fair value" for unvested stock options is estimated using an option-pricing model, such as Black-Scholes or binomial lattice model. A "modification" is broadly defined to include any change to an award's terms, including number of shares, exercise price, transferability, settlement provisions, and vesting conditions, and certain "inducements" to exercise and exchanges of awards or changes to award terms in connection with a business combination or an "equity restructuring," such as a stock dividend, stock split, spin-off, rights offering, or large nonrecurring cash dividend. See FAS 123(R).

13. Under FAS 123(R), companies can only recognize increases in award value. There are no modifications for reductions in value. FAS 123(R) treats most types of award modifications in the same manner and, in doing so, perhaps encourages companies to make a "value-for-value exchange" with little,

The new accounting standard has been effective for reporting periods that start after June 15, 2005, for public companies, except for small businesses with revenues of less than $25 million, which had until the first reporting period that started after December 15, 2005. Nonpublic companies were required to begin using the new accounting standard in fiscal years that began after December 15, 2005.[14] FAS 123(R) applies to all equity compensation granted, modified, repurchased, or cancelled after the applicable effective date, and to the nonvested portion of equity compensation outstanding as of the effective date, provided the awards were granted, modified, or settled in cash during fiscal years beginning after the original December 15, 1994, effective date of FAS 123.[15]

7.1.3   Federal Income Tax Considerations

Deferred Compensation Rules.   Code Section 409A has introduced sweeping new rules affecting the operation of deferred compensation arrangements, including equity compensation plans such as stock options. However, where the exercise price of an option is not less than the fair market value of the underlying stock on the grant date and there are no other deferral features involved that would delay recognition of income on the award beyond the exercise date, the stock option will generally be treated as exempt from the requirements of Section 409A.[16] Certain

---

if any, accounting effect when the award's fair value remains essentially unchanged.

14.   FAS 123(R).

15.   Id.

16.   Prop. Reg. 1.409A-1(b)(5)(i)(A), (b)(5)(ii); Notice 2005-1 (Dec. 20, 2004, modified Jan. 6, 2005), Q&A-4(d)(ii),(iii). An option to purchase stock other than the common stock of the corporation that is a service recipient (or its controlled group members) generally will provide for a deferral of compensation under Section 409A. See Prop. Reg. 1.409A-1(b)(5)(i)(C). The right to receive all or part of the dividends declared and paid on a number of shares underlying the stock right between the date of grant and the date of exercise of the stock right constitutes an offset to the exercise price of the stock option unless the right to the dividends is explicitly set forth as a separate arrangement. Prop. Reg. 1.409A-1(b)(5)(i)(E). The existence of a separate arrangement to receive dividends does not cause a stock right to fail to satisfy the requirements of the exclusion from the definition of deferred compensation under Code Section 409A. Id. In Notice 2006-4 (Dec. 23, 2005), the IRS clarified that the valuation rules for options and stock appreciation rights (SARs) set forth in the proposed regulations under Section 409A will become effective prospectively, when and if contained in the final regulations. Where "fair

modifications made to an existing stock option may cause the option to be treated, for purposes of Section 409A, as a new grant.[17] Although the repricing of an outstanding option will be treated as a new grant, the new grant may still continue to qualify for the Section 409A exemption if that grant does not have a below-market exercise or base price at the time of repricing.

Multiple repricings of the same option may indicate that the exercise price or base price is actually a floating or adjustable price, with the result that the option will fail to qualify for the Section 409A exemption from the date of the original grant.[18] The importance of ascertaining whether the option grant is subject to Section 409A should not be overlooked, because a failure to comply with its requirements will result in immediate recognition of taxable income, measured by the spread between the exercise price and the value of the underlying stock at the date of grant, as well as the imposition of additional tax penalties.[19]

Nontaxable Event. The federal income tax rules treat a repriced stock option as an option exchange, i.e., a cancellation and regrant, regardless of the actual form of repricing.[20] Generally, there are no federal income tax consequences for option holders on their exchange of underwater stock options because repricing is not a taxable event. However, the decision to reprice may still involve several significant income tax considerations for the five highest-paid officers of a public company as well as for holders of incentive stock options.

---

market value" for publicly held companies is generally determined on the basis of actual transactions in the stock on an established securities market, the proposed regulations provide three valuation methods presumed to result in a reasonable valuation for privately held companies. In Notice 2006-79 (Oct. 4, 2006), the IRS announced its intention to apply penalties under Code Section 409A to stock options and SARs granted by companies that had registered equity securities with the SEC that were either backdated or misdated in a manner that resulted in a below-market grant and which were not corrected to comply with 409A by December 31, 2006.

17. Prop. Reg. 1.409A-1(b)(5)(v).
18. Id.
19. Section 409A(a)(1)(A), (B); 409A(b)(4).
20. Treas. Reg. 1.162-27(e)(2)(vi)(B). For the purposes of this chapter, "options exchange" refers to a repricing by means of a cancellation of outstanding underwater options in exchange for the regrant of a new option at the then-current fair market value.

Five Highest-Paid Officers. In many instances, the participation in a re-pricing by the five highest-paid officers of a public company will trigger Code Section 162(m) considerations. Under Section 162(m), a publicly held company may deduct no more than $1 million in compensation paid to any of its five highest-paid officers. Stock options are treated as compensation includible for purposes of this limitation under Section 162(m) unless the options are considered to be "performance-based compensation" and have been approved by at least two "outside direc-tors" of the company's full board of directors.[21] Repriced options must also be approved in this same manner to be exempt from the Section 162(m) deduction limits.

For the Section 162(m) exemption to apply, the option plan must also specify the maximum number of shares for which options may be granted to any employee during a specified period of one or more years.[22] If the option is repriced during the same period in which it was granted, then, to allow one to determine the maximum number of shares for which options may be granted to an employee during the specified period, the plan would include the number of shares subject to the option after the repricing as well as the number of shares subject to the option before the repricing.[23] If repricing causes the individual limit to be exceeded, the Section 162(m) exemption would no longer apply to that individual.[24]

Incentive Stock Options. Whether publicly or privately held, companies repricing their incentive stock options must consider the holding period and share value dollar limitations of Code Section 422. To retain their status as incentive stock options, repriced options will be required to satisfy the two-years-after-grant and one-year-after-exercise holding period applicable to incentive stock options for such options to continue

---

21. Code Section 162(m), Treas. Reg. 1.162-27(e)(2). The definition of an "outside director" for this purpose differs from that used for Section 16 of the Securi-ties Exchange Act of 1934.

22. Treas. Reg. 1.162-27(e)(2)(vi)(A) requires that the plan under which the op-tion is granted state the maximum number of shares that may be granted during a specified period to any employee in order for the Section 162(m) performance-based compensation exception to apply.

23. Treas. Reg. 1.162-27(e)(2)(vi)(B) provides that in the case of a repricing, "both the option that is deemed to be cancelled and the option that is deemed to be granted reduce the maximum number of shares for which options may be granted to the employee under the plan."

24. Treas. Reg. 1.162-27(e)(2)(vi)(B).

to defer tax recognition.[25] Repricing will start over again the capital gains tolling period. Therefore, to obtain incentive stock option treatment, shares subject to the repriced option may not be disposed of within two years from the date of the repricing or within one year from the date of exercise of the repriced option. Also, to retain incentive stock option treatment, the aggregate fair market value (determined as of the grant date) of stock that is bought by exercising an incentive stock option may not exceed $100,000 in a calendar year.[26] Repricing may cause the number of shares subject to the option to increase. These additional shares would be counted against the $100,000 limit when the repriced options are exercisable.[27] Any repriced options exceeding this limit would be treated for tax purposes as nonqualified stock options.

7.1.4 Securities Law Issues

The securities laws, like the federal income tax rules, treat option repricing as an option exchange. In the case of a repricing where the exercise price of stock options held by "named executive officers" (generally the five highest-paid executives) was revised during the preceding fiscal year, the company must disclose (in reasonable detail) the repricing and its basis in its proxy statements.[28] Additionally, the repricing may trigger

---

25. See Temp. Reg. 14A.422A-1.

26. Code Section 422(d) provides that to the extent that the aggregate fair market value of the underlying shares of stock are exercisable by the optionee in any calendar year exceeds $100,000, such options are not be treated as incentive stock options.

27. Code Section 422(d)(2) discusses the ordering rule for purposes of applying the $100,000 per year limitation.

28. SEC Regulation S-K requires information disclosed in the form of a table if the issuer adjusted or amended the exercise price of previously awarded stock options or stock appreciation rights during the last fiscal year. Item 402(i); 17 C.F.R. 229.402(i). In August 2006 the SEC adopted final rules revamping the executive compensation disclosure rules for "named executive officers" (redefined to include the principal executive officer, principal financial officer and three other most highly compensated executive officers). Under the new rules, which generally apply to public filings made on or after December 15, 2006, a revised Summary Compensation Table will include disclosure of option repricings and modifications made in a given year, and include recognition of the incremental fair value of the award resulting from a repricing or modification. This is the same expense FAS 123(R) now requires to be recognized. The text of the final rules is available at www.sec.gov/rules/final/2006/33-8732.pdf.

extensive 10-year reporting for all officers and directors in the proxy statement.[29] As part of this report, the company must describe repricing of options held by any executive officer during the last 10 fiscal years.[30] Therefore, companies should consider whether to include "named executive officers" in a repricing of the company's stock options.

On March 21, 2001, the SEC issued an order under the Exchange Act "for issuer exchange offers that are conducted for compensatory purposes." The effect of this order is stricter advance filing requirements for public companies that reprice their stock options because exchange plans are considered to be tender offers (bids to buy company shares, usually at a premium), which require added disclosure.[31] However, they are exempt from the tender-offer requirement that they must be offered to all stockholders as long as the stock options are issued under the company's employee plans and are used for compensatory purposes.[32] In addition to the foregoing, the securities laws provide that the repricing of options is to be treated as a disposition of the existing options and the acquisition of new ones for purposes of Section 16 of the Exchange Act.[33] As such, repricing will trigger short-swing liability on gains unless at least two "non-employee directors" or the full board approved both the cancellation and regrant.[34] Repricing must also be reported by a person

---

29. See Item 402(i)(3)(i); 17 C.F.R. 229.402(i)(3)(i). The final rules governing executive compensation disclosures as adopted by the SEC in August 2006 eliminate the 10-year repricing table. Any material changes to awards, including repricings, are to be discussed in a supplemental narrative disclosure to the Summary Compensation Table and Grants of Plan-Based Awards Table.

30. Id.

31. See Press Release 2001-32 at www.sec.gov/news/press/2001-32.txt.

32. See Rule 13e-4 of the Securities Exchange Act of 1934. The SEC Exemptive Letter dated March 21, 2001, appears at www.sec.gov/divisions/corpfin/cf-noaction/repricingorder.htm.

33. See "Option Exchange Offers" at www.sec.gov/divisions/corpfin/repricings.htm.

34. Rule 16b-3(d) 1. A "non-employee director" is defined as a director who: (1) is not currently an officer or otherwise employed by the issuer or a parent or subsidiary of the issuer; (2) does not receive within the fiscal year compensation in excess of $60,000 for services as a consultant or in any capacity other than as a director of the issuer, or a parent or subsidiary of the issuer; (3) does not have an interest in any other transaction for which disclosure would be required in the issuer's proxy statement; and (4) is not engaged in a business relationship that would require disclosure under Item 404(b) or Regulation S-K. Rule 16b-3(b)(3)(i).

who is subject to Section 16 as the disposition of the existing option and the acquisition of new options.[35]

A repricing effected by an options exchange may trigger the registration requirements of Section 5 of the Securities Act if the repriced option includes terms that are less advantageous than the original option (such as a new vesting schedule or a decrease in the number of shares subject to the new options).[36] An exemption from this registration may be available under Section 3(a)(9) of the Securities Act if no commission or other remuneration is paid or given for the exchange of options.[37] Notice filings may also be necessary in connection with repriced options under some state blue sky laws.[38]

7.1.5 Timing the Repricing: Excess Parachute Payment Considerations

When a company is in a "change of control" situation, a repriced stock option may be treated as a "change-in-control stock option" for purposes of the excess parachute payment rules under Code Section 280G.[39] A change in control stock option is usually granted during the one-year period preceding the event.[40] As a result of the repricing, the entire option spread might be treated as a parachute payment, subjecting the company to loss of a tax deduction and the optionee to additional tax payments.[41]

7.1.6 Is Stock Option Repricing Fair to Shareholders?

An often-stated rationale for issuance of stock options is its ability to foster an "ownership" culture among employees. By aligning their interests

---

35. Section 16(a) of the Securities Exchange Act of 1934.
36. Section 5 of the Securities Act of 1933.
37. Section 3(a)(9) of the Securities Act of 1933.
38. The state blue sky laws should always be checked for each state where the stock option plan is offered.
39. Code Section 280G(b)(2).
40. Code Section 280G(b)(2)(C).
41. Code Section 280G(a). An excise tax of 20% of an "excess parachute payment" is imposed on the person who receives such a payment, as provided under Code Section 4999(a). For this purpose, an "excess parachute payment" is defined under the rules that deny a deduction to the corporation that makes an excess parachute payment. Code Section 4999(b).

with those of the company, employees who receive options benefit by any increase in the value of the company as a result of their individual and collective performance. Should these same employees suffer along-side shareholders when an economic downturn causes share values to decline? Many shareholders think so. In particular, institutional share-holders believe that option holders should be subject to the same risks in the volatility of underlying share price as shareholders.[42] Suffice it to say that companies expecting to undergo an option repricing should anticipate and prepare for negative feedback by shareholders.

7.2 Alternatives to Repricing

The repricing decision is easier to make today than several years ago as a result of the accounting changes introduced by FAS 123(R). However, other considerations may come into play in addition to accounting treat-ment when devising an effective strategy to deal with underwater stock options. Do any viable alternatives to repricing exist? Several alterna-tives that were popular before FAS 123(R) are no longer be preferable to straight repricing and, in fact, may be less so. The discussion below revisits these alternatives in light of recent developments.

7.2.1 Extension of the Expiration Date for Underwater Options

By extending the option exercise period, a company allows additional time for the share price to bounce back in order to self-correct the prob-lem. However, a company using this strategy must be careful in ascertain-

---

42. Institutional shareholders may insist upon no repricing if additional option grants are issued and may actually seek to add language that prohibits a repricing of new grants. With limited exceptions, the New York Stock Ex-change, Inc. (NYSE) and the National Association of Securities Dealers, Inc. (NASDAQ) now require listed companies to obtain shareholder approval of any equity compensation plan or material revision or amendment to an equity compensation plan before the issuance of listed securities under the plan. For this purpose, a "material revision" of an equity compensation plan includes the deletion or limitation of any provision prohibiting repricing of options. The NYSE rule provides that a plan that does not specifically permit repricing is deemed to prohibit repricing. NYSE 303A(8). NASDAQ recom-mends that the plans meant to permit repricings use explicit terminology to make this clear. NASD 4350(i); IM-4350-5. The final rules as approved by the SEC appear at www.sec.gov/rules/sro/34-48108.htm.

ing the length of extension that will be required because a disqualifying extension will result in Section 409A coverage retroactive to the original grant date.[43] A disqualifying extension will not be deemed to occur if the exercise period is not extended beyond the later of (1) the end of the calendar year in which the grant would have expired in the absence of such extension or (2) the 15th day of the third month following that normal expiration date.[44] If incentive stock options are involved, an extension of the exercise period beyond three months following termination of employment will cause the option to be treated as a nonqualified stock option for tax purposes.[45] For these reasons, this alternative may be appropriate when only a short-term extension is needed.

7.2.2 Grant/Cancellation of Options More Than Six Months Apart

Under FIN 44, as discussed above, the grant of new options and cancellation of underwater options in two separate and independent transactions spaced more than six months apart was a popular means of avoiding repricing, and thus variable accounting treatment. Under FAS 123(R), the cancellation of an out-of-the-money option results in recognition on the cancellation date of any still-unrecognized compensation cost, and the subsequent grant is treated as a new grant that will be recognized at its full cost rather than incremental cost.[46] As a result, under FAS 123(R) the six-month waiting period is no longer relevant; therefore, "six months and a day" exchange programs are no longer favored over straight repricing.

7.2.3 Acceleration of Next Grant or Issuance of Additional Grants

A company may issue a grant of options at current fair market value either as a new grant ahead of schedule or as an extra grant of options. However, with the mandatory recognition of compensation cost under FAS 123(R), such new or additional grants are treated as additional expense. As such, this alternative, which was designed to mitigate the

---

43. Prop. Reg. 1.409A-1(b)(5)(v).
44. Prop. Reg. 1.409A-1(b)(5)(v)(C).
45. Code Section 424(h)(3); Reg. 1.424-1(e)(4)(i).
46. FAS 123(R).

effects of underwater options without incurring variable accounting treatment that was attendant to repricing, no longer offers any advantages over a straight repricing and, due to the difference in recognition between full and incremental cost, may actually entail the recognition of more expense than what would occur under straight repricing.

7.2.4 Increasing Option Grant Frequency and Decreasing Size of Option Grants

The effects of a volatile stock market may be minimized by increasing the frequency of option grants while decreasing the size of each grant. Each grant would have the exercise price fixed to the prevailing market conditions. This repricing alternative usually works best in conjunction with the shortening of the option term, which, under FAS 123(R), would be considered a "modification" resulting in the recognition of an expense measured by the difference between the estimated fair value of the modified award and the original award at the modification date.[47] As such, this alternative today provides no accounting advantage over repricing.

7.2.5 Grant "Paired" Options with Six-Month-Plus Expiration Period

Under FIN 44, some companies avoided repricing and its attendant variable accounting treatment by granting options that expired at least six months and a day after the market value of the stock reached the exercise price of the original options. Like the "six months and a day" approach discussed above, this variation of it was rendered obsolete under FAS 123(R).

7.2.6 Issue Restricted Stock in Exchange for Cancelled Options

This alternative requires the company to issue restricted stock in exchange for the cancelled underwater options. Under FAS 123(R), the cancellation of an award accompanied by the concurrent grant of a replacement award is accounted for as a modification.[48] Since variable accounting is no longer a concern, this alternative offers no accounting advantage over repricing under FAS 123(R). However, because restricted

---

47. Id.

48. Id.

stock will maintain some value to an employee even if the company's stock price should fall below its fair market value on the grant date, companies wishing to avoid the underwater stock option problem in the future may want to consider issuing restricted stock or restricted stock units, at least on a selective basis, as part of an exchange program.

7.2.7 Buy Out Options with Cash

This alternative requires the company to buy out the underwater options with cash, perhaps at a discount from the options' Black-Scholes value.[49] Under FAS 123(R), cancellation of an award not accompanied by the concurrent grant of a replacement award is accounted for as a repurchase for no consideration.[50] There is no reversal of previously recognized compensation cost, and any previously measured but unrecognized cost is accelerated at the cancellation date.[51] Rather than avoiding recognition of expense, the cash award causes the entire compensation charge to be recognized in the year of the cash-out.

7.2.8 Sell Options to a Third Party

An employee may decide to sell his or her nonqualified stock options that are underwater to a third party, provided that the option plan or agreement permits it.[52] This alternative is not possible with incentive

---

49. Companies must establish the current "fair value" of their options when they are granted. FASB requires that companies use an option pricing model for valuing employee stock options that takes into consideration six specific variables. The most common option pricing model used by public companies is the Black-Scholes method, a mathematical formula that considers such factors as the volatility of returns on the underlying securities, the risk-free interest rate, the expected dividend rate, the relationship of the option price to the price of the underlying securities, and the expected option life. Under Code Section 409A, the cash-out of a grant for an amount equal to that otherwise payable upon exercise would not cause the existing grant to be treated as a modification. However, a cash-out of a grant at less than full value would cause the grant to be treated a modification, subjecting it to the 409A compliance rules.

50. FAS 123(R).

51. Id.

52. Option plans and agreements may and often do restrict the transfer of options. Code Section 422(b)(5) generally prohibits incentive stock options from being transferred during the optionee's lifetime.

stock options.[53] This alternative, though it allows the employee to recoup some value from the sold option, would create a new class of non-employee option holders. Many companies restrict transferability of their nonqualified stock option grants to prevent this from happening because they choose not to have outside investors holding their stock options.

7.2.9   Offer Non-Stock Incentives

A company may offer employees holding underwater options some form of non-stock compensation, such as a cash bonus, increased salary, or a non-cash perk, without cancelling the worthless options, as a means to "re-incentivize" its work force. This additional compensation would likely result in the recognition of expense. Each company considering this alternative must determine whether the type and amount of non-stock compensation that would be required to achieve the intended effect in lieu of a new option grant is feasible.

7.3   Conclusion

For many companies, stock options will continue to play a significant role as an incentive to attract and retain the best employees. Recent accounting and tax rule changes will likely make the repricing decision easier and, perhaps, preferable to various repricing alternatives that were designed to avoid the adverse accounting treatment that previously made repricing unacceptable. In a broader context, the mandatory recognition of stock options as an expense levels the playing field, thereby allowing companies to reconsider the use of other forms of equity compensation, including restricted stock, as part of an overall equity compensation program. The reduced popularity of stock options will lessen the impact of any future underwater stock option problem and perhaps make repricing an issue of less importance than what it once was. However, companies that continue to offer stock options as an integral part of their employees' compensation should anticipate their need for an effective repricing strategy to deal with the problem of underwater stock options during the next economic downturn.

---

53. Code Section 422(b)(5).

Stock Options in Divorce

William Dunn and Donna Yip

Contents

WHILE COMPENSATORY STOCK OPTIONS are not considered property for general tax purposes, they are generally viewed as assets subject to equitable distribution in matrimonial situations. As a result, property settlements in a divorce often address stock options held by one of the spouses and generally provide for one of the following outcomes: option retention, option transfer, or assignment of option proceeds. Each of these scenarios has the potential to produce different tax results. This chapter provides a general overview to these alternative outcomes and their attendant tax consequences and briefly addresses some of the specific issues that stock options in the context of divorce present at the state court level.

8.1   Retention

Retention, where the stock options remain in the hands of the working spouse but other assets are divided, provides for a straightforward tax analysis. The working spouse is generally taxed according to the rules

The authors thank Mark Poerio, a partner in the employment department of Paul, Hastings, Janofsky & Walker, LLP, for his review of this chapter.

applicable to the type of stock option retained, with no concern for the divorce. For nonqualified stock options (NSOs), the working spouse will be taxed at exercise for both income and Social Security tax purposes, subject to the normal reporting and withholding requirements that apply to such an exercise. For incentive stock options (ISOs), the normal rules[1] apply in determining whether a disqualifying disposition has occurred and thus what the resulting tax impact is to the optionee.

8.2 Option Transfer

Where options are transferred to a nonworking spouse, the tax analysis is more complicated. Generally, Treas. Reg. § 1.83-3 provides that the grant of an option to purchase certain property does not constitute a transfer of property for purposes of Section 83 of the Internal Revenue Code (the "Code"). Instead, the transfer of the shares subject to the option (e.g., exercise of the option) will generally constitute a transfer to which Section 83(a) and Section 83(b) apply. Thus, at exercise, if the property received with respect to the exercise of the option is not subject to a substantial risk of forfeiture, Section 83(a) will apply to tax the difference between the fair market value of that property received less the amount paid for it (i.e., the exercise price and the amount paid [if any] for the underlying option).

An exception to this general rule applies where the option is disposed of in an arm's length sale or other disposition of the option itself. In this situation, Section 83(a) and Section 83(b) apply to tax the transfer of money or other property received in the same manner as Section 83(a) and Section 83(b) would have applied to the transfer of property pursuant to an exercise of the options. This means that the optionee is taxed upon the option disposition date on the consideration received, even though the option has yet to be exercised. However, if the transaction is viewed not to be at arm's length, the compensatory element is held open, and the optionee is taxed when the option is ultimately exercised, even though he or she no longer holds the option.

In the case of a divorce, the distribution of property is occurring among adverse parties, and the transfers of any options are presumably occurring in an arm's length environment. If this scenario holds true, the employee spouse would presumably recognize income equal to the value of the option at the date the property settlement occurs rather than the date of exercise. Fortunately, the IRS now takes the position that the

---

1.   Code Section 422. See section 8.5 of this chapter.

arm's length disposition rules do not apply to the transaction, instead taking the position that the successor spouse steps into the shoes of the working spouse with respect to the option taxation. This position was first limited to those who reside in community property states, and it has now been expanded to address those who reside in non-community property jurisdictions.

In the case of community property states, the IRS had originally released PLR 9433010, which states that stock options held by the employee in a community property jurisdiction were considered owned by both him and his wife equally from the date of grant. The IRS concluded that no amount of income was required to be included in the gross income of the employee as a result of the division of the options pursuant to the parties' property settlement agreement. The IRS also concluded that no amount of income was required to be included in gross income of the employee upon the exercise by the spouse of the options. Rather, the difference between the exercise price and the fair market value on the date of exercise was included in the income of the spouse exercising the options.[2]

After those actions, the IRS released Revenue Ruling 2002-22, which brings the treatment of nonstatutory stock options and nonqualified deferred compensation in a community property jurisdiction into line with the treatment found in a non-community property jurisdiction. Although the ruling dealt with a non-community property jurisdiction fact pattern, the ruling states that the same holding would apply in a community property jurisdiction.

In Revenue Ruling 2002-22, the IRS concluded that Section 1041 confers nonrecognition treatment on any gain that a taxpayer might otherwise realize when transferring interests to a former spouse, including gain present in stock options. The ruling stated: "Although a transfer of nonstatutory stock options in connection with a marital property settlement may, as a factual matter, involve an arm's length exchange for money, property, or other valuable consideration, it would contravene the gift treatment prescribed by § 1041 to include the value of the consideration in the transferor's income under § 83. Accordingly, the transfer of nonstatutory stock options between divorcing spouses is entitled to nonrecognition treatment under § 1041."[3]

---

2. See also PLR 8751029; *Davis v. Comm'r*, 88 T.C. 1460 (1987) (exchanging interests in community property for other similarly classified property, i.e., stock options, is not taxable).

3. This ruling contrasts with FSA 20005006, in which the IRS concluded that a husband's transfer of one-half of the husband's option to his ex-wife was

Thus, an employee who transfers interests in nonstatutory stock options (as well as nonqualified deferred compensation) to a former spouse incident to divorce is not required to include an amount in gross income upon the transfer. Further, the IRS stated that the assignment of income doctrine does not apply to these transfers, and the employee is not required to include in gross income any income resulting from the former spouse's exercise of stock options or the payment of deferred compensation.[4] Instead, when the options are exercised, the former spouse must include in income an amount determined under Section 83(a) as if the spouse were the person who performed the services. The amount realized from payments of deferred compensation must be included in the former spouse's income in the year such payments are paid or made available. Thus, the former spouse, and not the taxpayer, is required to include an amount in gross income when the former spouse exercises the stock options or when the deferred compensation is paid or made available to the former spouse.

After releasing Rev. Rul. 2002-22, the IRS issued Notice 2002-31, which states that no payment of wages for employment tax purposes is deemed to be made upon a transfer of interests in nonstatutory stock options and nonqualified deferred compensation from an employee spouse to a nonemployee spouse incident to divorce. However, nonstatutory stock options would be subject to FICA and FUTA taxes at the time of exercise by a nonemployee spouse to the same extent as if the options had been retained and exercised by the employee spouse. Additionally, nonqualified deferred compensation also would remain subject to FICA

---

an arm's length disposition of the option and thus was a taxable event to the husband, not the wife. Both nonqualified options and ISOs were at issue, and the employee resided in a non-community property jurisdiction (an "equitable distribution" state). The husband was required to recognize ordinary income, in the year of such disposition, equal to the fair market value of the options when they were transferred to his ex-wife pursuant to the divorce decree. To determine this fair value, methodology such as the Black-Scholes test would presumably be used, although the ruling did not state which valuation approach is appropriate. According to the IRS, when the ex-wife subsequently exercised her option, there was no taxable event to the husband, and there were no tax consequences for the ex-wife. Rather, the ex-wife would be taxed on any gain (at the capital gains rate) on the subsequent sale of the underlying stock.

4. See also PLR 200442003, where the IRS cites Rev. Rul. 2002-22 and *Balding v. Commissioner*, 98 T.C. 368 (1992), and concludes that the "assignment of income doctrine" does not apply to the transfer at hand and that the employee spouse would be taxable for the Federal income tax when the company receives payments.

and FUTA taxes to the same extent as if the rights to the compensation had been retained by the employee spouse.

Revenue Ruling 2004-60 was then issued to modify Notice 2002-31; it concludes that nonqualified stock options and nonqualified deferred compensation transferred by an employee to a former spouse incident to a divorce are subject to the Federal Insurance Contributions Act (FICA), the Federal Unemployment Tax Act (FUTA), and income tax withholding to the same extent as if retained by the employee.[5] To the extent employment taxes apply, the wages would be considered the wages of the employee spouse. The employee portion of the FICA taxes would be deducted from the payment made to the transferee, and any FICA withholding from the payments would not reduce the amount includible in the gross income of the transferee.

Income recognized by a nonemployee spouse with respect to the exercise of nonqualified stock options would be subject to withholding under Code Section 3402. Amounts distributed to a nonemployee spouse from nonqualified deferred compensation plans also would be subject to withholding under Section 3402.

Social Security and Medicare wages and withholding would be reportable on a Form W-2 with the name, address, and Social Security number of the employee spouse; however, no amount would be includible in Box 1 and Box 2 of the employee's Form W-2 with respect to these payments. The income with respect to the exercise of a nonqualified stock option by the nonemployee spouse and distributions from nonqualified deferred compensation plans to the nonemployee spouse would be reportable in Box 3 as other income on a Form 1099-MISC with the name, address, and Social Security number of the nonemployee spouse. Income tax withholding with respect to these payments of wages would be included in Box 4, "Federal income tax withheld."

Income tax withholding on payments to a nonemployee spouse would be included on a Form 945 filed by the employer. Social Security tax and Medicare tax would be reported on the employer's Form 941, and FUTA tax would be reported on the employer's Form 940.

---

5.   Revenue Ruling 2004-60 states: "For periods before the effective date, employers may rely on a reasonable, good faith interpretation including the interpretations in the proposed revenue ruling in Notice 2002-31 and this revenue ruling. However, with respect to compensation transferred to a spouse incident to divorce, failure to treat nonstatutory stock option compensation, or amounts deferred under a nonqualified deferred compensation plan, as subject to FICA will not be considered a reasonable, good faith interpretation."

8.3 Assignment of Proceeds

Where the employee continues to hold the options but has promised their former spouse with a payment equal to the intrinsic value in the options at exercise, the outcome is less clear. Because this approach does not involve the actual transfer of the option, the favorable precedent found in the rulings cited above is unavailable. Therefore, normal assignment-of-income concepts likely apply to the transaction, meaning that for NSOs, the working spouse will be taxed at exercise for both income and Social Security tax purposes, subject to the normal reporting and withholding requirements that apply to such an exercise, while the other spouse will enjoy the value of the appreciation without tax consequence.

8.4 State-Level Issues

The issues that arise at the state court level are too broad to treat exhaustively in this chapter. However, there are several issues, in addition to the distinction between community and non-community property states (discussed above), worth raising here: (1) consideration as a basis of division, (2) the value of tax in the marital estate, and (3) the division of non-transferable options.

Several states[6] have made determinations on whether a portion of the stock options to be divided should be transferred on the basis of whether there has been consideration, i.e., services rendered, for such stock options. This is conceptually a nuance for community property states, where it is generally accepted that the stock options are marital property on the date of grant. Certain states simply inquire whether the stock options were granted in consideration of past or future services. Other states create a mathematical formula factoring in such variables, including the grant date, the date of separation, and the date the option can be exercised.[7]

Several states have addressed whether to consider the tax consequences of stock options in valuing the marital estate. On one hand, states like Alaska stipulate that the future tax consequences of exercising

---

6.   These states include, but are not limited to, California (see *In re Marriage of Nelson*, 177 Cal. App. 3d 170, 222 [1986]); Colorado (see *In re Marriage of Huston*, 967 P.2d 181 [Colo. Ct. App. 1998], and *In re Marriage of Miller*, 915 P.2d 1314 [Colo. 1996]; and Indiana (see *Hann v. Hann*, 655 N.E.2d 566 [Ind. Ct. App. 1995]).

7.   For example, California; see *In re Marriage of Nelson*, 177 Cal. App. 3d 170.

stock options should not be considered in valuing the marital estate.[8] On the other hand, states like Indiana[9] permit the inclusion of taxes payable after exercising a stock option in valuing the marital estate.

Although stock options are generally *prima facie* nontransferable, few states have reviewed the actual transferability aspect of the stock option. The Pennsylvania Supreme Court reviewed a specific case where the employee spouse could not transfer stock options to the nonemployee spouse despite a divorce decree requiring a distribution of property.[10] In this case, the court issued a domestic relations order requiring that the employee spouse pay the nonemployee spouse their share when the options were executed. The Illinois Appeals Court reviewed a similar case and authorized the trial court to retain jurisdiction until the options could be exercised or the options expired[11] and then to divide the property at such time.

While a single common-law rule regarding divorce and stock options cannot be derived from state precedents, it is clear that there are a variety of issues at the state court that may further obscure the divorce proceedings and that special attention to these state-level nuances is required.

8.5 Statutory Option Stock (Incentive Stock Options and Section 423 ESPPs)

The above information pertains only to NSOs. Special rules apply to "statutory option stock," i.e., shares acquired through ISOs and Section 423 employee stock purchase plan (ESPP) options.[12] Unlike the NSOs described above, these options are limited by a transferability condition; i.e., upon transfer, the shares lose their status as statutory qualified shares. Rev. Rul. 2002-22 concluded that the transfer of statutory options to a spouse incident to a divorce results in the disqualification of the

---

8. *Broadribb v. Broadribb*, P.2d (Alaska 1998).

9. *Hiser v. Hiser*, 692 N.E.2d 925 (Ind. Ct. App. 1998) (these states also include Michigan; see also *Everett v. Everett*, 489 N.W.2d 111 (1992).

10. *Fisher v. Fisher*, 769 A.2d 1165 (Pa. 2001).

11. *In re of Moody*, 457 N.E.2d at 1027 (Ill. App. 1991); see also *In re Marriage of Frederick*, 218 Ill.App. 3d 533, 578 N.E.2d 612 (1991).

12. "Statutory option stock" is the terminology used by Code Section 424 and refers to statutory shares, i.e., "any stock acquired through the exercise of an incentive stock option or an option granted under an employee stock purchase plan."

options,[13] which would result in those shares being subject to NSO tax treatment.

ISOs are statutory options offered by a corporation to certain employees that allow for tax-favored treatment if the requirements in Code Section 422 are met. Generally, to receive tax-favored treatment, ISO shares cannot be sold before two years after grant and one year after exercise. Where such conditions are met, Section 421(a)(1) stipulates that "no income shall result at the time of the transfer of such share to the individual upon his exercise of the option with respect to such share."

The Tax Court reaffirmed the findings of Rev. Rul. 2002-22 in 2005,[14] where the petitioners proposed a method of dividing ISOs incident to a divorce and were able to preserve ISO status. During the divorce proceedings, the spouses entered into an agreement to split the grants awarded to the employee spouse proportionally.[15] Pursuant to a court order, the employee spouse would retain all legal and beneficial ownership of the ISOs consistent with the statutory nontransferability and lifetime exercise rules of Section 422. The employee spouse would exercise the non-employee spouse's ISOs only according to the non-employee spouse's written instruction and only on that spouse's paying or making arrangements for the payment of the transaction. Such shares would be transferred immediately, and the non-employee spouse would be subject to all applicable taxes. The Tax Court ruled that such a scheme recognizing community property interest in the ISOs, requiring the employee to exercise ISOs according to the non-employee's instruction, and requiring that the employee designate the non-employee spouse as the beneficiary of the non-employee's pro-rata portion of the ISOs would not violate the non-transferability and lifetime exercise rules imposed by Section 422.

Another common form of stock option available to an employee is delivered through an ESPP. ESPPs allow employees to purchase company stock, generally at a discount to its fair market value and almost always using payroll deductions to fund the purchase price and using relatively short option periods.[16] Most ESPPs are qualified under Code

---

13. Disqualification as an ISO or treatment under ESPP, as stipulated in Code Sections 422(b)(5) and 423(b)(9) respectively.

14. Private Letter Ruling 200519011 (Jan. 13, 2005).

15. Proportionally to the time of vesting and the date of separation.

16. Unlike ISOs, ESPPs can be granted with a purchase price that is lower than the stock's value at the date of grant (a 15% discount is permitted). Purchase periods are usually less than a year, with six months being the most common.

Section 423 and are similar to ISOs in that both regimes impose no tax at the share purchase date and instead tax the optionee at the time that he or she disposes of the shares received upon exercise of the ESPP purchase right. Like ISO shares, Section 423 ESPP shares must be held at least two years from grant and one year from exercise to convert pre-exercise appreciation into capital gain.[17]

Under virtually all ESPP plans, the option rights cannot be transferred to a spouse during the option period (usually termed the "purchase period"). Therefore, no divorce issues arise out of the ESPP option itself.[18] However, stock acquired by the employee as a result of his or her ESPP purchase is included in the marital estate and therefore may be transferred in a divorce settlement. Section 424(c)(4) provides that in the case of transfers of shares acquired under an ESPP between spouses incident to divorce,[19] the transfer shall not be treated as a disposition for tax purposes, and the recipient shall take the same tax treatment as applied to the optionee. Therefore, the spouse who receives and then subsequently disposes of the shares must follow the ESPP share disposition rules to determine the share's ultimate tax treatment, and the employee who transferred the shares has no residual tax consequences.

8.5   Section 409A Considerations

The American Jobs Creation Act of 2004 included new Internal Revenue Code Section 409A, which addresses the tax treatment of deferred compensation. To clarify this new provision, the IRS first published Notice 2005-1 and then followed with proposed Section 409A regulations. In the notice and proposed regulations, the IRS states that certain NSOs, ISOs, and ESPPs are generally exempt from nonqualified deferred compensation treatment and thus are not subject to Section 409A.[20] Instead,

---

17. Note, however, that any discount that exists at the time the ESPP is granted is treated as ordinary income upon disposition, even if the holding period is met. Revenue Act of 1964. P.L. 88-272, Sen. Rprt. No. 88-830. (1964). See also *Kast v. Comm'r*, 78 T.C. 1154 (1982).

18. Like ISOs, any Section 423 ESPP option that might be transferred incident to divorce (within the meaning of Code Section 1041) or pursuant to a domestic relations order would no longer qualify as a statutory option as of the day of such transfer.

19. Transfers described in subsection (a) of Code Section 1041.

20. The exemption from 409A is generally available only for stock options that meet specific conditions, notably, (1) having an exercise price that is at or

NSOs and ISOs remain under the governance of Code Sections 83 and 422 respectively. For this reason, the guidance discussed elsewhere in this chapter continue to apply to these options, despite the presence of these new rules.

---

above the fair market value of the underlying shares on the grant date, and (2) omitting any feature allowing for tax deferral beyond the date of exercise for NSOs, or a disposition of the underlying shares for ISOs and ESPPs.

Designing and Implementing an Employee Stock Purchase Plan

Barbara Baksa and Timothy J. Sparks

Contents

T HIS CHAPTER SUMMARIZES THE principal features of employee stock purchase plans (ESPPs), especially those that are designed to qualify under Section 423 of the Internal Revenue Code (the "Code"), and highlights some of the practical considerations involved in putting an ESPP into place. The purpose of an ESPP is to encourage broad-based employee ownership of employer stock. Through an ESPP that qualifies under Sections 421 and 423 of the Code, an employee subject to U.S. tax law can purchase stock at a discount from fair market value and, if certain holding period requirements are met, receive preferred tax treatment upon sale of the ESPP shares.

9.1   Operation of an ESPP

Section 423 sets the basic operational parameters of an ESPP, which are discussed in greater detail below. In general, under a typical ESPP, employees are given an "option" to purchase employer stock at a favorable price at the end of an "offering period." While Section 423 does not require that the shares be purchased through accumulated payroll deductions, most employers find this approach administratively simpler than having all of the plan participants pay for the stock on the same day.

Before the beginning of each offering period, eligible employees must indicate whether they will participate in the plan. If so, the employee typically completes a subscription agreement or enrollment form indicating the percentage or dollar amount of compensation to be deducted from his or her paycheck throughout the offering period. During the offering period, the company withholds amounts from participants' compensation and credits the amounts to participant record-keeping accounts established for this purpose.

Under most ESPPs, the purchase price is set at a discount from fair market value. While some plans provide that the discount is to be applied to the value of the stock on the purchase date (e.g., 85% of the fair market value on that date), it is more common to provide that this discount is applied to the value of the stock on the first day of the offering period or on the last day, *whichever is lower* (this is generally called a "look-back" provision).

Most plans permit participants to withdraw from the ESPP before the last day of the offering period (the "exercise date"). If a participant does not withdraw from the plan, amounts held for his or her account under the plan are applied automatically to the purchase of shares on the exercise date for the maximum number of shares at the applicable option price. ESPP purchases often take place through a transfer agent of the company or through a brokerage account established for that purpose.

The original subscription agreement setting forth the payroll deduction percentage can continue as long as the plan remains in effect, unless the participant withdraws from the plan, becomes ineligible to participate, or terminates employment. Many plans permit participants to increase or decrease their payroll deduction percentage at any time during the offering period.

9.2   Section 423's Requirements

To qualify under Section 423 of the Code, an ESPP must meet the following requirements:

- *Employees only.* Only employees of the plan sponsor (or its parent or subsidiary corporations) may participate in the ESPP. Thus, for example, consultants and non-employee directors may not participate in an ESPP.

- *Shareholder approval.* An ESPP must be approved by the shareholders of the plan's sponsor within 12 months before or after the ESPP is adopted by the board. Once an ESPP has been approved by shareholders, no further shareholder approval is required except for an increase in the number of plan shares (other than an increase pursuant to an evergreen provision—see below) or an amendment to allow employees of certain related corporations (e.g., a subsidiary) to participate.

- *No 5% shareholders.* Any employee who owns 5% or more of the stock of the plan sponsor may not participate in the ESPP.
- *Eligibility.* All eligible employees must be allowed to participate in the ESPP, although certain categories of employees may be excluded:
  — employees employed less than two years;
  — employees whose customary employment is 20 hours or less per week;
  — employees whose customary employment is for less than five months in a calendar year; and
  — "highly compensated" employees (as defined in Section 414(q) of the Code).
- *Equal rights and privileges.* All ESPP participants must enjoy the same rights and privileges under the plan, except that the amount of stock that may be purchased may be based on compensation differences (e.g., a percentage of compensation).
- *Purchase price.* The purchase price may not be less than the lesser of 85% of the fair market value of the stock (1) at the beginning of the offering period or (2) on the purchase date.
- *Maximum term.* The maximum term of offering periods under an ESPP may not exceed 27 months unless the purchase price is based solely on the fair market value at the time of purchase, in which case the offering period may be as long as five years. There is no maximum term applicable to the ESPP itself, although most ESPPs have a ten-year term.
- *$25,000 limit.* Under all ESPPs of the employer company and its parent and subsidiary corporations, an employee may not purchase more than $25,000 worth of stock (determined based on the fair market value on the first day of the offering period) for each calendar year in which the offering period is in effect.
- *Nontransferability.* An employee's right to purchase stock under the ESPP may not be transferred except by will or the laws of descent and distribution and may be exercisable during the employee's life only by the employee.

9.3 Designing an ESPP

Within the broad framework of Section 423 there is a good deal of flexibility in plan design:

9.3.1 Number of Shares

There is no limit per se on the number of shares that can be issued under an ESPP. The number of shares reserved under an ESPP should take into account the number of shares available to employees under other stock-based programs, the value of the stock, the duration of the offering, limits on employee contributions, eligibility requirements, and so on. In our experience, it is common for employers to reserve as little as 1% and as much as 8.5% of their outstanding shares for their ESPPs, with an average of about 3.5%. Some employers include an "evergreen" or automatic stock replenishment provision in their ESPP. With such a provision, the number of shares available for issuance under the plan increases automatically, typically each year, based on a specified percentage of the employer's outstanding shares (e.g., 2.5% per year). For tax reasons, the annual increase should be subject to a fixed and determinable limit (e.g., 250,000 shares). An evergreen provision avoids having to continually seek shareholder approval of plan share increases. This can also help the employer avoid additional compensation charges for financial accounting purposes that can apply when the plan runs out of shares during an offering period (see "Grant Date" under "Accounting Considerations" below). While shareholders, particularly institutional shareholders, do not generally view evergreen provisions favorably, approval of such a provision in an ESPP is apparently more palatable to shareholders than an evergreen provision in the employer's stock option plan.

Some employers limit their ESPP share consumption by imposing a cap on the number of shares that can be issued in any one offering period. Such a feature allows employers to plan for future share increases and the associated shareholder approval.

9.3.2 Dilution

Other than the number of shares in the plan, the two factors primarily responsible for the dilutive effect of an ESPP are the purchase price of the stock and the duration of the offering period. As a rule, the longer the offering period, the more dilutive the plan, since employees become more likely to purchase their shares at a substantial discount. For example, assume that the fair market value of the employer's stock on the date of grant is $30, and with a 15% discount, the purchase price would be $25.50 (85% of $30). Assume further that at month 24, the fair market value of the stock is $48. By allowing employees to purchase the shares at 85% of the value on the date of grant (i.e., $25.50), the 15% discount would increase, in this example, to a discount of 47% of the value on the date of purchase. The dilutive effect is even more pronounced in plans that include a feature (discussed in greater detail below) under which participants automatically flip into a new offering period in the event of a decline in the value of the company's stock.

9.3.3 Offering Periods

ESPPs typically permit participants to purchase shares at the end of an "offering period," which typically runs from 3 to 27 months. Most plans have offering periods of either 6 months or some multiple thereof (e.g., 12 months or 24 months). Plans with offering periods of more than six months typically include interim "purchase periods." For example, if the offering period is 24 months, employees might be allowed to purchase shares at the end of each of the four 6-month purchase periods within the 24-month offering period. In this situation, the purchase price in any one purchase period is usually based on the fair market value on the first day of the offering period or the last day of the particular purchase period, whichever is lower. Plans with offering periods longer than 6 months are more difficult to administer, both because of the interim purchase periods and the fact that in most plans of this kind there are overlapping offering periods (e.g., a new 24-month offering commences every 6 months).

Some ESPPs include an offering period "reset" provision. These plans typically include offering periods that are 12 or 24 months long and begin every 6 months. For example, a 24-month offering period plan might include four 6-month purchase periods (i.e., purchases occur every 6 months during the offering period). Under a reset provision, if the company's stock declines in value, at the end of a purchase period the employees are considered to have automatically withdrawn from that offering period and enrolled in the next 24-month offering period. This feature gives the employee the lowest possible purchase price, since the purchase price is reset as of the first day of the new offering period.

Some plans offer 12- or 24-month offering periods without interim purchases or otherwise restrict the transferability of purchased shares. These plans preclude employees from selling their shares immediately after purchase and are intended to foster greater employee stock ownership.

9.3.4 Contribution Limits

Section 423 limits purchases under an ESPP to $25,000 worth of stock in any one calendar year, valued as of the first day of the offering period. Under this rule, if a plan has a 12-month offering period beginning each January 1, and the value of the stock on a particular January 1 is $10, then no employee may purchase more than 2,500 shares ($25,000 divided by $10) in that offering period.

Where the offering period extends over more than one calendar year, the limit is $25,000 worth of stock for each calendar year in which the offering period is in effect. In addition, the amount of stock that employees have accrued the right to purchase under the offering remains available until the end of the offering (not just until the end of the calendar year in which it was accrued). In other words, the unused limit from each calendar year of the offering can be carried forward and increases the limit available in future years under the offering. Assume an employee enrolls in a 24-month offering that begins on July 1, 2006, with purchases occurring every six months under the offering. For the first purchase that occurs on December 31, 2006, the employee has accrued the right to purchase up to $25,000 worth of stock. If, however, the employee only purchases $10,000 worth of stock on this date, the remaining $15,000 accrued under the limit carries forward to the next year of the offering, so that in 2007, the employee would be able to purchase $40,000 worth of stock. This is the $25,000 worth of stock that the employee would normally accrue the right to purchase during this year, plus the remaining $15,000 worth of stock that he or she did not purchase in 2006. Since the same offering extends into 2008, any remaining amount available under the limit in 2007 further carries forward. If the employee only purchased $18,000 worth of stock in 2007, the remaining $22,000 available under the limit for 2007 carries forward, and the employee will be able to purchase $47,000 worth of stock in the purchase that occurs on June 30, 2008. Thus, where an offering spans three calendar years, an employee will be able to purchase $75,000 worth of stock in the offering ($25,000 for each calendar year). Note, however, that the right to purchase stock under the limit does not accrue until each calendar year under the offering begins. Thus, in the example above, it is not permissible to allow the employee to purchase $75,000 worth of stock on December 31, 2006, because at this point the offering has only been outstanding in one calendar year, and thus the employee has only accrued the ability to purchase the first $25,000 worth of stock.

Furthermore, the amount of stock that the employee has accrued the right to purchase under the limit is available only until the end of the offering. Once the employee begins participation in the new offering, he or she loses the right to any amounts accrued above $25,000 in the prior offering. Let us say that in our example above, the employee purchases only $10,000 worth of stock on June 30, 2008 (the last purchase under the offering). Going into this purchase, the employee had accrued the right to purchase $47,000 worth of stock, but once the offering ends, the employee loses the right to any amounts accrued under this offering. Thus, for the next purchase on December 31, 2008, which occurs under a new offering that begins on July 1, 2008, the employee will be limited to $25,000 worth of stock.

Other than this limit, there is no *statutory* limitation in employee contributions. However, most plans limit employee contributions to a fixed percentage of compensation, generally 10% to 15%. For most plan participants, this limit usually falls well below the statutory $25,000 limitation.

9.3.5 Compensation

Closely related to the percentage limitation is the plan definition of compensation. Generally, base pay is the simplest, but another definition can be used if base pay does not accurately reflect the makeup of the employees' compensation. However, the definition of compensation cannot operate to discriminate against certain employees. For example, defining compensation as base salary above a certain level (e.g., above $30,000) would violate the equal rights and privileges requirement (discussed above).

9.3.6 Eligibility

Generally, all employees may participate in an ESPP. Section 423 permits a plan to exclude employees who have been employed for less than two years or who are employed for less than 20 hours per week or five months per year. Also, owners of 5% or more of the common stock of a company by statute are not permitted to participate. Most companies impose either no service requirements or require only a brief employment period to participate, such as three months. Any service requirement should be considered in light of employee turnover, competitive practices, and the eligibility requirements of other company plans.

Offering periods often commence every six months. As a result, new hires may have to wait up to six months to participate in an ESPP, in addition to any service requirement.

9.3.7 Participation by Non-U.S. Employees

Often, employers with employees working outside of the U.S. wish to extend ESPP participation to such employees. Before expanding an ESPP outside the United States, however, employers should become familiar with the applicable laws and regulations of each of the foreign countries where participation will be extended. A discussion of these laws and regulations is beyond the scope of this chapter.

Employers will also need to consider the impact of such participation on qualification of their ESPP under Section 423. Among other things, Section 423 requires (1) that all otherwise eligible employees of any corporation whose employees participate be allowed to participate in the ESPP, and (2) that such participants be allowed to participate on the same terms and conditions. These requirements can by problematic with respect to non-U.S. participants. Local laws sometimes impose requirements that are unique to employees in a particular country, which could violate the equal rights and privileges requirement under Section 423. Similarly, problems can arise where the non-U.S. employees work out of branch offices or divisions, since the non-U.S. employees will be considered employees of the U.S. employer for purposes of Section 423.

As an alternative to adding non-U.S. employees to the ESPP, many employers implement mirror ESPPs for their non-U.S. employees. These plans, which are not intended to qualify under Section 423, give employers more flexibility in designing the plan to meet the particular requirements of each country and with respect to each employee group. Moreover, it preserves the 423 plan for the benefit of U.S. employees who can benefit from the favorable tax treatment offered under tax-qualified plans.

9.3.8 Maximum Number of Shares

In addition to the $25,000 limit discussed above, most plans establish a limit on the number of shares that may be purchased by any one participant in an offering period. This satisfies a rather loose Internal Revenue Service (IRS) requirement that applies where the number of shares that will be purchased is not known until the last day of the offering period.

The IRS takes a position that a plan must establish a maximum cap as of the first day of the offering period. Most plans define the maximum cap with reference to a formula or based on a specific number of shares.

9.3.9   Interest

Money contributed by the plan by employees becomes part of the employer's general assets. In the event the employee terminates employment, this money is refunded, typically without interest. A few employers provide that money returned to employees is credited with interest at some nominal rate, such as 5%.

9.4   Federal Income Tax Considerations for Section 423 ESPPs

If a plan meets all the requirements discussed above, an employee who purchases stock under the ESPP will not recognize income for federal income tax purposes on the purchase but will instead defer the tax consequences until the employee sells or otherwise disposes of the stock.

   If stock that was purchased under an ESPP is held for more than one year after the date of purchase *and* more than two years after the beginning of the offering period, or if the employee dies while owning the shares, a portion of the overall gain will be taxed as ordinary income upon the sale (or other disposition). The amount of ordinary income equals the lesser of: (1) the actual gain (the amount by which the market value of the shares on the date of sale, gift, or death exceeds the purchase price), or (2) the purchase price discount. For purposes of this calculation, the "purchase price discount" is always determined using the stock price at the beginning of the offering period. For example, if the ESPP purchase price is 85% of the lesser of the beginning or ending stock price, the "purchase price discount" is 15% of the beginning stock price. And if the purchase price is 85% of the ending stock price (i.e., if the plan has no "look-back" provision), the "purchase price discount" is still 15% of the beginning stock price. Or if it is 90% of the ending stock price, the "purchase price discount" is 10% of the beginning stock price. All additional gain upon the sale of stock is treated as long-term capital gain. If the shares are sold and the sale price is less than the purchase price, there is no ordinary income, and the employee has a long-term capital loss for the difference between the sale price and the purchase price.

If the stock is sold, or is otherwise disposed of, including by way of gift, within either of the Section 423 holding periods (a "disqualifying disposition"), the employee recognizes ordinary income at the time of sale or other disposition taxable to the extent that the fair market value of the stock at the date of purchase was greater than the purchase price (i.e., the "spread" at purchase). This amount is considered ordinary compensation income in the year of sale or other disposition even if no gain is realized on the sale or disposition. This would be the case, for example, in the event of a gift. The difference, if any, between the proceeds of sale and the fair market value of the stock at the date of purchase is a capital gain or loss, which is long-term if the stock has been held more than one year. Ordinary income recognized by the employee upon a disqualifying disposition constitutes taxable income that must generally be reported on a Form W-2.

Subject to the limitations of Code Section 162(m) (the $1 million deduction limit), the employer receives a tax deduction only to the extent that a participant recognizes ordinary income on a disqualifying disposition. The employer does not receive a deduction if the participant meets the holding period requirements. Since the purchase price is typically expressed as a discount from fair market value, compensation recognized by a participant will not be considered "performance-based" within the meaning of Section 162(m), and will therefore apply against the $1 million deduction limitation under that section. To enable the employer to take full advantage of its tax deduction, participants should be required to notify the employer in writing of the date and terms of any disposition of stock purchased under an ESPP.

The appendix to this chapter illustrates the tax treatment of employees under a Section 423 ESPP.

9.4.1 Tax Withholding

The American Jobs Creation Act, enacted in 2004, exempts Section 423 ESPPs from tax withholding and also excludes purchases under these plans from the definition of wages for FICA/FUTA tax purposes. (Even transactions that occurred before the enactment of the American Jobs Creation Act are exempted from withholding for federal income, Social Security, and Medicare tax purposes, under a moratorium established in 2002 by IRS Notice 2002-47.) Therefore, employers are not required to withhold federal income tax, Social Security, or Medicare on either purchases or dispositions of shares acquired under a qualified ESPP. Note, however, that state tax treatment may differ from the federal treatment described here.

9.4.2 Information Statements

Section 6039 of the Code requires that the employer provide participants with an information statement by January 31 of the year following the year in which they first transfer shares purchased under an ESPP. The statement is required only for the first transfer of the shares, not subsequent transfers. The statement must include the name and address of the corporation; the name, address, and tax identification number of the participant; the number of shares transferred; the date the shares were purchased; and the type of option under which the shares were acquired.

9.5 Federal Income Tax Considerations for Non-Section 423 ESPPs

In some cases, an ESPP may not qualify under Section 423, either by design or as a result of plan operation. In light of FAS 123(R) and the loss of favorable accounting treatment for Section 423 ESPPs (discussed below), some employers are exploring alternative plan designs that fall outside of Section 423. For example, an employer may wish to limit participation or provide a stock "match" in lieu of a discount or provide a purchase discount that is greater than the discount allowed under Section 423.

9.5.1 General Rule

In the case of a broad-based ESPP that does not qualify under Section 423, stock purchased will be treated, for tax purposes, as though it had been acquired under a nonstatutory stock option. As a result, a plan participant will not recognize income by virtue of participating in the plan but instead will recognize ordinary compensation income for federal income tax purposes at the time of purchase measured by the excess, if any, in the value of the shares at the time of purchase over the purchase price. Subject to the deduction limitation under Code Section 162(m), the company will be entitled to a tax deduction in the amount and at the time that the plan participant recognizes compensation income with respect to shares acquired under the plan.

If the participant is also an employee of the company, the compensation income recognized at the time of purchase will be treated as wages and will be subject to tax withholding by the company and reporting (e.g., on Form W-2). Upon a resale of shares by the participant, any difference between the sales price and the purchase price (plus any compensation income recognized with respect to such shares) will be a capital gain or loss and will qualify for long-term capital gain or loss treatment if the shares have been held for more than one year. Capital losses are allowed in full against capital gains and up to $3,000 of other income.

9.5.2 Code Section 409A (Nonqualified Deferred Compensation Plans)

The American Jobs Creation Act of 2004 added new Section 409A to the Internal Revenue Code. Section 409A applies to nonqualified deferred compensation plans (NDCPs) and provides that compensation deferred under a NDCP is includible in gross income in the year of deferral, unless (1) certain requirements are met or (2) the compensation is subject to a substantial risk of forfeiture. Failure to comply with Section 409A with respect to a deferred amount results in current taxation of the deferred amount, interest, penalties, and an additional 20% tax.

An NDCP is broadly defined under Section 409A as any arrangement that provides for the deferral of compensation to a year later than the year in which the service provider (e.g., the employee) acquires a legally binding right to the compensation. Section 423 ESPPs are not subject to Section 409A, nor are options with an exercise price that is set at or above the grant date fair market value. However, options granted with an exercise price less than the grant date fair market value (i.e., "discount options") are subject to Section 409A. As a result, ESPPs with a discount feature that do not qualify under Section 423 must be considered in the context of Section 409A.

As a general matter, Section 409A subjects the holder of discount options to taxation as and to the extent the option vests, unless the option satisfies the requirements of Section 409A. One way to accomplish this is to fix the option exercise date at the time of grant, thereby avoiding any gap (i.e., deferral) between the vesting date and the exercise date.

Although typical ESPPs involve the grant of discount options, this should not be fatal under Section 409A since ESPP options become exercisable on predetermined dates (i.e., the options "vest" and are exercised at the same time). As a result, it should be possible to design non-Section 423 ESPPs without running afoul of Section 409A.

9.6 Accounting Considerations

Beginning in 2006, employers were required to account for ESPPs under Statement of Financial Accounting Standards No. 123 (revised 2004), *Share-Based Payment* ("FAS 123(R)"). Under FAS 123(R), ESPPs can be considered compensatory or noncompensatory. Plans that are noncompensatory are implemented for a purpose other than compensation (e.g., to raise capital or distribute stock to employees) and consequently do not result in any income statement expense. Plans that are compensatory will result in compensation expense in much the same manner as traditional stock options and other forms of stock compensation. To qualify as noncompensatory under FAS 123(R), a plan must meet the following requirements:

1. The plan must not incorporate any "option-like" features.

2. The plan must allow for the participation of substantially all full-time employees meeting limited employment qualifications on an equitable basis.

3. The plan cannot provide for a discount from fair market value for the purchase price that exceeds the reasonable costs of raising capital or stock must be offered to all shareholders under the same terms.

If a plan does not qualify as noncompensatory (and most traditional plans cannot, even under the revised requirements), then it is necessary to estimate the "fair value" of the participation rights or "options" that are granted to participants in the plan.

9.6.1 "Option-Like" Features Limitation

To be noncompensatory under FAS 123(R), an ESPP may not contain any "option-like" features, such as a provision permitting a participating employee to cancel participation before a purchase date or a provision establishing the purchase price as an amount based on the lesser of the fair market value of the company's stock on the date of enrollment or the date of purchase (referred to in FAS 123(R) as a "look-back option").

There are two limited exceptions to this restriction. First, a plan may contain a provision under which employees are permitted a short period of time (not to exceed 31 days) after the purchase price has been fixed in which to enroll in the plan. Second, the plan may contain a provision that permits a participating employee to cancel participation before a purchase date and receive a refund of amounts previously paid where the purchase price is based solely on the fair market value of the company's stock on the purchase date.

9.6.2 Purchase Discount Limitation

Under FAS 123(R), there are no restrictions on the discount that can be offered under a noncompensatory ESPP, provided that the stock sold under the plan is offered to all shareholders of that same class of stock under the same terms as those that apply under the plan. If this is not the case, then the discount cannot exceed the cost of raising capital in a public offering. A discount from fair market value of 5% or less is considered to be per se reasonable and does not have to be justified. Where the discount from fair market value is more than 5%, however, the company would have to demonstrate that the cost of raising capital is equal to or exceeds the discount for the plan to be considered noncompensatory. This must be demonstrated not only upon implementation of the plan but also on an ongoing basis (at least annually), making a greater-than-5% discount impractical for most companies. Where the greater discount cannot be justified, the entire discount (not just the portion of the discount that exceeds 5%) is treated as compensatory.

9.6.3 Plans with "Look-Back" Features

An ESPP where the purchase price of the stock is based on 85% of the lesser of the fair market value of the company's stock at the beginning of the offering (the date of "grant") or the date of purchase (the date of "exercise") is considered to provide for so-called "look-back" options. Under FAS 123(R), these plans are considered compensatory in nature and require the determination of a "fair value" estimate at the time of enrollment (or "grant") for the participation rights (or "options") granted to participating employees.

9.6.4 ESPP Fair Value

The fair value of each participation right or "option" is to be estimated at the grant date (typically the enrollment date—see discussion below) by dividing the right into its components and valuing the instrument as a combination position.

Component 1—Discount. The first component represents the inherent discount in the purchase price formula. A participation right or "option" with an exercise price that equals 85% of the value of the underlying stock on the exercise date is considered to always be worth 15% of the stock price upon exercise. (For a stock that pays no dividends, the "option" is the equivalent of 15% of a share of stock.)

Component 2—Look-back. The second component represents the value of the look-back provision. This value reflects 85% of an at-the-money call option with the specific characteristics of the participation right being granted, as estimated using a standard option-pricing model. The look-back, which is essentially an option to purchase stock in the future at a price set on the enrollment date, is viewed as economically equivalent to a call option (which gives the holder the right to buy stock at a specified price). The look-back is represented by an at-the-money option (rather than a discounted option) because the value of the discount has already been included under the first component; it is for this reason as well that only 85% of the call option value is included in the ESPP option fair value.

Component 3—Additional Shares. While the foregoing reflects the accounting treatment for one common type of ESPP, it does not adequately address the accounting treatment for a variety of plans with "look-back" options that contain additional, and often different, features. In December 1997, the Financial Accounting Standards Board issued FASB Technical Bulletin No. 97-1, which provides guidance on how to account for many of the more common types of ESPPs with a "look-back" option and one or more of the following features: multiple purchase periods, price reset mechanisms, and the ability to change the withholding amount or percentage after the enrollment date.

One of the more significant topics addressed by Technical Bulletin No. 97-1 is the differing accounting treatment for ESPPs that establish a maximum on the enrollment date as to the number of shares of stock that can be purchased (identified as a "Type A Plan" in the Bulletin) and those that permit the employee to purchase as many shares as the full amount of the employee's withholdings will permit, regardless of whether the company's stock price is lower on the purchase date than on the enrollment date (identified as a "Type B Plan" in the Bulletin).

The example given previously for estimating the fair value of a participation right or "option" on the enrollment date is for a Type A Plan.

In the case of a Type B Plan, the prior example is modified to take into consideration the fact that, under this type of plan, the number of shares that an employee may purchase is not fixed. Instead, if the purchase price declines during the period, employees are permitted to purchase additional shares. For example, assume an employee enrolls in an ESPP with a 15% discount and a look-back when the market value is $10 per share. Over the course of the offering, the employee contributes $1,000 to the ESPP. If the stock price increases during the offering, the employee can purchase a maximum of 117 shares. But let us say the fair market value declines to $8 on the purchase date. This reduces the purchase price to $6.80, enabling the employee to purchase a maximum of 147 shares (30 more than he or she could have purchased if the fair market value had increased). These additional shares serve to preserve or "lock in" the gain that existed on the employee's enrollment date. In our example, the spread or gain on the employee's enrollment date is $176 ($1.50 multiplied by 117 shares). If, after the fair market value declines to $8, the employee is limited to only purchasing 117 shares, his or her actual gain on the purchase will be only $140 ($1.20 multiplied by 117 shares). Allowing the employee to purchase the additional 30 shares ensures that he or she realizes the same gain that existed on the employee's enrollment date, or $176 ($1.20 multiplied by 147 shares). This is essentially the benefit provided by a put option, which enables the option holder to sell stock at a guaranteed price, thereby ensuring that the holder receives a minimum amount of gain regardless of market fluctuation. Therefore, under FAS 123(R), the additional shares employees can purchase if the fair market value declines during the offering period is represented by a third component in the valuation: 15% of the fair value of an at-the-money put option. (Only 15% of the fair value of a put option is included because the guarantee relates only to 15% discount.)

Calculating the Fair Value

As a consequence of the above factors, the fair value estimate includes three separate components. As under a Type A Plan, the first component is to reflect the inherent discount in the purchase price formula. A participation right or "option" with an exercise price that equals 85% of the value of the underlying stock on the exercise date is considered to always be worth 15% of the stock price upon exercise. (For a stock that pays no dividends, the "option" is the equivalent of 15% of a share of stock.) The second component, which is to be estimated using a standard option-pricing model, is to reflect 85% of a call option with the specific characteristics of the participation right being granted. The third component, which is to be estimated using a standard option-pricing model, is to reflect 15% of a put option using the same measurement assumptions that were used to value the call option component. The sum of these three components would be multiplied by the number of shares being issued under the plan and would result in a compensation cost estimate that would be recognized in the company's income statement.

Important Note: The preceding discussion assumes an ESPP with a 15% discount. If the discount is a different amount, the percentage of the call and put option included in the ESPP option fair value would be adjusted proportionately. For example, for an ESPP with a 10% discount, the fair value would include 10% of the fair market value on the enrollment date (component 1), 90% of the fair value of a call option (component 2), and, if applicable, 10% of the fair value of a put option (component 3).

Example 1

Assume that a six-month offering begins under an ESPP when the fair market value is $10 per share. The purchase price under the offering is 85% of the lower of the fair market value on the enrollment date or the purchase date, and there is no limit on the number of shares that participants can purchase should the price decline during the period. After considering expected terminations, the company anticipates that $850,000 in contributions will be applied to purchase shares under the offering. Participants have essentially been granted an option: the grant date is their enrollment date and the purchase date is the date the option will be exercised (thus, the option has an expected term of six months). The fair value of the option is calculated as in table 9-1.

It is not necessary to know the actual purchase price (or the actual number of shares to be purchased) to value the option granted under the ESPP. Instead, the third component of the valuation (the value of the put option) represents the economic benefit the employee would receive should the price decline, allowing him or her to purchase additional shares.

Example 2

Where there are multiple purchases in an offering, each purchase can be valued as a separate option. If an offering was 24 months in length with purchases occurring every 6 months, at the outset of the offering,

Table 9-1

Component 1 (discount)	$1.50	(15% of enrollment/grant date fair market value)
Component 2 (look-back)	$1.25	(85% of at-the-money call option)*
Component 3 (additional shares)	$.20	(15% of at-the-money put option)*
ESPP option fair value	$2.95	
Expected shares to be purchased	100,000	($850,000 in contributions divided by $8.50 price)
Aggregate option fair value	$295,000	

* The option fair value was computed using the Black-Scholes module, assuming 50% volatility, a 3% risk-free interest rate, and no dividend yield.

four options would be valued: a 6-month option, a 12-month option, an 18-month option, and a 24-month option.

For example, assume a 12-month offering begins when the market value is $10 per share, with purchases occurring every 6 months. The purchase price under the offering is 85% of the lower of the fair market value on the enrollment date or the purchase date, and there is no limit on the number of shares that the employee can purchase should the price decline during the period. After estimating terminations, the company expects that contributions of $850,000 will be applied to each purchase under the offering. The total expense for the offering is computed as in tables 9-2 and 9-3.

Grant Date

FAS 123(R) requires a grant date valuation; i.e., the fair value of the right to participate in an ESPP is determined on the grant date. Under FAS 123(R), the grant date occurs when four conditions have been met:

1. The employer and employee have a mutual understanding of the key terms and conditions of the award.
2. The employer is contingently obligated to issue equity instruments or transfer assets to an employee who renders the requisite services.
3. The employee begins to benefit from, or be adversely affected by, subsequent changes in the price of the employer's equity shares.
4. The required approvals for the grant have been obtained.

Table 9-2. Value of 6-Month Option

Component 1 (discount)	$1.50	(15% of enrollment/grant date fair market value)
Component 2 (look-back)	$1.25	(85% of at-the-money call option)*
Component 3 (additional shares)	$.20	(15% of at-the-money put option)*
Six-month option fair value	$2.95	
Expected shares to be purchased	100,000	($850,000 in contributions divided by $8.50 price)
Aggregate option fair value	$295,000	

Table 9-3. Value of 12-Month Option

Component 1 (discount)	$1.50	(15% of enrollment/grant date fair market value)
Component 2 (look-back)	$1.80	(85% of at-the-money call option)*
Component 3 (additional shares)	$.30	(15% of at-the-money put option)*
Six-month option fair value	$3.60	
Expected shares to be purchased	100,000	($850,000 in contributions divided by $8.50 price)
Aggregate option fair value	$360,000	
Aggregate offering fair value	$655,000	($295,000 value of 6-month option plus $360,000 value of 12-month option)

In most cases, all of these conditions will be met on the enrollment date, thereby establishing the grant date for valuation purposes. In some cases, however, employees may be permitted to enroll in a plan that has not yet been approved by the company's shareholders. When a new plan is implemented (or an existing plan is amended in a manner that requires shareholder approval), Section 423 simply requires that shareholder approval be obtained within one year of when the board adopts the plan (or amendment). This will defer the grant date to the date shareholder approval is obtained (for FAS 123(R) purposes only; the grant date for tax purposes will remain the enrollment date). Until that date, the plan will be subject to liability treatment, and any fluctuations in the fair market value of the company's stock (both increases and decreases) will have a commensurate effect on the fair value of the offering.

Where a company experiences a shortage of shares under the plan in the midst of an offering period, the grant date can also be deferred. If participants are permitted to purchase shares that were allocated to the plan (and approved by the company's shareholders) after the enrollment date, the grant date for these shares will be the date the shareholders approved the share allocation. The shares will be subject to liability treatment until the allocation is approved by the shareholders. This treatment can be avoided by limiting purchases to only those shares that were already allocated the plan and approved by shareholders on the enrollment date.

9.6.5 Automatic Reset and Rollover Mechanisms

Many ESPPs that have multiple purchases within a single offering period include a reset or rollover provision that is triggered when the fair market value has declined during the period. These provisions require that if the fair market value of the stock on the purchase date is less than the fair market value at the beginning of the offering, all employees enrolled in that offering are automatically withdrawn from the plan and immediately reenrolled in a new offering period. Under a reset provision, the employees are reenrolled for only the remainder of the current offering (for example, if the reset mechanism is triggered 6 months into a 24-month offering period, the employees are reenrolled for the remaining 18 months only). Under a rollover provision, the employees are reenrolled in new offering period equal to the length of the original period (for example, if the offering was originally 24 months in length, the employees are reenrolled in a new 24-month offering regardless of when the rollover mechanism is triggered).

Technical Bulletin No. 97-1 addresses both reset mechanisms (a "Type D Plan") and rollover mechanisms (a "Type E Plan"), requiring that both be treated as a modification of the original option. To account for the modification, the employer recognizes all of the cost associated with the original offering period but now also recognizes the incremental cost of the new offering period. The incremental cost is equal to the fair value of the new offering less the fair value of the original offering at the time the reset or rollover mechanism was triggered.

Example 3

Assume the same facts as in Example 2, but assume that the fair market value on the first purchase date is $8 per share, triggering a reset provision in the plan. All participants are automatically withdrawn after the first purchase and re-enrolled at $8 per share for the remaining 6 months of the offering. This is viewed as a modification, i.e., a cancellation of the original offering and the start of a new offering. The company must continue to recognize the $660,000 of expense computed for the original offering, but it now must also recognize the incremental expense of the new offering. The incremental expense is computed as in tables 9-4 and 9-5 (assuming 50% volatility, 5% risk-free interest rate, and no dividend yield on the underlying stock).

Table 9.4. Fair Value of New 6-Month Offering

Component 1 (discount)	$1.20	(15% of current fair market value)
Component 2 (look-back)	$1.00	(85% of at-the-money call option.)*
Component 3 (additional shares)	$.15	(15% of at-the-money put option)*
Six-month option fair value	$2.35	
Expected shares to be purchased	125,000	($850,000 in contributions divided by $6.80 price)
Aggregate option fair value	$293,750	

* Both options are assumed to have an $8 exercise price, since both are granted on the reset date when the market value is $8 per share. The fair market value of the underlying stock assumed for valuation purposes is also $8 per share, the value on the reset date.

In computing the fair value of the cancelled 12-month offering, since the 6-month purchase was completed before the reset, only the value of the 12-month purchase period is applied against the value of the new offering. The value of the 12-month offering is re-computed based on current conditions, as in table 9-5.

The aggregate incremental expense for the new offering is $93,750. This is the fair value of the new offering ($293,750) less the current fair value of the cancelled offering ($200,000). This incremental expense is recognized over the remaining six-month term of the new offering, along with any remaining unamortized expense from the original offering.

9.6.6 Increases in Contribution Rates

Technical Bulletin No. 97-1 treats increases in contribution rates that occur during an offering period as modifications of the original option. By

Table 9-5. Fair Value of Cancelled 12-Month Offering

Component 1 (discount)	$1.20	(15% of current fair market value)
Component 2 (look-back)	$.45	(85% of underwater call option)*
Component 3 (additional shares)	$.35	(15% of in-the-money put option)*
Six-month option fair value	$2.00	
Expected shares to be purchased	100,000	($850,000 in contributions divided by $8.50 price)
Aggregate option fair value	$200,000	

* The exercise price of both options is assumed to be $10 per share, the fair market value when the offering originally began. This means that the call option is underwater (since it provides the right to buy stock at $10 when the current fair market value is only $8), and the put option is in the money (since it provides the right to sell stock at $10 when the current fair market value is only $8). The expected term assumed for both options is 6 months, since there are only 6 months remaining under the offering at the time the reset occurs.

allowing employees to increase their contributions and thereby purchase additional shares under the offering, the employer is considered to have modified the terms of the original option. To account for the modification, the employer recognizes all of the cost associated with the original option but now also recognizes the incremental cost of the new option. The incremental cost is equal to the fair value of the new option less the fair value of the original option at the time the increase occurred.

Example 4

Assume the same facts as in Example 1, but also assume that midway through the offering, when the fair market value is $12 per share, a number of participants increase their contribution rate such that the company now anticipates $900,000 in contributions will be applied to purchase shares under the offering. This increase is viewed as a modification that will result in incremental expense, computed as in tables 9-6 and 9-7.

The incremental expense resulting from the increase in contribution rates is $22,646. This is the fair value of the new offering ($407,646) less the current fair value of the cancelled offering ($385,000). The incremental expense will be recognized over the remaining three months of the offering, along with any unamortized amounts remaining from the original $295,000 of expense computed for the offering. Thus, the total expense

Table 9-6. Fair Value of the New Offering

Component 1 (discount)	$1.80	(15% of current fair market value)
Component 2 (look-back)	$2.00	(85% of in-the-money call option)*
Component 3 (additional shares)	$.05	(15% of underwater put option)*
ESPP option fair value	$3.85	
Expected shares to be purchased	105,882	($900,000 in contributions divided by $8.50 price)
Aggregate option fair value	$407,646	

* The exercise price of both options is assumed to be $10 per share, the fair market value when the offering originally began. This means that call option is in the money (since it provides the right to buy stock at $10 when the current fair market value is higher than this amount) and the put option is underwater (since it provides the right to sell stock at $10 when the current fair market value is higher than this amount). The expected term assumed for both options is three months, since there are only three months remaining under the offering at the time the increase in contribution rates occurs.

Table 9-7. Fair Value of Cancelled Offering

Component 1 (discount)	$1.80	(15% of current fair market value)
Component 2 (look-back)	$2.00	(85% of in-the-money call option)
Component 3 (additional shares)	$.05	(15% of underwater put option)
ESPP option fair value	$3.85	
Expected shares to be purchased	100,000	($900,000 in contributions divided by $8.50 price)
Aggregate option fair value	$385,000	

for the offering will be $317,646 ($295,000 original expense plus $22,646 incremental expense).

When contribution rates are increased, the fair value of the cancelled and new offerings will always be the same on a per-share basis. Looking at Example 4, you can see that the only factor that changes in the before-and-after valuations is the number of shares involved in the valuation. This is because an increase in the contributions does not change the price the participants will pay for the stock or any of the other factors required for valuation; the increase only changes the number of shares participants can purchase. Therefore, the incremental value of the increase can be determined by simply computing the fair value of the additional shares as of the date the increase occurs, as in table 9-8.

Table 9-8. Fair Value of the Additional Shares

Component 1 (discount)	$1.80	(15% of current fair market value)
Component 2 (look-back)	$2.00	(85% of in-the-money call option)*
Component 3 (additional shares)	$.05	(15% of underwater put option)*
ESPP option fair value	$3.85	
Additional shares to be purchased	5882	($50,000 added contributions divided by $8.50 price)
Incremental fair value	$22,646	

9.6.7 Decreases in Contribution Rates and Withdrawals

Under FAS 123(R), the employer is not required to recognize expense for shares that are forfeited under an ESPP. Therefore, if a plan participant terminates his or her employment and consequently forfeits the right to participate in the ESPP, the shares that the employee would have been able to purchase had he or she not terminated are not treated as a cost to the employer.

Employees' decisions to withdraw from the plan or reduce their rates of contribution, however, are not considered forfeitures because these decisions are voluntary. Just as an employer must recognize expense for an employee stock option that expires unexercised, the employer must recognize expense for the ESPP as if the withdrawals and decreases in contribution rates had not occurred. The shares that the employees could have purchased, if they had not withdrawn or decreased their contribution rate, are treated as a cost to the employer.

9.6.8 A Bit of Accounting History

Before FAS 123(R), employers were permitted to choose whether to account for their stock compensation plans, including their ESPP, under the original FAS 123 or APB Opinion No. 25.

Issued in October 1972, APB Opinion No. 25, *Accounting for Stock Issued to Employees* ("APB 25") first established the principles that employers would apply to account for stock compensation programs. Just as under FAS 123(R), APB 25 provides that employees do not have to recognize compensation expense in connection with stock issued through "noncompensatory plans." Under APB 25, however, the conditions required for a plan to receive noncompensatory were significantly less onerous than under FAS 123(R). To be noncompensatory under APB 25, the plan had to meet the following conditions:

1. Substantially all full-time employees meeting limited employment qualifications must be allowed to participate (employees owning a specific percentage of the outstanding stock and executives may be excluded).

2. Stock must be offered to eligible employees equally or based on a uniform percentage of salary or wages (the plan may limit the number of shares of stock that an employee may purchase through the plan).

3. The time permitted for exercise of an option or purchase right must be limited to a reasonable period, generally presumed to be no longer than 27 months.

4. The discount from the market price of the stock cannot be greater than would be reasonable in an offer of stock to stockholders or others, generally presumed to be no greater than 15%.

APB 25 goes on to say that "an example of a noncompensatory plan is the "statutory" employee stock purchase plan that qualifies under Section 423 of the Internal Revenue Code." As a result, virtually all Section 423 ESPPs were treated as noncompensatory, and therefore did not result in any compensation expense, under APB 25.

In 1995, the FASB issued the first version of FAS 123. The treatment of ESPPs under the original FAS 123 was substantively the same as their treatment under FAS 123(R). FAS 123 was intended to supersede APB 25 in its entirety but, for political reasons, FASB was unable to require this. Instead, FAS 123 originally permitted employers to elect to adopt its provisions or to continue to rely on APB 25 and simply disclose, on a pro forma basis, the impact FAS 123 would have on their financial statements, if adopted. Most employers elected to remain under APB 25 with only pro forma disclosure of the FAS 123 impact. It was not until the issuance of FAS 123(R) in 2004 that FASB was able to require employers to adopt the new standard. Now all employers are required to account for their stock compensation programs, including their ESPPs, under FAS 123(R).

Employers were permitted to adopt FAS 123(R) using a modified prospective approach or with retrospective restatement. Those employers that adopted using the modified prospective approach did not restate fiscal periods ending before they adopted FAS 123(R) for the new standard. Thus, these employers may be continuing to rely on APB 25 to account for their ESPP in these historical periods.

9.7 Additional Considerations

9.7.1 Shareholder Approval

Section 423 of the Code requires that an ESPP be approved by company shareholders within 12 months of its adoption by the board of directors. No further shareholder approval is required unless the company amends the plan to increase the number of shares available for issuance or changes the designation of corporations whose employees may participate in the plan (unless the plan provides that such designations may be made from time to time).

9.7.2 Federal Securities Law

For public companies, shares issued under an ESPP are typically registered with the Securities and Exchange Commission (SEC) on Form S-8. Registration of shares by means of Form S-8 is relatively straightforward. Form S-8 consists of two parts, a prospectus and an information statement. The prospectus is intended to be distributed to participants but is not filed with the SEC. The information statement, which must be filed with the SEC, largely consists of documents, such as annual financial reports, that have been prepared by the company for other purposes and are incorporated in the S-8 by reference.

As a result of the 1996 changes to Rule 16b-3 of the Securities and Exchange Act of 1934, ESPP transactions (other than sales of shares purchased under any ESPP) are exempt from Section 16(b) of the Exchange Act (i.e., the short-swing profit rules). Transactions under any ESPP are exempt from the reporting requirements of Section 16(b) as well.

APPENDIX
Illustration of Section 423 ESPP Tax Treatment

The following examples illustrate the federal income tax consequences when a participant sells stock purchased under a Section 423 ESPP. They assume a purchase price of 85% of the lower of (1) market value on the enrollment date or (2) market value on the purchase date.

Example 1—Qualifying Disposition: The participant sells stock one or more years after the purchase date *and* two or more years after the enrollment date (i.e., a qualifying disposition). The tax consequences at a variety of sale prices are shown below:

Assumptions:

Enrollment date market value	$ 5.00	$ 5.00	$ 5.00	$ 5.00	$ 5.00	$ 5.00
Purchase date market value	10.00	10.00	10.00	4.00	4.00	4.00
Purchase price	4.25	4.25	4.25	3.40	3.40	3.40
Sale price	12.00	8.00	2.50	10.00	3.75	3.00
Actual gain (loss)	$ 7.75	$ 3.75	$ (1.75)	$ 6.60	$ .35	$ (.40)

Tax Consequences:

Ordinary income (the lesser of 15% discount at enrollment date or sale price minus purchase price)	$ .75	$ .75	$ —	$ .75	$ .35	$ —
Long-term capital gain (or loss) (sale price, less ordinary income, less purchase price)	$ 7.00	$ 3.00	$ (1.75)	$ 5.85	$ —	$ (.40)

Example 2—Disqualifying Disposition: The participant sells stock within one year after the purchase date or within two years after the enrollment date (i.e., a disqualifying disposition). The tax consequences at a variety of sale prices are shown below:

Assumptions:

Enrollment date market value	$ 5.00	$ 5.00	$ 5.00	$ 5.00	$ 5.00	$ 5.00
Purchase date market value	10.00	10.00	10.00	4.00	4.00	4.00
Purchase price	4.25	4.25	4.25	3.40	3.40	3.40
Sale price	12.00	8.00	2.50	10.00	3.75	3.00
Actual gain (loss)	$ 7.75	$ 3.75	$ (1.75)	$ 6.60	$ .35	$ (.40)

Tax Consequences:

Ordinary income (market value on date of purchase minus purchase price)	$ 5 .75	$ 5.75	$ 5.75	$ .60	$ .60	$ .60
Capital gain (or loss)* (sale price, minus ordinary income, minus purchase price)	$ 2.00	$ (2.00)	$ (7.50)	$ 6.00	$ (.25)	$(1.00)

*If shares are held for more than one year, the capital gain or loss is long-term.

A Layperson's Glossary of Employee Stock Plan Terminology

Alisa J. Baker

A S WITH ANY SPECIALIZED field, the world of employee stock plans has its own vernacular. Stock options and related plans are governed, as well as influenced, by a wide array of laws, regulations, rules, and standards, including tax laws and concepts, securities laws, and accounting principles. Following is a glossary of many of the more commonly used words and phrases in this field. All references to the "Code" in this glossary refer to the Internal Revenue Code of 1986, as amended (which itself is defined below). Any other abbreviations used in the definitions are also defined.

10% Owner

In general: Beneficial owner of more than 10% of a class of equity securities of an issuer that is registered under Section 12 of the Exchange Act.

For ISOs: An employee who, at the time of grant, owns stock possessing more than 10% of the total combined voting power of all classes of stock of the employer corporation or of its parent or subsidiary corporation. Under Section 422(b)(6) of the Code, such an employee is not eligible to receive an ISO unless, as provided in Section 422(c)(5) of the Code, at the time such option is granted the option price is at least 110% of the fair market value of the company's stock subject to the option and such option by its terms is not exercisable after the expiration of five years from the date such option is granted.

Acceleration

With respect to unvested shares, speeding up the vesting schedule (that is, decreasing the period over which vesting restrictions lapse).

Administrator

See "Plan Administrator."

Affiliate

Under Rule 144, a person who directly or indirectly controls, is controlled by, or is under common control with the issuer. As a rule, executive officers and directors are deemed to be affiliates. Affiliates are subject to certain limitations as to volume and timing with respect to sale of unregistered (restricted) stock of the issuer.

Alternative Minimum Tax (AMT)

In general: "Alternative" method of computing federal income tax that recaptures certain preferences and adjustments that are otherwise excluded from gross income.

For ISOs : The difference, if any, between the option price and the fair market value of the stock of the corporation on the date of exercise of an ISO is an AMT adjustment, and therefore—although it is otherwise excluded from gross income in the year of exercise—it will be added back when computing alternative minimum taxable income (AMTI). If an ISO produces AMT, it may result in a tax credit against ordinary income tax in future years.

AMEX (American Stock Exchange)

The second largest organized stock exchange, on which corporate securities are traded. Because the listing requirements of this exchange are considered to be less stringent than those of the New York Stock Exchange, the exchange generally trades the securities of small-to-medium-sized corporations.

Annual Meeting

A meeting of a corporation's directors, officers, and shareholders/stockholders, held for the purpose of communicating the operating and financial results of the business for the prior fiscal year, the corporation's prospects for the future, and major decisions of management, and for deciding matters requiring the approval of the corporation's shareholders/stockholders. Generally, the election of the corporation's board of directors occurs at the annual meeting. Shareholders/stockholders who are not able to physically attend the annual meeting may vote on the election of directors and other matters brought before the meeting by submitting a proxy before the meeting authorizing a third party to vote their shares of stock.

Anti-dilution Adjustment

A change to the terms, conditions, and/or price of a security to prevent a diminution in value as the result of a change in the capital structure of a corporation. Typically, an employee stock option plan will provide for an appropriate adjustment in the number and kind of securities subject to the plan and to all outstanding employee stock options in the event of a change in the capitalization of the corporation.

APB 25

Accounting Principles Board (APB) Opinion No. 25, issued in 1972, set out the accounting standards for both compensatory and noncompensatory options before FAS 123(R), which supersedes it.

Authorized but Unissued

The difference between the number of securities of a given class authorized for issuance under a corporation's charter documents and the number of securities of that class that are issued and outstanding.

Available for Grant

The incremental difference between the number of shares of stock authorized for issuance under a stock option plan and the number of shares already subject to option. Cancelled shares that are added back to the plan and any increase in the number of shares available for issuance pursuant to the plan are included in the calculation of shares "available for grant."

Backdating

The practice (whether or not fraudulent) of setting an option exercise price that is less than fair market value on the grant date. The term "backdating" has been used to describe practices as varied as intentional discounting (i.e., intentionally stating that the option was granted on a date different than the actual grant date), misdating (unintentionally stating the incorrect grant date price), "spring-loading" (granting options before good news breaks), "bullet-dodging" (granting options after bad news breaks), "forward-dating" (approving options with a grant date set after approval), and 30-day pricing (approving options with grant price to be set at the average or best price in a 30-day window). Backdating may raise accounting, SEC disclosure, and tax issues (particularly under Section 409A of the Code).

Basis

See "Tax Basis."

Beneficial Owner

Under the Exchange Act generally: a person who, directly or indirectly, through any contract, arrangement, understanding, relationship or otherwise, has or shares voting power (which includes the power to vote or to direct the voting of) a security and/or investment power (which includes the power to dispose of or to direct the disposition of) such security.

For Section 16: a person who, directly or indirectly, through any contract, arrangement, understanding, relationship, or other means has or shares a direct or indirect pecuniary interest in equity securities. Securities are "beneficially owned" for these purposes if the holder is entitled to the economic benefits resulting from a transaction in them, whether or not the holder is the record, or registered, owner of the securities.

Blackout Period

The period, as determined by a corporation, during which the securities of the corporation may not be sold by certain designated individuals, typically the corporation's insiders. Generally, the period runs from some predetermined time following the release of the corporation's quarterly or annual financial results until 24 to 48 hours following the release of the subsequent period's financial results. Also, a period during which the ability of participants or beneficiaries in a corporation's pension plan to direct or diversify assets credited to their accounts, to obtain loans from the plan, or to obtain distributions from the plan is temporarily suspended, limited, or restricted.

Black-Scholes Option Pricing Model

A mathematical formula used for valuing employee stock options that considers such factors as the volatility of returns on the underlying securities, the risk-free interest rate, the expected dividend rate, the relationship of the option price to the price of the underlying securities, and the expected option life. Developed in 1973 by three economists, the model was originally created to value options traded on European commodity exchanges.

Blue Sky Laws

State securities laws governing the purchase and sale of securities. The phrase "blue sky" originates from a federal case that described such laws as aimed against "speculative schemes which hold no more basis than so many feet of blue sky."

Board of Directors

A group of individuals elected by a corporation's shareholders to set the policies and oversee the affairs (but not the day-to-day management) of the corporation.

Broker/Brokerage Firm

An individual or a company that acts as an intermediary between a buyer and seller of securities. A broker receives compensation, in the form of a commission, for assisting in or effecting the purchase or sale of securities. A broker is "registered" with the NASD and the exchange on which the securities are traded. Brokers are also regulated under federal and state securities laws.

Cancellation

In the context of an employee stock option plan, a transaction (usually triggered by a specific event, such as an optionee's termination of employment) in which an outstanding employee stock option is rescinded and the unexercised shares of stock subject to such option are returned to the pool of shares reserved for issuance under the plan.

Capital Asset

Property that meets the definition in Section 1221 of the Code, as follows: property held by a taxpayer, other than (1) stock in trade, inventory or property held primarily for sale to customers in the ordinary course of business, (2) real property or depreciable property used in a trade or business, (3) a copyright, a literary, musical, or artistic composition or similar property of a taxpayer who created such property, (4) accounts or notes receivable acquired in the ordinary course of a trade or business, or (5) publications of the United States government received at a discount. In general, securities (including stock purchased upon exercise of an option) are a capital asset.

Capital Gain

The increase in value, or profit, realized from the sale or exchange of a capital asset; that is, the excess of the proceeds received from the transaction over the basis of the asset. Capital gains can be short-term (where the capital asset was held for one year or less) or long-term (where the capital asset was held for more than one year). Generally, long-term capital gains are taxed at rates more favorable than those applicable to ordinary income.

Capital Loss

The decrease in value realized from the sale or exchange of a capital asset; that is, the excess of the basis of the asset over the proceeds received from the transaction.

Capitalization

The total value of all securities that have been issued by a corporation. A corporation's capitalization may include both equity securities and debt securities.

Cashless Exercise

Form of stock option exercise in which the option price for the number of shares of stock being purchased is paid with consideration other than cash. Common cashless exercise methods include stock swap, net exercise, delivery of a promissory note, and (broker-assisted) same-day-sale transaction. Frequently used to refer to an arrangement between a corporation and a third party, such as a securities brokerage firm or a financial institution, whereby the third party will provide funds, on a temporary basis, to an employee to exercise an employee stock option, immediately upon which some or all of the shares of stock acquired upon exercise of the employee stock option will be sold to repay the funds advanced to initiate the transaction.

Change in Capitalization

An adjustment to the capital structure of a corporation—for example, due to a stock dividend, stock split, or reverse stock split—that results in either an increase in the number of outstanding securities, with a corresponding reduction in the value of each security, or a decrease in the number of outstanding securities, with a corresponding increase in the value of each security.

California Commissioner's Rules

Regulations implementing the California Securities Act of 1968.

Change in Control

A transaction that alters the ownership of a corporation, including a merger, consolidation, stock sale, or asset sale. With respect to options, events that constitute a change in control are generally defined in the plan.

Cliff Vesting

Form of vesting in which an installment of shares vests on a single date rather than ratably over a period of months. For example, for a four-year option, a typical cliff vesting schedule might provide that 25% of the total shares vest on the first anniversary of the grant date, with the remainder vesting monthly over the following three years of employment.

Code

The Internal Revenue Code of 1986, with such modifications, revisions, and additions as are made from time to time.

Collateral

Property given as security for a loan (e.g., a promissory note).

Common Stock

Basic unit of corporate ownership interest that typically confers on the holder of the security the right to vote, select directors, receive dividends, and share in the residual assets upon the dissolution or winding up of the business. Unlike preferred stock, common stock has no preference to dividends or to any distribution of assets by the corporation.

Compensation Committee

Committee of the board of directors that evaluates and approves executive compensation (including equity compensation plans).

Compensation Expense (for Equity)

For financial reporting purposes, the "cost" recognized by a corporation on its financial statements with respect to the issuance of its securities in connection with a stock-based compensation plan or arrangement. Under FAS No. 123(R), the amount of compensation expense associated with an employee stock option represents the "fair value" of the employee stock option calculated as of the date of grant of the option using a mathematical option pricing model (such as the Black-Scholes Option Pricing Model).

Compensation Income (for Equity)

Gross income recognized and taxed as ordinary income by a service provider in connection with the transfer of equity from the service recipient (e.g., exercise of an NSO, disqualifying disposition of an ISO, or purchase or receipt of restricted stock).

Confirmation of Exercise

A written statement issued by a corporation to an optionee setting forth specific information about a stock option exercise transaction. In the case of an exercise of an ISO, this statement is sometimes used to provide the information required by Section 6039 of the Code to be provided to an employee.

Constructive Receipt

For tax purposes, income has been constructively received (and is subject to taxation) at the first time that the taxpayer has an unrestricted right to receive such property, regardless of whether or not he chooses to do so. Note that Section 409A of the Code essentially treats any "nonqualified deferred compensation" that does not satisfy specific requirements to be constructively received as of the date the taxpayer had a legal right to the payment. See also Section 83 of the Code, which takes the same concept and applies it to property.

Corporate Tax Deduction (for Equity)

The amount realized on exercise of an option (or other compensatory transfer of equity) that is deductible on the corporate income tax return as a trade or business expense under Section 162 of the Code (subject to the application of Section 162(m)). Generally, the amount of deductible compensation expense is equal to the amount of compensation income recognized by the employee for federal income tax purposes.

Corporation

A legal entity that is separate from, and independent of, the persons who formed and/or own the business. A corporation possesses the attributes of (1) limited liability (that is, its shareholders/stockholders are not personally liable for the debts of the corporation), (2) centralized management (that is, responsibility for managing the business and affairs of the corporation resides with designated directors and officers rather than with the owners, the shareholders/stockholders), (3) continuity of life (that is, the corporation has a perpetual existence that is not affected by the death or departure of its shareholders/stockholders), and (4) free transferability of interest (that is, the shareholders/stockholders have the ability, subject to any contractual limitations, to freely transfer or otherwise dispose of their shares of stock without affecting the corporation's status).

Derivative Security

A security that takes, or "derives," its value from another instrument. For purposes of Section 16 of the Exchange Act, a derivative security includes any option, warrant, convertible security, stock appreciation right or similar right with an exercise or conversion privilege at a price related to an equity security, or similar securities with a value derived from the value of an equity security.

Director

An individual elected by the shareholders/stockholders of a corporation to serve on the corporation's board of directors who performs the functions of a director set forth in the corporation's charter documents and bylaws.

Discount Stock Option

A stock option granted with an option price that is less than the fair market value of the corporation's stock on the date of grant. By virtue of the requirement under Section 422 (b)(4) of the Code that an ISO must have an option price that is not less than the fair market value of the corporation's stock on the date of grant, a discount stock option will necessarily be a non-qualified stock option. Under FAS 123(R), discounting that is disclosed properly at the time of grant is less of an issue than it was under APB 25. However, undisclosed discounting may raise serious SEC disclosure issues. Discounting in general may cause tax issues under Section 409A of the Code.

Disposition

Sale, gift, or other transfer of property (such as shares of stock) by a person.

Disqualifying Disposition

Disposition of shares of stock acquired upon the exercise of an ISO or Section 423 ESPP option before meeting the statutory holding period set out in Section 421 of the Code of period of one year from exercise and two years from grant. In the year of the disqualifying disposition, the employee recognizes compensation income equal to the difference, if any, between the option price and the fair market value of the stock of the corporation on the date of exercise (or, if unvested at the time of exercise, at the time of vesting). Any post-exercise appreciation recognized by the employee as a result of the disposition is taxable as capital gain. Under Section 422(c)(2) of the Code, the amount included as ordinary income on a disqualifying disposition will be the lesser of the actual gain at sale or the spread on exercise (or vesting).

Early Exercise

The exercise of an option before the time that the shares issued pursuant to such option have vested under the option's vesting schedule.

EDGAR (Electronic Data Gathering, Analysis, and Retrieval System)

The automated computer system developed and implemented by the SEC for the filing of registration statements, periodic reports, and other filings mandated under the federal securities laws by issuers registered under Section 12 of the Exchange Act.

Employee

An individual who performs services for an employer, subject to the control of the employer as to the type of work and manner of performance. Employee status is distinct from that of an independent contractor. For income tax purposes, withholding of income taxes on wages applies only to employees.

Employee Stock Option

See "Option" or "Stock Option."

Employee Stock Option Agreement

See "Option Agreement."

Employee Stock Option Plan

See "Option Plan."

ESPP (Employee Stock Purchase Plan)

Type of stock option plan that provides for ongoing stock purchases by employees pursuant to a subscription agreement. May be a tax-qualified statutory option plan under Section 423 of the Code, or may result in nonstatutory option treatment under Section 83. Tax-qualified plans generally include a discount from market price, determined as of either the first day or the last day of the applicable exercise period. See "Section 423 Plan."

Employer

Person who directs and controls the performance of services by an employee.

Employment (or "Payroll") Taxes

Generally, a term used to describe taxes imposed under FICA and FUTA. These taxes are assessed against employers and, in the case of FICA taxes, employees with respect to the wages paid to such employees.

Equity

Term that refers to an ownership interest in a corporation. Equity also represents the amount of capital invested by the shareholders/stockholders plus the retained earnings of the business. The term is also used to denote the capital stock of a corporation.

Equity Compensation

Use of equity (rather than or in addition to cash) to compensate a service provider. The most common forms of equity compensation include restricted stock, stock options, and "phantom" stock.

Equity Security

A stock or similar security, or a security that is convertible, with or without consideration, into such a security, which provides an equity interest in the corporation.

Evergreen Provision

A replenishment feature in a stock plan that automatically increases at regular intervals the number of shares reserved under the plan.

Exchange Act

See "Securities Exchange Act of 1934."

Exercise

Purchase of stock pursuant to an option.

Exercise Date

The date on which an employee stock option is exercised.

Exercise Notice

Form completed and submitted by an optionee to the issuer that provides notice of the optionee's intention to exercise an option. Generally, an exercise notice requires the optionee to identify the option being exercised, indicate the number of shares of stock being purchased, provide payment of the aggregate option price for the shares of stock being purchased in a form permitted under the option agreement, make certain representations to the corporation concerning the optionee's investment intent, and agree to certain restrictions imposed on the shares of stock.

Exercise Price

The consideration in money or property that, pursuant to the terms of an employee stock option agreement, is the price at which the shares of stock subject to an employee stock option may be purchased. The exercise price is typically expressed on a per-share basis. Also referred to "option price" or "strike price."

Expiration Date

The last date on which an employee stock option may be exercised by an optionee. This date is typically set forth in the option agreement for the employee stock option and usually ranges from five to ten years following the date of grant of the employee stock option. Also refers to the date on which an employee stock option plan expires.

Fair Market Value

For tax purposes, the value of a share of stock on any given date. In a privately held company, fair market value is determined by the corporation's board of directors. In a public company, fair market value is determined with reference to the price posted on the applicable stock market (generally this is closing price, but it depends on how the plan was drawn up).

Fair Value

For accounting purposes, the value of an option determined in accordance with FAS 123(R), using a pricing model such as Black-Scholes or a lattice model.

FASB (Financial Accounting Standards Board)

A private sector organization recognized by the Securities and Exchange Commission as the source for generally accepted accounting principles for corporations that offer and sell securities in the United States.

FAS 123

Statement of Financial Accounting Standards No. 123, "Accounting for Stock-Based Compensation." FAS 123 requires companies to place a "fair value" on employee stock options not otherwise covered by APB 25 as of the date of grant and to either reflect such value as a charge to earnings during the service period or disclose the amount that would have been charged in a footnote to the company's financial statements.

FAS 123(R)

Statement of Financial Accounting Standards No. 123 (revised 2004), "Share-Based Payment." The Financial Accounting Standards Board's revision of its FAS 123 accounting standard. Mandates that compensation expense for options and awards granted to employees is determined at grant and is generally not adjusted for subsequent events (with the exception of forfeitures), provided that the option or award can only be settled in stock.

FICA: Federal Insurance Contributions Act

A series of employment taxes imposed on employees and employers with respect to employee wages, including Social Security and Medicare taxes.

FUTA: Federal Unemployment Tax Act

An employment tax imposed on employers with respect to employee wages.

Fiscal Year

The annual accounting period for a corporation. A fiscal year is a period of 12 consecutive months. It frequently coincides with the calendar year, but can conclude at the end of a different month. For example, a fiscal year can run from October 1 to September 30.

Form 3

The initial ownership report for directors, officers, beneficial owners of more than 10% of a class of an issuer's registered equity securities, and any other person subject to Section 16 of the Exchange Act. A Form 3 requires information on the number of non-derivative securities and derivative securities beneficially owned at the time the reporting person becomes subject to Section 16 and, except in the case of an issuer's first registration of a class of equity securities pursuant to Section 12 of the Exchange Act, must be filed with the SEC within 10 days of that date. A Form 3 must be filed with the SEC even if the reporting person does not own any securities of the issuer at the time the filing is required.

Form 4

Change in beneficial ownership report for directors, officers, beneficial owners of more than 10% of a class of an issuer's registered equity securities, and any other person subject to Section 16 of the Exchange Act. A Form 4 requires information on any change in beneficial ownership of non-derivative securities and derivative securities by a reporting person that is not eligible for deferred reporting. With limited exceptions, a Form 4 must be filed with the SEC within two business days after the date of execution of the transaction that results in a reportable change in beneficial ownership.

Form 5

Annual change in beneficial ownership report for directors, officers, beneficial owners of more than 10% of a class of an issuer's registered equity securities, and any other person subject to Section 16 of the Exchange Act. A Form 5 requires information on holdings and changes in beneficial ownership by a reporting person of non-derivative securities and derivative securities that are exempt from current reporting. A Form 5 must be filed with the SEC within 45 days after the end of the issuer's fiscal year.

Form 1099

Information report that must be provided to the service provider by the service recipient with respect to any non-wage compensation income earned or received during the taxable year covered by the report.

Form 10-K

An annual disclosure report for issuers subject to the reporting requirements of Section 13(a) or 15(d) of the Exchange Act. The report contains information about the business and management of the issuer, legal proceedings involving the issuer, management compensation, and the issuer's latest audited financial statements. Form 10-K must be filed within 60 days after the end of an issuer's fiscal year.

Form 10-Q

A quarterly report for issuers subject to the reporting requirements of Section 13(a) or 15(d) to the Exchange Act. The report contains information about the business and management of the issuer, and other specified information. Form 10-Q must be filed within 35 days after the end of an issuer's first three fiscal quarters.

Form S-8

Form of registration statement under the 1933 Act that may be used by issuers subject to the reporting requirements of Section 13(a) or 15(d) of the Exchange Act to register securities issuable to participants in an employee benefit plan, such as an employee stock option plan.

GAAP (Generally Accepted Accounting Principles)

Substantive rules for the practice of accounting as established by the body of opinions and decisions issued by the FASB.

Grace Period

Period of time provided under an option agreement for the exercise of an employee stock option following termination of the optionee's employment. Typically, this period of time ranges from 30 days until the expiration of the original option term, may vary depending upon the reason for the termination of employment, and is limited to the exercise of shares of stock that were vested as of the date of termination.

Grant Date

The date upon which an employee stock option is formally approved by the company's board of directors. The grant gives rise to certain contractual rights and obligations on the part of the optionee and the corporation.

Golden Parachute

Under Section 280G of the Code, the value of certain compensation-related benefits (including options) receive by an employee contingent upon a change in control.

Holding Period

For tax purposes: The length of time stock must be held before transfer for any gain to be eligible for capital gain treatment. For statutory option purposes, the period is one year from exercise and two years from grant (set out in Section 421 of the Code); for general capital gains purposes, the period is one year from the date of transfer of capital property (Sections 1221–1223 of the Code). The tax holding period begins on the date the property is first transferred (regardless of whether purchased with a note or subject to contractual restrictions).

For Rule 144 purposes: The length of time unregistered stock must be held before transfer. If purchase is with a note, the securities holding period begins only when the note is paid off or fully collateralized with property other than the underlying stock.

IASB (International Accounting Standards Board)

Voluntary global accounting standards-setting organization whose member nations include the U.S., Australia, Canada, France, Germany, Japan, New Zealand, and the U.K. IASB standards are intended to establish GAAP on an international basis.

Immaculate or Net Exercise

An exercise technique that permits the optionee to buy shares with no cash down by agreeing to allow the issuer to withhold (at exercise) that number of shares with a value equal to the full exercise price. The optionee receives only the balance of the shares and pays ordinary income tax on the full exercise price, which is equivalent to the difference between the amount paid for the withheld shares (zero) and their fair market value at exercise.

Income Tax Regulations

Rules promulgated by the Internal Revenue Service implementing and interpreting the statutory provisions of the Code, which have the force of law. Congressional authority for the issuance of regulations is set forth in Section 7805 of the Code.

Independent Contractor

A service provider who is not an employee.

Indexed Stock Option

A stock option with an option price that is periodically adjusted in relation to a market, industry or peer group performance (such as the Standard & Poor's 500). Economically, for the stock option to have value to the optionee, the corporation's stock must outperform the designated performance indicator. While it is possible that the stated option price can be decreased if the designated performance indicator declines over the option term, many employee stock option plans do not permit the option price to drop below the fair market value of the corporation's stock on the date of grant. Since the option price for this type of employee stock option changes over time, for financial reporting purposes it is considered a "variable" award that results in periodic compensation expense until the option price is finally fixed.

Insider

A general term referring to persons who, by virtue of their positions within a corporation, have access to confidential information about the corporation. Frequently used to denote the directors, officers, beneficial owners of more than 10% of a class of an issuer's registered equity securities, and persons otherwise subject to Section 16 of the Exchange Act.

IPO (Initial Public Offering)

A corporation's first offering of securities to the general public under a registration statement prepared and filed with the Securities and Exchange Commission in accordance with the 1933 Act. The offering must also be made in compliance with the requirements of the securities laws of the various states where the securities will be offered for sale and sold.

Insider Trading

A person's wrongful use or wrongful communication, whether directly or indirectly, of confidential information to purchase or sell securities.

In-the-Money

Term used to describe an employee stock option where the current fair market value of the shares of stock subject to the option is greater than the exercise price.

Internal Revenue Code (the "Code")

The Internal Revenue Code of 1986, as amended; the key federal statute providing for the taxation of individuals, corporations, and other persons.

IRS (Internal Revenue Service)

An agency of the federal government, under the supervision of the Department of the Treasury, that is responsible for administering the federal tax laws, including the Code.

ISO (Incentive Stock Option)

An employee stock option that meets the requirements of Section 422(b) of the Code and, therefore, qualifies for the preferential tax treatment under Section 421 of the Code. Generally, an ISO does not give rise to federal income tax consequences for the employee either at the time of grant or at exercise. Instead, the employee is subject to taxation at the time of disposition of the shares of stock acquired upon the exercise of the ISO.

ISO Amount Limitation

A dollar limitation to the amount of stock that can receive preferential tax treatment under an ISO grant. As set forth in Section 422(d) of the Code, to the extent that the aggregate fair market value of the shares of stock with respect to which ISOs are exercisable for the first time by an employee during any calendar year (under all plans of the employee's employer corporation and its parent and subsidiary corporations) exceeds $100,000, such stock options shall be treated as non-qualified stock options to the extent of the amounts in excess of $100,000. For purposes of applying this rule, options are to be taken into account in the order in which they were granted. In addition, for purposes of applying this rule, the fair market value of any shares of stock is to be determined as of the time the ISO with respect to such shares of stock was granted.

Issuer

A corporation that issues securities.

Leave of Absence

A temporary, approved absence from employment. For purposes of applying the ISO rules, a leave of absence is not considered an interruption of the employment relationship if the leave is shorter than 91 days or the employee's right to reemployment is guaranteed by statute or contract.

Legend

Statement printed on a stock certificate to indicate that the securities represented by the certificate are subject to limitations or restrictions on transfer. Generally, used to denote that the securities were issued in a private placement and, therefore, are "restricted securities" and "legended stock" for purposes of the federal securities laws. May also reflect a contractual restriction that has been placed on the securities by the issuer as a condition to their original issuance.

"Lock-Up" Restrictions

Transfer restrictions imposed by the underwriters of a public offering of securities on the directors, officers, principal shareholders, and, possibly, others associated with the issuer in order to maintain an orderly trading market in the issuer's securities.

Lattice Models

Models for determining the fair value of employee stock options that use a decision-tree approach of possible future outcomes. A value is arrived at based on the weighted probability of all possible future outcomes. There are many different kinds of lattice models including binomial models and trinomial models, among many others.

Mark to Market

For variable award accounting purposes, a measurement of option expense taken periodically over the life of the option (i.e., from date of grant/modification until the option is either exercised or is no longer outstanding). Under APB 25, variable award expense is measured based on the difference between the exercise price and its fair market value, with subsequent changes to fair market value marked to market. Under FAS 123, variable award expense is measured as the difference between fair value and the amount (if any) paid on date of grant, with subsequent changes to fair value marked to market.

Measurement Date

For accounting purposes, the first date on which both the number and the price of shares subject to an option are known. The measurement date for a fixed award is the date of grant, while the measurement date for a variable award is the date of vesting (or expiration).

Modification

For purposes of fixed vs. variable award accounting: Such changes as cancellation/reissuances of options, extensions/renewals of option terms, and the addition of accelerated vesting (including acceleration at the company's discretion). The modification of an already outstanding fixed option will change treatment for unexercised shares from fixed to variable.

For purposes of a statutory option: A beneficial change to the terms of an option (including by way of example, the number of shares, an extension of the term, pricing, or the method of financing). Under Section 424 of the Code, the underlying option will be disqualified from statutory option treatment unless it is treated as a new option as of the date of the modification.

National Association of Securities Dealers, Inc. (NASD)

A self-regulatory organization subject to the Exchange Act, comprised of brokers and dealers in the over-the-counter (OTC) securities market. The NASD was established in the late 1930s to regulate the over-the-counter securities market.

NASDAQ

A computerized network showing quotations and transaction information with respect to securities traded in the over-the-counter market which meet the size and trading volume requirements to be quoted on the system. NASDAQ tends to reflect prices for the more active OTC-traded securities.

Net Exercise

See "Immaculate Exercise."

New York Stock Exchange (NYSE)

The oldest organized stock exchange.

No-Action Letter

Interpretive letter issued by the SEC to a specific requestor, indicating the SEC staff's advice regarding the application of specific securities forms or rules; available to the public.

Non-approved Plan

A stock option plan that has not been approved by the shareholders.

NQSO, NSO (Nonstatutory [or Nonqualified] Stock Option)

A stock option that does not satisfy the requirements of a statutory stock option under the Code. The spread (if any) on exercise of an NSO is includable in ordinary income and subject to tax under Section 83 of the Code.

Non-Recourse Loan

Term used to describe a loan or other obligation that does not provide for personal liability against the debtor. In the event of a default on the obligation, the creditor is limited to recovery on the collateral provided for in the loan.

Nontransferability Restriction

Term used to describe a restriction imposed on a security that precludes its transfer or conveyance to a third party.

Offering Period

With respect to an ESPP, the period starting with the grant or offering date and ending with the exercise date.

Officer

Corporate officials responsible for managing the day-to-day operations of a corporation. For purposes of Section 16 of the Exchange Act, an issuer's president, principal financial officer, principal accounting officer (or if there is no such accounting officer, the controller), any vice-president of the issuer in charge of a principal business unit, division or function, any other officer who performs a policy-making function or any other person who performs similar policy-making functions for the issuer.

Option/Stock Option

A contractual right granted to an individual to purchase a specified number of shares of stock of the granting corporation at a specified price for a specified period of time. As set forth in the regulations to Section 83 of the Code, the term "option" includes the right or privilege of an individual to purchase stock from a corporation by virtue of an offer of the corporation continuing for a stated period of time, whether or not irrevocable, to sell such stock at a pre-determined price, such individual being under no obligation to purchase. Such a right or privilege, when granted, must be evidenced in writing. The individual who has such right or privilege is referred to as the "optionee."

Option /Stock Option Agreement

A written contract setting forth the terms and conditions of an employee stock option grant. While no particular form of words is necessary, the written agreement should express, among other things, an offer to sell at the option price and the period of time during which the offer shall remain open. Typically, the written agreement also contains the complete name of the individual receiving the stock option, the effective date of the stock option, the type of stock option granted, such as ISO or NSO, the number of shares of stock covered by the option, the option price, and the vesting schedule for the shares of stock covered by the option.

Option Date

See "Grant Date."

Option/Stock Option Plan

A formal program adopted by a corporation, often in writing, that provides for the grant of employee stock options to one or more individuals upon the terms and conditions set forth in the plan document and the issuance of shares of stock of the corporation upon the exercise of such stock options.

Option Price

See "Exercise Price."

Option Term

The period of time granted to an individual to exercise an employee stock option. Generally, the term of an employee stock option ranges from five to 10 years.

Optionee

The recipient of a stock option. In the case of an ISO, the optionee must be an employee of the granting corporation or a parent corporation or subsidiary corporation of the granting corporation at both the time of grant of the stock option and the time of exercise of the stock option (or have been an employee within three months of the date of exercise). In the case of an NSO, the optionee may be either an employee of the granting corporation or, if provided in the employee stock option plan, a non-employee (such as a non-employee director or a consultant or other independent contractor providing services to the granting corporation or a parent corporation or subsidiary corporation of the granting corporation.

One Million Dollar Cap

Under Section 162(m) of the Code, the maximum amount of certain kinds of compensation paid to "covered employees" that may be deducted by a publicly traded corporation.

Out-of-the-Money or Underwater

When the option price is greater than the current fair market value of the shares of stock subject to the stock option.

Outstanding Option

An employee stock option which has been formally granted by a corporation and not cancelled, exercised, or expired. The shares of stock underlying an employee stock option have their own status, which is affected by exercise and expiration of the stock option as well as cancellation.

Overhang

Used as a measure of dilution, this is the percentage of company stock represented by all potentially grantable shares under the plan. It is calculated by adding the total number of shares represented by outstanding, unexercised stock options to the number of additional shares available for grant and then dividing that sum by the total number of shares of common stock outstanding.

Over-the-Counter (OTC) Market

The public trading market for securities which are not traded on either the AMEX or the NYSE. It is composed of brokerage firms making a market and executing transactions in non-listed securities. The over-the-counter market operates primarily through telephone transmissions rather than through the auction-style market found at the exchanges.

Par Value

A dollar amount assigned to shares of stock by the corporation's charter documents. It may be used to compute the dollar accounting value of common shares on a corporation's balance sheet. Many corporations issue no-par stock. Par value has no relation to fair market value.

Parent Corporation

A corporation that owns a controlling interest in the securities of another corporation. For purposes of the ISO rules, any corporation (other than the employer corporation) in an unbroken chain of corporations ending with the employer corporation if, at the time of grant of the employee stock option, each of the corporations other than the employer corporation owns stock possessing 50% or more of the total combined voting power of all classes of stock in one of the other corporations in such chain.

Performance-Based Stock Option

An employee stock option granted with terms that provide that the stock option will be exercisable as to the shares of stock subject to the stock option only upon the attainment of one or more performance-based objectives (that is, objectives other than merely continued service with the corporation). For financial reporting purposes, a performance-based stock option is considered a "variable" award that results in a periodic compensation expense for the corporation until the stock option vests or is settled.

Plan Administrator

In general: An individual or committee of individuals authorized under an employee stock option plan to administer and carry out the objectives, purposes, terms, and conditions of an employee stock option plan. The plan administrator usually selects the individuals to whom stock option grants are to be made, determines the number of shares of stock to be covered by a particular grant, sets the option price at which the grant is made, approves the form or forms of written agreement to accompany each grant, and determines all other terms and conditions of the grant (consistent with the employee stock option plan). Typically, the plan administrator will have the power to establish, amend, and rescind rules and policies deemed necessary or appropriate for the proper administration of the employee stock option plan, to make all necessary determinations under the plan, to construe and interpret the provisions of the plan, and to amend or terminate the plan and, under certain circumstances, outstanding stock option grants. Often a corporation's board of directors will act as the administrator of the employee stock option plan or will delegate responsibility for administering the plan to a subcommittee of the board of directors.

For purposes of Section 16 of the Exchange Act: The plan administrator of an employee stock option plan of an issuer with a class of equity securities that has been registered under Section 12 of the Exchange Act will often be composed of individuals who qualify as "non-employee" directors for purposes of Rule 16b-3.

For purposes of Section 162(m) of the Code: The plan administrator of an employee stock option plan of a "publicly-held corporation" (as that term is defined under Section 162(m)(2)) must be comprised of individuals who qualify as "outside" directors (as that term is defined in the income tax regulations) in order for compensation to be eligible for the "performance-based compensation" exception to that provision.

Plan Expiration Date

The date after which shares of stock may no longer be granted, awarded, or issued pursuant to the terms and conditions of a stock plan.

Post-Termination Exercise Period

Period of time provided under an option agreement for the exercise of an employee stock option following termination of the optionee's employment. Typically, this period of time ranges from 30 days until the expiration of the original option term, may vary depending upon the reason for the termination of employment, and is limited to the exercise of shares of stock that were vested as of the date of termination.

PLR

See "Private Letter Ruling (PLR)."

Preferred Stock

Equity securities of a corporation that carry certain rights, preferences, and privileges superior to the common stock. Preferred stock generally receives an investment return at a specific rate whenever dividends are declared, and it has priority to the earnings and assets in the event of a sale or liquidation of the corporation before distributions may be made to the common shareholders.

Premium-Priced Stock Option

An employee stock option with an option price that is greater than the fair market value of the corporation's stock on the date of grant.

Private Letter Ruling (PLR)

A ruling issued by the IRS to a specific taxpayer, indicating the IRS interpretation of the tax law with respect to a stated set of facts. PLRs include private letter rulings and technical advice memoranda, and are available to the public, although they may not be cited as precedent and do not bind the IRS other than as to the taxpayer requesting the ruling Other forms of non-precedential IRS rulings include field service memoranda and IRS Chief Counsel Advisory memoranda.

Privately (or "Closely") Held Company

A corporation the securities of which are not publicly traded. Because there is no public market for the corporation's stock, the fair market value of the corporation's stock is typically based upon an independent appraisal conducted by one or more third parties or determined by the board of directors based on all of the relevant facts and circumstances.

Promissory Note

A written promise to pay a specified amount of money at a specified time in the future; may be unsecured or secured with collateral acceptable to the holder of the note. If recourse is not limited specifically to the underlying collateral, holder will be entitled to recourse against all of the assets of the maker.

Prospectus

A written document used as a selling piece in an offering of securities that contains certain specified information about the issuer, its business and financial condition, and the terms and conditions of, and risks associated with, the offering. A prospectus is a condensed version of the registration statement filed with the SEC in connection with the offering of securities.

Proxy

A grant of authority to vote the securities of another person. Also refers to the person authorized to vote the securities on behalf of another and/or the written document granting the authority.

Proxy Notice

A written notice to a shareholder/stockholder providing notification of the date, time, and place of a corporation's annual meeting of shareholders/stockholders and describing the matters to be submitted for the approval of the shareholders/stockholders at such meeting.

Proxy Solicitation

A request to be empowered to vote the securities of another person. Typically, a corporation will solicit the authority to vote the securities of its shareholders/stockholders at the corporation's annual meeting of shareholders/stockholders.

Proxy Statement

Solicitation materials relating to an issuer's annual meeting of shareholders, which must be delivered in advance of the meeting. Generally, these materials describe the agenda items for the meeting and contain certain specific information about the directors and principal shareholders/stockholders of the corporation, the compensation of management, and detailed information on proposals to be submitted to the shareholders/stockholders for approval.

Public Company

A company whose stock is publicly traded on a recognized stock exchange; subject to the registration, disclosure, and related rules enforced by the SEC.

Public Offering

An offering of securities to the general public under a registration statement prepared and filed with the SEC in accordance with the 1933 Act and any applicable blue sky laws.

Pyramid Exercise

A transaction in which an optionee exercises a minimum number of shares of stock underlying an employee stock option for cash and then immediately tenders such shares of stock back to the corporation at their appreciated value to exercise additional shares of stock under the stock option. Through a series of successive stock swaps in this manner, the optionee is able to fully exercise the shares of stock subject to the employee stock option. In this manner, the employee stock option can be fully exercised with a minimum cash investment. This results in the optionee receiving shares of stock with an aggregate value equal to the total amount of appreciation in value inherent in the stock option at the time that the transaction is initiated.

Qualifying Disposition

For purposes of stock purchased pursuant to a statutory stock option, a disposition made after satisfying the statutory holding period set out in Section 421 of the Code of two years from grant and one year from exercise.

Readily Ascertainable Fair Market Value

Under Section 83 of the Code, an option must have a "readily ascertainable fair market value" in order to be taxed at the time of grant. In order to have a readily ascertainable fair market value, the income tax regulations require that the stock option either be actively traded on an established securities market or, if not actively traded on an established securities market, the fair market value of the stock option be measurable with reasonable accuracy. The income tax regulations further provide a series of conditions that must be satisfied in order for an employee stock option to meet the "reasonably accurate measurement" test, including, among other things, free transferability of the stock option and the absence of restrictions that could significantly affect the value of the stock option or the underlying shares of stock. Since employee stock options are virtually always non-transferable and subject to vesting restrictions, such stock options seldom would have a readily ascertainable fair market value at the time of grant. As a result, the compensatory element of the acquisition of the employee stock option will not be subject to taxation under Section 83 of the Code until the stock option is exercised.

Realization

Tax concept that describes when gain (whether or not reduced to cash) is treated as compensation. Generally, a gain is considered "realized" when it has been received by a person for such person's use, benefit or disposal. For example, the exercise of an employee stock option to purchase shares of stock that have appreciated in value will be considered a realization of gain since the optionee has taken the final steps to obtain the benefits of economic gain that had previously accrued to the optionee. Realized gain is not necessary taxed at the time of the realization: see "recognition."

Recapitalization

An internal reorganization of the capital structure of the corporation. Typically, a reorganization involves a change to the type or number of securities outstanding. Sometimes the transaction will involve an amendment to the corporation's charter documents.

Recognition

Tax concept that describes when realized gain becomes taxable. Most realized gains are taxable at the time reported; however, tax recognition of some realized gains may be deferred under the Code. For example, Section 1036 of the Code is a non-recognition provision that provides that any gain realized from an exchange of shares of stock of a corporation for other shares of stock of the same corporation (such as in a stock swap exercise of an employee stock option) is not to be recognized at the time of the exchange. Instead, typically an adjustment to the basis of the property involved is made to preserve any unrecognized gain or loss, which may eventually be subject to taxation at a later time.

Record Date

A date set by the corporation for purposes of determining stock ownership for purposes of voting, dividends, and adjustments resulting from a change in capitalization (for example, a stock split, a stock dividend or a reverse stock split).

Recourse

Term used to describe a loan or other obligation that provides for personal liability against the debtor. In the event of a default on the obligation, the creditor can seek to foreclose on the personal assets of the debtor.

Registration

The formal process for the issuance of securities under federal and/or state securities laws that permit the public sale of securities.

Regrant

The reissuance or replacement of a previously granted employee stock option, often with terms and conditions that differ from those in the original stock option.

Regulation D

Exemption promulgated by the SEC under the 1933 Act for the private placement of securities that permits limited offerings of securities made in compliance with the conditions of the regulation and exempts such offerings from the registration requirements of the 1933 Act.

Regulation G

Provision promulgated by the Board of Governors of the Federal Reserve System to regulate the extension of credit by persons other than banks or brokers and dealers in connection with the purchase or carrying of marginable securities. Generally, this provision would apply to the extension of credit by certain corporations in connection with the purchase of shares of stock under an employee stock option plan.

Regulation T

Provision promulgated by the Board of Governors of the Federal Reserve System to regulate the extension of credit by brokers and dealers in connection with the purchase or carrying of securities.

Reload Option

A stock option granted to an individual who has exercised an option (typically by a stock swap) that restores the original number of shares under option; the terms of the option (e.g., the price) need not be the same as those of the swapped option.

Replacement Grant

A new employee stock option grant that is intended to replace a previously granted stock option, often with terms and conditions that differ in some respect from those contained in the original stock option. Frequently, when an employee stock option is repriced, the transaction will take the form of a cancellation of the original employee stock option and the grant of a new "replacement" stock option.

Reporting Person

A general term referring to directors, officers, beneficial owners of more than 10% of a class of an issuer's registered equity securities, and any other person otherwise subject to Section 16 of the Exchange Act.

Repricing

The adjustment of the option price of an outstanding employee stock option to reflect a decline in the value of the corporation's stock subject to the stock option. Typically, a stock option "repricing" takes the form of either an amendment of an outstanding stock option to reduce the exercise price or a cancellation of an outstanding employee stock option in exchange for the grant of a new stock option that has an option price equal to or greater than the current fair market value of the corporation's stock. The repricing of employee stock options is subject to extensive regulation and may trigger, among other things, significant income tax, securities law, and accounting consequences.

Repurchase

The reacquisition of shares of stock from an individual by a corporation. Depending on the nature of a corporation's repurchase rights, the corporation may pay the original cost of the shares of stock to the individual or the fair market value of the shares of stock at the time of repurchase.

Repurchase Option/Right

Contractual right reserved by the issuer to repurchase shares from employees (or service providers) at the time of their termination of employment (or service contract) or on another specified event. In general, the issuer will always reserve the right to repurchase unvested shares at their original purchase price. In privately held companies, the issuer may also reserve the right to purchase vested shares at their then-fair market value. Note that many forms of repurchase rights will expire under their terms at the time of an IPO.

Restricted Stock

For securities law purposes, shares of stock issued in a transaction that was not registered under the 1933 Act in reliance on an exemption. Resale of such shares is generally subject to Rule 144 (or subsequent registration).

Revenue Procedure

A notice published by the IRS giving administrative guidance on the application of tax laws; intended to be relied upon by taxpayers.

Revenue Ruling

A ruling published by the IRS that states the IRS audit position on the application of the tax law to specific facts; establishes precedent that may be relied upon.

Reverse Stock Split

Generally, a change in the capitalization of a corporation that decreases the number of securities outstanding and adjusts the value of the securities upward.

Right of First Refusal

Contractual restriction imposed on shares of stock that entitles a corporation to match any third party offer to purchase the shares of stock subject to the restriction on the same terms and conditions as the third party offer.

Rule 144

Rule promulgated by the SEC as a "safe harbor" for the resale of "restricted securities" (that is, securities that were acquired other than in a public offering) and "control securities" (that is, securities owned by affiliates of the corporation).

Rule 16b-3

Rule promulgated by the SEC that provides that transactions between an issuer that has registered a class of equity securities under Section 12 of the Exchange Act (including an employee benefit plan sponsored by the issuer) and a director or officer of the issuer that involve equity securities of the issuer will be exempt from the operation of the "short-swing profits" recovery rule of Section 16(b) of the Exchange Act if the transaction satisfies the applicable conditions set forth in the rule.

Run Rate

Used as a measure of dilution, this is the number of options granted annually (less option cancellations) as a percentage of total shares issued and outstanding.

Sale

A transaction involving the disposition of property, such as shares of stock, in exchange for the receipt of consideration for such property.

Same-Day Sale (or "Broker Same-Day Sale")

A form of cashless exercise of an employee stock option in which an individual sets the sale price with a broker on the exercise date (in the case of options) or the purchase date (in the case of a purchase under a Section 423 plan), has the shares delivered directly to the broker, and, on delivery of the shares, receives payment for the shares sold.

Section 12 Registration

Registration of a class of an issuer's equity securities under Section 12 of the Exchange Act. Registration under Section 12 is required if securities of the class are listed on a national securities exchange or are held by 500 or more individuals and the issuer has total assets exceeding $10 million, as of the last day of the issuer's most recent fiscal year.

Section 16(a) of the Exchange Act

Provision of the Exchange Act that requires the directors and officers of an issuer that has registered a class of its equity securities under Section 12, as well as the beneficial owners of more than 10% of any class of the issuer's registered equity securities, to file periodic reports with the Securities and Exchange Commission disclosing their holdings and changes in beneficial ownership of the issuer's equity securities.

Section 16(b) of the Exchange Act

Provision of the Exchange Act that requires the directors and officers of an issuer that has registered a class of its equity securities under Section 12, as well as the beneficial owners of more than 10% of any class of the issuer's registered equity securities, to return over to the issuer any profits realized from the purchase and sale, or sale and purchase, of the issuer's equity securities within a period of less than six months.

Section 83 of the Code

Provision of the Code that governs the taxation of property (including stock) received in connection with the performance of services. Section

83 provides that the difference between the fair market value of such transferred property and the amount (if any) paid for such property must be recognized on the first date that the property is freely transferable or not subject to a substantial risk of forfeiture (i.e., vested). Section 83 governs the federal income tax consequences of the grant and exercise of a non-qualified stock option.

Section 83(b) Election

Under Section 83(b), a taxpayer may elect to treat the spread (if any) on transfer of property as vested for purposes of federal income tax (and the capital gains holding periods) on the date of transfer, even if such property is otherwise unvested for non-tax purposes. If the spread on transfer is minimal, ordinary income tax attributable to the spread may be significantly reduced from what it would otherwise be at the time of vesting. The election is a technical device and requires the taxpayer to file a written statement with the IRS no later than 30 days after the date of transfer of property.

Section 162(m) of the Code

Provision of the Code that limits the ability of publicly traded corporations to deduct as an ordinary and necessary business expense certain employee remuneration in excess of $1 million paid to specified "covered employees" of the corporation.

Section 423 Plan

An employee stock purchase plan (ESPP) that qualifies under Section 423 of the Code.

Section 6039 of the Code

Provision of the Code that requires corporations to provide, by January 31 of the following year, certain specified information to employees who have exercised an ISO or transferred stock under a Section 423 plan.

SAR/SSAR

See "Stock Appreciation Right (SAR)."

Securities Act of 1933 (1933 Act)

A federal statute governing the offer and sale of securities in interstate commerce; prescribes registration, disclosure, and anti-fraud rules.

Securities and Exchange Commission (SEC)

An agency of the federal government created under the Exchange Act that administers the federal laws regulating the offer and sale of securities within the United States.

Securities Exchange Act of 1934 (Exchange Act)

A federal statute that requires stock exchanges to register with (or qualify for an exemption from registration) as a prerequisite to doing business; includes reporting, proxy solicitation, tender offer, and insider trading rules.

Security

General term, used to describe instruments, such as shares of stock, bonds, and debentures, as well as other instruments that have one or more characteristics of a security. The traditional definition of a security is an instrument that involves an investment where the return is primarily or exclusively dependent on the efforts of a person or persons other than the investor.

Share

An individual unit of a class of equity securities that represents the basic ownership interest of a corporation, usually denoted by a share certificate.

Share (or Stock) Certificate

A document that evidences ownership of a specific number of securities of a corporation. The certificate typically contains an alpha-numeric identifier, the name of the issuing corporation, the number of securities represented by the certificate, and the name and address of the shareholder/stockholder.

Shares Outstanding

The equity securities of a corporation that have been issued to, and are currently held by, the shareholders/stockholders of the corporation. In the context of an employee stock plan, the shares of stock of a corporation that have been sold and issued to, and are currently held by, the participants in the plan.

Share Reserve

The number of shares of stock that have been authorized and reserved by a corporation's board of directors for issuance pursuant to an employee stock option plan.

Shareholder/Stockholder

A person who owns one or more of the outstanding shares of stock of a corporation. These shares of stock may be either shares of common stock or shares of preferred stock. "Shareholder" and "stockholder" are synonymous; however, the corporate laws of different states assign the term to corporations incorporated in their jurisdictions. For example, Delaware corporations have stockholders; California corporations have shareholders.

Shareholder Approval

Authorization by shareholders of a corporate transaction or event. Generally, shareholder/stockholder approval is sought in connection with the adoption of an employee stock option plan and, in certain instances, with the amendment of such plans.

Short-Swing Profits Recovery Rule

Under Section 16(b) of the Exchange Act, a rule requiring directors and officers of an issuer that has registered a class of its equity securities under Section 12, as well as the beneficial owners of more than 10% of any class of the issuer's registered equity securities, to disgorge to the issuer any profits realized from the purchase and sale, or sale and purchase, of the issuer's equity securities within a period of less than six months.

Social Security Tax

An employment tax for retirement income imposed on employees and employers under the Federal Insurance Contributions Act with respect to the wages paid to employees.

Spread

For shares purchased under an option, the difference, if any, between the option price and the fair market value of the shares on the date of exercise (or, if exercise is for unvested shares, on the date of vesting).

Statutory Holding Period

Holding period established by Sections 422 and 423 of the Code for ISOs and ESPP options: one year from exercise and two years from grant.

Statutory Stock Option

An employee option accorded favorable tax treatment under Sections 421–424 of the Code; that is, an ISO or Section 423 ESPP option.

Stock

The basic form of equity issued by a corporation (other than a limited liability corporation). A corporation may issue different classes and series of stock, including common and preferred stock, as well as voting and nonvoting stock.

Strike Price

See "Exercise Price."

Stock Appreciation Right (SAR)/Stock-Settled Stock Appreciation Right (SSAR)

A contractual right granted to an individual that gives the recipient the right to receive a cash amount equal to the appreciation on a specified number of shares of stock over a specified period of time. An SSAR pays out the appreciation in the form of stock rather than cash.

Stockbroker

An individual that acts as an intermediary between a buyer and seller of securities. A stock broker receives compensation, in the form of a commission, for assisting in or effecting the purchase or sale of securities. A stock broker is "registered" with the National Association of Securities dealers and the exchange on which the securities are traded. Brokers are also regulated under federal and state securities laws.

Stock Certificate

A document that evidences ownership of a specific number of securities of a corporation. The certificate typically contains an alpha-numeric identifier, the name of the issuing corporation, the number of securities represented by the certificate, and the name and address of the shareholder/stockholder.

Stock-for-Stock Exercise

See "Stock Swap Exercise."

Stock Option Committee

Committee of the board of directors of a corporation responsible for decisions pertaining to employee stock option grants under the corporation's employee stock option plan.

Stock Option Plan

See "Option Plan"

Stock Option Repricing

See "Repricing."

Stock Split

A change in the capitalization of an issuer that increases or decreases the number of securities outstanding, and adjusts the value of the securities accordingly, without a corresponding change in the assets or capital of the issuer. Generally, used to denote a change in capitalization that increases the number of securities outstanding and adjusts the value of the securities downward.

Stockholder

See "shareholder."

Stock Swap

A transaction in which already-owned shares of stock are exchanged in lieu of cash to pay the option price for the exercise of a stock option.

Street Name Issuance

The registration of a security in the name of a securities brokerage firm as a nominee for the beneficial owner of the securities. Securities are often held in "street name" to expedite transfers of the securities when the securities are sold, since no delivery of the certificate or signature of transfer by the beneficial owner is required.

Subsidiary

A corporation that is majority owned or wholly owned by another corporation. For purposes of the ISO rules, any corporation (other than the employer corporation) in an unbroken chain of corporations beginning with the employer corporation if, at the time of grant of a stock option, each of the corporations other than the last corporation in the unbroken chain owns stock possessing 50% or more of the total combined voting power of all classes of stock in one of the other corporations in such chain.

Substantial Risk of Forfeiture

Tax concept under Section 83 of the Code that describes a situation in which an individual's rights to the full enjoyment of property is conditional upon the future performance of substantial services.

Swapped Shares

The number of shares of stock tendered to the corporation in a stock swap exercise. The swapped shares are assigned a value, typically the fair market value of the corporation's stock on the date of exercise. To complete the transaction, the optionee must deliver to the corporation a certificate or certificates covering enough previously issued and presently owned shares of stock to pay the aggregate option price for the share of stock being acquired through the stock option exercise.

Tandem Stock Option

An employee stock option that also provides the optionee with a related right, such as a stock appreciation right, covering an equivalent number of securities. Generally, the exercise of one right affects the holder's ability to exercise the other right. For example, to the extent that an optionee exercises the employee stock option portion of a tandem employee stock option/stock appreciation right, the related stock appreciation right is cancelled, and vice versa.

Tax Basis

A tax concept representing the actual and constructive "cost" of property to a taxpayer; for purposes of stock purchased under an option, the tax basis is equal to the amount paid on exercise plus any amount included in ordinary income prior to disposition.

Tax Deferral

The ability to postpone the payment of taxes from the date of a specific transaction until a later date. For example, assuming that a stock option designated as an ISO satisfies the conditions of Section 422(b) of the Code, upon exercise of such ISO the employee is permitted to defer the recognition of taxable income in connection with the acquisition of the shares of stock received upon exercise of the stock option until the disposition of such shares of stock.

Tax Offset Bonus

A cash bonus payable to an employee upon the exercise of a non-qualified stock option to cover, or "offset," the withholding taxes due as a result of the exercise. Generally, the amount of the bonus will be based upon a percentage of the total amount of compensation income recognized by the optionee plus additional amounts needed to "gross up" the bonus to fully offset the tax effect of the transaction on an after-tax basis.

For financial reporting purposes, the use of a tax offset bonus to reimburse an employee for the withholding taxes due on the exercise of a non-qualified stock option will result in "variable" accounting treatment for the transaction. That is, the corporation will record a compensation expense for financial reporting purposes equal to the amount of the cash bonus plus the entire difference between the option price and the fair market value of the corporation's stock on the date of exercise.

Tax Regulations

Rules promulgated by the Internal Revenue Service implementing and interpreting the statutory provisions of the Code. Congressional authority for the issuance of regulations is set forth in Section 7805 of the Code. While such rules are not law, they represent the Internal Revenue Service's interpretation of the proper application of the law and are presumed to be valid.

Tax Withholding

The retention of certain amounts from an employee's wages or compensation by a corporation to satisfy income tax and/or employment tax obligations.

Term

The stated period of time within which an option may be exercised (before it expires). Generally, the term of an employee stock option will be a period of up to 10 years. Also may refer to the duration of an employee stock option plan, during which time the plan administrator may grant stock options to eligible participants in the plan.

Termination Date (Option)

The date on which an option terminates, which may be either at the end of a stated term or at the time of the optionee's termination of employment (or service contract) with the company.

Termination of Plan

The termination of a stock option plan resulting from either the affirmative decision of the plan administrators to wind up the plan, the exhaustion of the plan share reserve or the expiration of the stated plan term.

Time-Accelerated Stock Option

A form of employee stock option that provides for a fixed, service-based vesting schedule with certain vesting accelerators tied to the achievement of specified performance criteria. If properly structured, for financial reporting purposes, the amount of compensation expense associated with the stock option is measured at the date of grant. This type of arrangement enables a corporation to grant an employee stock option that, from a practical standpoint, operates as a performance-based award but which receives "fixed" accounting treatment rather than the "variable" accounting treatment that is typically associated with performance-based arrangements.

Time-Accelerated Restricted Stock Award Plan (TARSAP)

A form of restricted stock purchase award that provides for a fixed, service-based vesting schedule with certain vesting accelerators tied to the achievement of specified performance criteria. If properly structured, for financial reporting purposes, the amount of compensation expense associated with the award is measured at the date of grant. This type of arrangement enables a corporation to grant an award that, from a practical standpoint, operates as a performance-based award but which receives "fixed" accounting treatment rather than the "variable" accounting treatment that is typically associated with performance-based arrangements.

Tax Withholding with Shares

An exercise feature that allows the optionee to request that the corporation withhold some of the shares of stock being acquired upon the exercise of the stock option in order to satisfy the optionee's withholding tax liability arising in connection with the transaction. The traded shares are assigned a value, usually the fair market value of the corporation's stock on the date of exercise. This value is divided into the total taxes due to determine the number of shares of stock required to be withheld. The number of shares of stock exercised is then reduced by the number of shares of stock to be withheld and only the net balance is issued to the optionee.

Trade Share Value

The value assigned to an exercised share that is traded back to the corporation to satisfy a withholding tax liability arising in connection with a stock option exercise. Commonly the trade share value is equal to the fair market value of the corporation's stock on the date of exercise.

Transfer

Conveyance of property, such as shares of stock, from one individual to another individual, followed by recording the ownership of the property on the records of the issuer.

Transfer Agent

An institution selected by an issuer to issue and transfer share certificates representing the ownership of the outstanding securities of the issuer. An agent of the corporation responsible for registering shareholder/stockholder names on the corporation's records. The transfer agent maintains a current list of shareholders/stockholders for purposes of distributing dividends, reports, and other corporate communications.

Transferable Stock Option (TSO)

An NSO that permits the optionee, under the terms and conditions set forth in the option agreement, to transfer the option to one or more third parties. Because of the limitation on transferability set forth in Section 422(b)(5) of the Code, an ISO cannot be a transferable stock option. Most corporations that permit transferable stock options limit the group of permissible transferees to immediate family members of the optionee or to entities (such as trusts or partnerships) for the benefit of immediate family members. A number of federal income and gift tax issues must be considered in connection with the implementation and use of transferable stock options.

Transfer Date

The date upon which securities are considered to have been transferred from one person to another.

Treasury Shares (Treasury Stock)

Shares of the capital stock of a corporation that were previously issued by the corporation and have been reacquired and are being held in "treasury" rather than retired. Substantively, treasury shares are equivalent to authorized but unissued shares. However, the corporation may reissue treasury shares without having to satisfy the minimum consideration requirements of state corporate law. Several states do not recognize the concept of treasury shares.

Underwater or "Out of the Money"

Terms used to describe an employee stock option where the option price is greater than the current fair market value of the shares of stock subject to the stock option.

Unvested Shares

Shares of stock that an individual has not yet earned and, therefore, may not transfer to a third party. Entitlement to the shares of stock is subject to the satisfaction of one or more contingencies (generally service-based) that are attached to the receipt of the shares of stock.

Vesting

With respect to shares of stock, the process through which shares are earned over a period of employment (or provision of services); for purposes of Section 83 of the Code, shares become vested on the first date they are transferable or not subject to a substantial risk of forfeiture. Conditions for vesting are generally stated in either the option grant (for stock options) or the restricted stock purchase agreement (for stock purchase).

Vesting Period

In general, the time period over which shares become vested, as set out in the option grant or purchase agreement.

Vesting Schedule

The specific schedule that dictates vesting. For an option, the vesting schedule may be the same as the exercise schedule (i.e., the option may only be exercised as to shares that are already vested) or may be different (i.e., the option may be exercised "early" as to shares that are not already vested). If early exercise is permitted, the shares themselves will be subject to vesting (see "repurchase option").

"Window" Period

A period of time during which, under a corporation's trading policy, it is permissible for a director, officer or employee to trade in the corporation's securities if the individual is in compliance with the terms of the policy (that is, the individual is not in actual possession of material, non-public information concerning the corporation). Typically, these periods run from ten days to two months following the release of quarterly or annual financial information by the corporation.

Withholding

The retention of certain amounts from an employee's wages or compensation by a corporation to satisfy the income tax and/or employment tax obligations of the employee that arise in connection with the exercise of a non-qualified stock option.

W-2 Income

See "Form W-2 Income."

Wages

Under Section 3401 of the Code, remuneration (in any form) paid to an employee in connection with services rendered to the employer.

Index

Expiration, 45, 87
  extension of date, 212–3

F

Fair market value, 8–9
FAS 123(R). *See* Financial Accounting
  Standards Board
Federal securities laws, 31–102
Financial Accounting Standards
  Board
  FAS 123(R), 9–10, 14, 79, 132, 134,
    146, 151, 154–5, 174–5, 202–6,
    212–5
    ESPPs, 240–53
  FAS 128, 176
  Technical Bulletin No. 97-1, 247,
    248–9
Foreign private issuers, 34, 36–7, 78,
  85
Form 1099-MISC, 27, 221
Form W-2, 27, 221, 237
Form W-9, 15
Forms 3, 4, 5, 8-K, 10-K, and 10-Q. *See*
  Securities Exchange Act of 1934
Formula plans, 135
Fractional shares, 10

G

Gifts, 45, 86
Google, 35
Granting stock options, 4–10, 86
  acceleration or addition of grants,
    213–4
  agreements, 7–8, 12
  fixed schedules, 5
  frequency, 214
  internal approval, 6–7
  number of shares granted, 5–6
  paired options, 214
  participation, 5
  policies and procedures, 4–5
  size, 5–6, 214
  term, 10

I

Imputed interest, 17
Incentive stock options (ISOs), 3–4,
  17, 168–70
  $100,000 limit, 209
  calculating gain on exercise, 19
  death, 182–5
  disqualifying dispositions, 28–9
  divorce, 223–5
  employment requirement, 25–6
  evergreen plans, 192–5
  holding period, 28
  leaves of absence, 25–6
  maximum term, 10
  repricing, 208–9
  shareholder approval, 4, 195
  tax treatment, 28
Initial public offerings (IPOs), 56–7,
  123–77
  cheap stock, 140–2
  financial statement disclosures,
    154–5, 174–7
  lockup periods, 138
  plan amendments, 126–32
    contractual restrictions, 127
    dispositions of options, 135–8
    eligibility criteria, 126
    exercise methods, 127–8
    individual grant limits, 127
  planning considerations, 126–38
  registration statements,
    preparation of, 142–153
  regulatory considerations after,
    155–77
  regulatory considerations before,
    138–55
    Section 16 insiders, 138–40
  shares eligible for future sale, 153
Insider trading, 59–64, 170–4
  during blackout periods, 61–2
  policies, 61, 171–2
Insider Trading and Securities Fraud
  Enforcement Act, 174

About the Authors

Alisa J. Baker of Levine & Baker LLP specializes in counseling individuals and companies on the full range of compensation-related matters, including equity and executive compensation, executive contract negotiation, strategic stock planning and plan design, and option litigation consulting. For the last two decades, Alisa has been a frequent writer and speaker on issues related to her practice. She has authored or coauthored two books published by NCEO: *The Stock Options Book* and *The Law of Equity Compensation*.

Barbara Baksa is the executive director of the National Association of Stock Plan Professionals (NASPP). She is a frequent speaker on equity compensation-related topics and has spoken at NCEO, NASPP, and other industry events. In addition to her speaking engagements, she has authored several white papers on equity compensation-related topics and has contributed chapters to four books on equity compensation. Barbara is a Certified Equity Professional (CEP) and serves on the Certified Equity Professional Institute's Advisory Board.

Mark A. Borges is a principal with Compensia, Inc., a management consulting firm providing executive compensation advisory services to compensation committees and senior management of knowledge-based companies. From April 2003 until September 2007, he was a principal for Mercer in the firm's Washington Resource Group in Washington, D.C. Previously, Mr. Borges was a special counsel in the Office of Rulemaking, Division of Corporation Finance, with the U.S. Securities and Exchange Commission. Before that, he was general counsel for ShareData, Inc. Mr. Borges practiced law with the firms of Ware & Friedenrich (now DLA Piper) from 1987 to 1992 and Pillsbury, Madison & Sutro (now Pillsbury Winthrop) from 1982 to 1987, specializing in equity compensation and insider trading matters as well as venture capital finance. From 1981 to 1982, he served as law clerk to the Honorable Marion T. Bennett of the United States Court of Claims in Washington, DC. A California native, Mr. Borges graduated from Humboldt State University in 1976. He received his J.D. from Santa Clara University in 1979 and an L.L.M. in Taxation from New York University in 1981. He is a member of the American Bar Association.

William Dunn is a partner in PricewaterhouseCoopers's Global Human Resource Solutions (GHRS) practice, where he co-leads the executive compensation tax practice. Mr. Dunn and his team consult with clients on a variety of executive compensation issues, including the use of stock-based compensation plans; compensation issues associated with business reorganizations; and deferred compensation planning, including the use of asset protection strategies. He and other PricewaterhouseCoopers professionals in the GHRS practice serve as client advocates in executive compensation matters, where they act as the liaison between the firm's clients, the IRS National Office, the Treasury Department, Congress, and other global regulatory authorities in matters relating to rulings, tax legislation, and regulatory guidance. Mr. Dunn has a master's degree in taxation from the American University, Washington, D.C., and a bachelor's degree from the University of Maryland, College Park, MD. He is a Certified Public Accountant and is a member of the American Institute of Certified Public Accountants.

Daniel N. Janich is the managing principal of Janich Law Group. He has extensive experience counseling businesses and executives on all aspects of employee benefits and executive compensation, including tax, securities law, and ERISA. He also litigates employee benefits and executive compensation claims. A former chair of the Chicago Bar Association's Employee Benefits Committee, Mr. Janich is currently associate senior editor of *Employee Benefits Law* and management co-chair of the Reporting and Disclosure Subcommittee of the ABA Labor and Employment Law Section's Employee Benefits Committee. He is also a Fellow of the American College of Employee Benefits Counsel. Mr. Janich received a B.A. degree cum laude in history from Marian College, Indianapolis; a J.D. degree from The John Marshall Law School, Chicago; and an LL.M. in Taxation degree from DePaul University, Chicago.

Thomas LaWer is a principal at Compensia, a compensation consulting firm, in its Silicon Valley (California) office. Tom advises compensation committees, boards of directors, and senior management regarding executive and board pay, reward strategies, equity compensation programs, and corporate governance issues related to compensation programs. Before joining Compensia, Tom was a partner in the law firm of Greenberg Traurig and one of the leaders of its national executive compensation group. Tom received his J.D. from the University of Chicago Law School and received a B.S. in Economics from the Wharton School of Business of the University of Pennsylvania. Before law school, Tom was a Certified Public Accountant at KPMG in New York City.

Mark Poerio is a partner with the law firm of Paul, Hastings, Janofsky & Walker LLP, where he is responsible for the Global Executive Compensation and Employee Benefits practice. In 2006, Mr. Poerio co-chaired task forces focused on advising Paul Hastings clients about the SEC's amended executive compensation disclosure rules, about compliance with new Code Section 409A, and about responses to the stock option backdating scandals. His team routinely handles issues ranging from multi-country stock plan design and implementation to golden parachute tax planning to the negotiation of executive employment, severance, and succession agreements. Mr. Poerio graduated with honors from both Cornell Law School (1980) and the University of Virginia (1980). He is a member of the state bars of Massachusetts, New York, and the District of Columbia.

Eric Orsic is a partner and **William J. Quinlan, Jr.** is counsel in the international law firm of McDermott Will & Emery LLP, resident in its Chicago office. Mr. Orsic is a member of the firm's Public Companies Group and the Corporate and Securities Department. Mr. Quinlan is a member of the firm's Executive Compensation Group and its Corporate and Securities Department. Both have worked extensively with both public and private companies in the design and structuring of executive compensation packages, including stock and stock-based compensation plans.

Timothy J. Sparks is the president and cofounder of Compensia, a consulting firm that provides counsel to boards, compensation committees, and senior management on issues concerning executive and board pay, reward strategy, and corporate governance as it relates to compensation plans. Before cofounding Compensia, Tim was a cofounder and executive vice president of Callisma, Inc., a leading network services consulting company, which was acquired by SBC in 2003. Tim joined

Callisma after 14 years at Wilson Sonsini Goodrich & Rosati, in Palo Alto, California, where he was the head of the firm's Employee Benefits and Compensation Group. Tim received a B.S. in business administration from U.C. Berkeley and a J.D. from U.C. Hastings College of the Law. Tim serves on the Advisory Board of the National Association of Stock Plan Professionals.

Matthew Topham is a partner in the corporate securities/mergers & acquisitions department of Preston Gates & Ellis LLP. He has experience in mergers and acquisitions involving both public and private companies, initial public offerings, state and federal securities law filings, and venture capital financings. He has counseled firm clients on a variety of employment-related issues and has experience drafting employment contracts, independent contractor agreements, nondisclosure agreements, and equity incentive plans for both public and private corporations and limited liability companies.

Donna L. Yip is an associate in the labor and employment department at Proskauer Rose LLP. She works with companies and boards; private equity and hedge funds; and CEOs, senior executives, and management groups (in numerous business sectors) on a full range of executive compensation matters. She has a Juris Doctor from Emory University, Atlanta, GA, and a bachelor's degree from the University of Richmond, Richmond, VA. She is a member of the Connecticut and New York state bars.

About the NCEO

The National Center for Employee Ownership (NCEO) is widely considered to be the leading authority in employee ownership in the U.S. and the world. Established in 1981 as a nonprofit information and membership organization, it now has over 2,500 members, including companies, professionals, unions, government officials, academics, and interested individuals. It is funded entirely through the work it does.

The NCEO's mission is to provide the most objective, reliable information possible about employee ownership at the most affordable price possible. As part of the NCEO's commitment to providing objective information, it does not lobby or provide ongoing consulting services. The NCEO publishes a variety of materials on employee ownership and participation, holds dozens of seminars, Webinars, and conferences on employee ownership annually, and offers a variety of online courses. The NCEO's work includes extensive contacts with the media, both through articles written for trade and professional publications and through interviews with reporters. It has written or edited several books for outside publishers. The NCEO maintains an extensive Web site at www.nceo.org.

See the following page for information on membership benefits and fees. To join, see the order form at the end of this section, visit our Web site at www.nceo.org, or telephone us at 510-208-1300.

Membership Benefits

NCEO members receive the following benefits:

- The bimonthly newsletter *Employee Ownership Report*, which covers ESOPs, equity compensation, and employee participation.

- Access to the members-only area of the NCEO's Web site, which includes a searchable database of well over 200 NCEO members who are service providers in this field, plus many other resources, such as a searchable newsletter archive and a discussion forum; a stock plan glossary; legislative/regulatory updates; and case studies organized by plan type and company type.

- Substantial discounts on publications, online courses, and events produced by the NCEO.

- Free access to live Webinars on ESOPs and related topics.

- The right to contact the NCEO for answers to general or specific questions regarding employee ownership.

An introductory NCEO membership costs $90 for one year ($100 outside the U.S.) and covers an entire company at all locations, a single professional offering services in this field, or a single individual with a business interest in employee ownership. Full-time students and faculty members who are not employed in the business sector may join at the academic rate of $40 for one year ($50 outside the U.S.).

Selected NCEO Publications

The NCEO offers a variety of publications on all aspects of employee ownership and participation. Below are some of our main publications.

We publish new books and revise old ones on a yearly basis. To obtain the most current information on what we have available, visit us on the Web at www.nceo.org or call us at 510-208-1300.

Equity Compensation

- *The Stock Options Book* is a straightforward, comprehensive overview covering the legal, accounting, regulatory, and design issues involved in implementing a stock option or stock purchase plan.

    $25 for NCEO members, $35 for nonmembers

- *Selected Issues in Equity Compensation* is more detailed and specialized than *The Stock Options Book,* with chapters on issues such as repricing, securities issues, and evergreen options.

    $25 for NCEO members, $35 for nonmembers

- *Beyond Stock Options* is a complete guide, including annotated model plans, to phantom stock, restricted stock, stock appreciation rights, performance awards, and more. Includes a CD with plan documents.

    $35 for NCEO members, $50 for nonmembers

- *The Decision-Maker's Guide to Equity Compensation* describes the various types of equity compensation, how they work, and how to decide much to give and to whom. Includes a CD with an audiovisual presentation on sharing equity.

  $35 for NCEO members, $50 for nonmembers

- *Accounting for Equity Compensation* is a guide to the accounting rules that govern equity compensation programs in the U.S.

  $35 for NCEO members, $50 for nonmembers

- *The Stock Administration Book* is a comprehensive guide to administering stock options and other equity compensation plans. It includes a CD with templates for immediate use.

  $50 for NCEO members, $75 for nonmembers

- *The Law of Equity Compensation* reviews and analyzes case law, statutory, and regulatory law developments in recent years.

  $25 for NCEO members, $35 for nonmembers

- *Equity-Based Compensation for Multinational Corporations* describes how companies can use stock options and other equity-based programs across the world to reward a global work force. It includes a country-by-country summary of tax and legal issues as well as a detailed case study.

  $25 for NCEO members, $35 for nonmembers

- *Incentive Compensation and Employee Ownership* takes a broad look at how companies can use incentives, ranging from stock plans to cash bonuses to gainsharing, to motivate and reward employees.

  $25 for NCEO members, $35 for nonmembers

- *Tax and Securities Sources for Equity Compensation* is a compilation of statutory and regulatory material relevant to the study of equity compensation.

  $35 for NCEO members, $50 for nonmembers

- *Equity Compensation in a Post-Expensing World* presents strategies for companies in the new accounting environment.

  $25 for NCEO members, $35 for nonmembers

Employee Stock Ownership Plans (ESOPs)

- *The ESOP Reader* is an overview of the issues involved in establishing and operating an ESOP. It covers the basics of ESOP rules, feasibility, valuation, and other matters, and includes brief case studies.

  $25 for NCEO members, $35 for nonmembers

- *Selling to an ESOP* is a guide for owners, managers, and advisors of closely held businesses, with a particular focus on the tax-deferred Section 1042 "rollover" for C corporation owners.

  $25 for NCEO members, $35 for nonmembers

- *Leveraged ESOPs and Employee Buyouts* discusses how ESOPs borrow money to buy out entire companies, purchase shares from a retiring owner, or finance new capital.

  $25 for NCEO members, $35 for nonmembers

- *ESOP Valuation* brings together and updates where needed the best articles on ESOP valuation that we have published in our Journal of Employee Ownership Law and Finance, described below.

  $25 for NCEO members, $35 for nonmembers

- *ESOPs and Corporate Governance* covers everything from shareholder rights to the impact of Sarbanes-Oxley to choosing a fiduciary.

  $25 for NCEO members, $35 for nonmembers

- *Model ESOP* provides a sample ESOP plan, with alternative provisions given to tailor the plan to individual needs. It also includes a section-by-section explanation of the plan and other supporting materials.

  $50 for NCEO members, $75 for nonmembers

- *Executive Compensation in ESOP Companies* discusses executive compensation issues, special ESOP considerations, and the first-ever survey of executive compensation in ESOP companies.

  $25 for NCEO members, $35 for nonmembers

- *S Corporation ESOPs* introduces the reader to how ESOPs work and then discusses the legal, valuation, administrative, and other issues associated with S corporation ESOPs.

  $25 for NCEO members, $35 for nonmembers

- *The ESOP Communications Sourcebook* provides ideas for and examples of communicating an ESOP to employees and customers. It includes a CD with communications materials, including many documents that readers can customize for their own companies.

  $35 for NCEO members, $50 for nonmembers

- *The Inside ESOP Fiduciary Handbook* provides an overview of the issues involved in being a fiduciary at an ESOP company.

  $10 for NCEO members, $15 for nonmembers

- *How ESOP Companies Handle the Repurchase Obligation* has essays and recent research on the subject.

  $25 for NCEO members, $35 for nonmembers

Other

- *Section 401(k) Plans and Employee Ownership* focuses on how company stock is used in 401(k) plans, both in stand-alone 401(k) plans and combination 401(k)–ESOP plans ("KSOPs").

  $25 for NCEO members, $35 for nonmembers

- *Employee Ownership and Corporate Performance* reviews the research that has been done on the link between company stock plans and various aspects of corporate performance.

  $15 for NCEO members, $25 for nonmembers

- *The Journal of Employee Ownership Law and Finance* is the only professional journal solely devoted to employee ownership. Articles are written by leading experts and cover ESOPs, stock options, and related subjects in depth.

  One-year subscription (four issues):
  $75 for NCEO members, $100 for nonmembers

To join the NCEO as a member or to order publications, use the order form on the following page, order online at www.nceo.org, or call us at 510-208-1300. If you join at the same time you order publications, you will receive the members-only publication discounts.

Order Form

This book is published by the National Center for Employee Ownership (NCEO). You can order additional copies online at our Web site, *www.nceo.org;* by telephoning the NCEO at 510-208-1300; by faxing this page to the NCEO at 510-272-9510; or by sending this page to the NCEO at 1736 Franklin Street, 8th Floor, Oakland, CA 94612. If you join as an NCEO member with this order, or are already an NCEO member, you will pay the discounted member price for any publications you order.

Name

Organization

Address

City, State, Zip (Country)

Telephone   Fax   Email

Method of Payment: ❑ Check (payable to "NCEO")   ❑ Visa   ❑ M/C   ❑ AMEX

Credit Card Number

Signature   Exp. Date

Checks are accepted only for orders from the U.S. and must be in U.S. currency.

Title	Qty.	Price	Total

Tax: California residents add 8.75% sales tax (on publications only, not membership)	Subtotal $
Shipping: In the U.S., first publication $5, each add'l $1; elsewhere, we charge exact shipping costs to your credit card, plus a $10 handling surcharge; no shipping charges for membership	Sales Tax $
	Shipping $
Introductory NCEO Membership: $90 for one year ($100 outside the U.S.)	Membership $
	TOTAL DUE $